"Long entombed within the amber prose of King James scholars, Luke the Evangelist here emerges as a deeply human teacher, by turns poetic and even puzzled, yet always profound. Mark Whitters, a superb scholar and perceptive humanist, has found new words and a new way to lead us to a deeper understanding of the words and the way of Jesus of Nazareth."

—*Mark C. Carnes*
Barnard College, Columbia University

"In *Memoirs of How It All Began*, Whitters bridges the yawning gap between scholarship and everyday life and between divine revelation in Scripture and subjective spirituality. Like a skilled movie producer, Whitters takes the old written movie about Jesus' life first produced by the Evangelist Luke and remakes it for a contemporary audience. Beyond vividly portraying Christ crucified before their eyes, Whitters compels the audience to enter the Lukan story as performers and to react to the dramatic characters and unfolding events. This prequel to Whitters's *Memoirs of an Unfinished Tale* is sure to capture the attention of modern audiences, and I give it two-thumbs up!"

—*Troy W. Martin*
Saint Xavier University

"Memoirs of How It All Began will immerse readers of the Gospel of Luke in a creative experience of the text. While remaining rooted in excellent scholarship, it acts as a bridge between 'then' and 'now', offering a new and rewarding way into the Gospel. Highly recommended, especially for study groups!"

—*Leslie Baynes*
Missouri State University

"Most believers recognize their need for help with reading Scripture, yet the commentaries they read leave them more confused than before. In *Memoirs of How It All Began*, Whitters takes the Gospel of Luke and recasts it as a holy play. Where you and I see disconnected tales, Whitters see paragraphs in a story and the plot of a spiritual mystery. He invites us to participate in the production of the true story of the God who became Man. As we participate as performers, that story becomes real in our lives. I wholeheartedly recommend *Memoirs of How It All Began* for individuals or groups."

—*Samuel C. Williamson*
Founding Director, Beliefs of the Heart

"Picture, if you will, that Luke took pen in hand for a third rendering of the drama of Jesus intervening in the course of human history and God's Spirit animating the simple people of field, village, and religious center. Dr. Mark Whitters takes pen in hand and deftly portrays the layers of paradox (and pun) as God turns the world on its head in showering light, mercy, and peace on common people in a way that would pale the efforts of the religious and political powers of that day. Something God continues doing to this very day! Come discover your part in this 'drama' of renewal and redemption!"

—*Bob and Deb Clark*
Faculty Ministry, InterVarsity Christian Fellowship, Madison, WI

"*Memoirs of How It All Began* is a captivating account of the Gospel of Luke. Whitters provides the requisite background that illuminates the Gospel. I found the background and the footnotes to be very helpful in setting the context for my study of Luke. The questions that he crafts tease out applications of Luke's Gospel for us in our busy lives. In *Memoirs of How It All Began*, Jesus is the performer and he invites the disciples and us (Theophilus included) into his performance! What a great invitation!"

—*Anthony M. Musumba*
University of Mary

Memoirs of How It All Began

Memoirs of How It All Began

A Performance Interpretation of the Gospel of Luke

With Application Questions
for Study and Discussion

Mark F. Whitters

CASCADE *Books* · Eugene, Oregon

MEMOIRS OF HOW IT ALL BEGAN
A Performance Interpretation of the Gospel of Luke

Cascade Books
An Imprint of Wipf and Stock Publishers
199 W. 8th Ave., Suite 3
Eugene, OR 97401

www.wipfandstock.com

PAPERBACK ISBN: 978-1-5326-6046-7
HARDCOVER ISBN: 978-1-5326-6047-4
EBOOK ISBN: 978-1-5326-6048-1

Cataloguing-in-Publication data:

Names: Whitters, Mark F., author.

Title: Memoirs of how it all began : a performance interpretation of the gospel of Luke. / Mark F. Whitters.

Description: Eugene, OR: Cascade Books, 2019. Includes bibliographical references and index.

Identifiers: ISBN 978-1-5326-6046-7 (paperback) | ISBN 978-1-5326-6047-4 (hardcover) | ISBN 978-1-5326-6048-1 (ebook)

Subjects: LCSH: Bible. Luke—Commentaries. | Bible. Luke—Criticism, interpretation, etc. | Bible. Luke—Drama.

Classification: BS2595.2 W55 2019 (print) | BS2595.2 (ebook)

Manufactured in the U.S.A.   NOVEMBER 21, 2019

Contents

Figures and Illustrations | *viii*
Acknowledgments | *ix*
Preface | *xi*

Introduction | 1
    Greetings, Reader! | 1
    Invitation
Chapter One: Preparation for Performance | 3
    Part One: Advance Publicity (1:1–4) | 3
    Part Two: Jesus Auditions | 19
Chapter Two: Introduction and Supporting Cast | 31
    Introduction | 31
    Supporting Cast | 41
    Reacting Game Excursus: Jesus on the Cusp of Fame (7:19–35) | 62
Chapter Three: Taking the Show on the Road | 67
    Entertaining with Parables and *Mystēria* (8:22–25) | 67
    Persistence Despite Disasters: A Disciple's Testimony (8:26–37) | 70
    Persistence Despite Demons: A Disciple's Testimony | 71
    Reacting Game Excursus: Jesus and Legion (8:26–37) | 74
    Persistence Despite Disease (8:40–56) | 76
    Persistence Despite Death | 77
    Persistence Despite Despotism: Herod's Testimony (9:1–9) | 79
    The Show Returns Home (9:10–17) | 81
    More Training and Rehearsal (9:18–26) | 83
    Down Time for Jesus? Phase One (9:28–36) | 83
    Down Time for Jesus? Phase Two (9:51–56) | 86
Chapter Four: Preparations for the Big Show | 90
    Mobilization (10:1–12; 13–20; 21–24) | 90

Excuses (10:25–34; 38–42) | 95

Getting Ready through Prayer (11:1–4) | 99

Getting Ready for Spiritual Opposition (11:14–23; 24–28) | 102

Getting Ready for Public Opposition (11:29–32) | 105

An Afterthought | 107

Getting Ready for Institutional Opposition (11:49–51) | 108

Another Afterthought (11:53–54) | 112

How Ready Are We for the Kingdom? (12:1–12) | 113

Three Tests: Internal, External, and Final | 113

Back to the Crowds (12:13–21) | 117

Possessions (12:22–34) | 119

Long-Term Strategy (12:35–36) | 122

In the Meantime (12:49–53) | 124

Back to the Crowds (12:54–59; 13:1–9; 18–21) | 126

Chapter Five: Almost on the Big Stage | 133

The Perils of Traveling (13:22–30) | 133

Will Arrival Bring Blessing or Curse? (13:31–35) | 135

Rest Stop: Sabbath (Again) (14:1–6) | 138

Rest Stop (Continued) (14:7–11) | 141

Rest Stop (Conclusion) (14:12–24) | 142

Traveling Again: A Hard-Sell Pitch to the Public (14:25–35) | 144

Traveling Again: A Soft-Sell Pitch in Three Parts (15:1–10) | 146

A Soft-Sell Pitch: Finale (15:15–32) | 149

Reacting Game Excursus for Large Group | 152

The Hook in the Soft-Sell Pitch (16:1–13) | 155

A Story to Interpret the Hard-Sell and Soft-Sell Pitches to the Public (16:19–31) | 158

Coaching before Curtain Call (17:1–4, 5–6, 7–10) | 161

A Choral Interlude: All Are Off-Key but One! (17:11–19) | 165

Waiting for the Kingdom | 167

Unlikely Recruits: Tax Collectors (18:9–14) | 169

Unlikely Recruits: Children (18:15–17) | 171

Likely Recruits Unlikely! (18:18–30; 31–34) | 172

Chapter Six: Visitation on Big Stage | 176

Jericho: The Blind Man and Zacchaeus (19:1–10) | 177

"Spoiler Alert" Parable: Fake News about a Happy Ending (19:11–27) | 179

Visitation to the City (19:28–40) | 182

Visitation Results Predicted (19:41–44) | 184

Visitation Performed (19:45–48) | 186

Visitation Dialogues (20:1–8; 9–19) | 188

Reacting Game Excursus: Ideas for Developing a Game
(20:9–19) | 191

Dialogue about Caesar (20:20–26) | 192

Dialogue about Marriage and the Afterlife (20:27–40) | 194

Dialogues Follow-Up (20:41–47; 21:1–4) | 198

Dialogue Conclusion: Jesus's Parting Prediction (21:5–19; 20–28;
29–38) | 199

Chapter Seven: The Final Act | 206

Part One: Spotlight Theater on Three Characters | 206

Spotlight: Judas (22:1–6) | 206

Spinning Things Differently (22:7–13) | 209

The "Hour" to Celebrate? (22:14–23) | 210

Party Games (22:23–30) | 213

Game Losers (22:31–34) | 215

My Soul's "Et Tu, Brute" Moment [Jesus] (22:35–38) | 216

Spotlight: Jesus (22:39–46) | 217

The Angel in the Garden (22:47–53) | 219

Betrayal with a Kiss (22:54–62) | 221

Spotlight: Peter (22:54–62) | 222

Reacting Game Excursus: Eavesdropping in the Passion of Luke
(22:39–62) | 224

Part Two: Farce or Tragedy? | 229

Scene 1 (22:63–71) | 229

Scene 2 (22:63–71) | 230

Scene 3 (23:1–5) | 231

Scene 4: Which Interpretation? (23:8–12) | 232

Scene 5 (23:13–25) | 233

Scene 6: Which Interpretation? (23:26–31) | 235

Scene 7: Which Interpretation? (23:32–43) | 236

Scene 8 (23:44–49) | 239

Final Scene: Sabbath (23:50–56) | 241

Chapter Eight: The End Game | 243

Reacting Game Excursus: Theophilus Wants a Report about What
Happened after Jesus Died and Was Buried (23:1–48) 243

Conclusion | 253

Index | 255

Scripture Index | 259

Figures and Illustrations

Figure 1: *The Narrator* (by Jamie Treadwell) xiii
Figure 2: *Mary & Elizabeth Meet* (by Jamie Treadwell) 8
Figure 3: *A Reed Shaking in the Wind* (by Garrett Shireman) 59
Figure 4: *The Good Samaritan* (by Garrett Shireman) 97
Figure 5: *The Barren Fig Tree* (by Yvette Rock) 128
Figure 6: *Lazarus and Dives* (by Jamie Treadwell) 159
Figure 7: *Jesus Weeps over Jerusalem* (by Garrett Shireman) 185
Figure 8: *Emmaus Walkers* (by Yvette Rock) 246

Acknowledgments

As with my first recreation of Luke (*Memoirs of an Unfinished Tale*), this new "prequel" depended on the support and contribution of colleagues and friends. In the former category are Larry Lahey and Troy Martin, who read over most or all of the book and suggested many changes and new (and undoubtedly better) interpretations of the Gospel of Luke. Though academics, they helped to see the text with the eyes of faith.

In the latter category are a trio of artists whose contributions are noticeable at various places in the pages that follow. Two of them, Yvette Rock and Jamie Treadwell, helped with illustrations in my first volume and now in this one. They were joined by Garrett Shireman. All of these friends are connected in one way or another to reach youth, especially in an urban context.

Finally, I cannot fail to mention my debt to Dave O'Connor and Ed Conlin who have managed to live out community with me for well over a decade of work in the city of Detroit. They are now joined by another forbearing confrere, Brian LaLonde. They all manage to tolerate my ideas and put up with my projects in the academic world. A special salute to Dave O'Connor, who, after nineteen years in Detroit, will soon depart for similar life and work in Manila. As the proverb says, "There are friends who pretend to be friends, but there is a friend who sticks closer than a brother" (Prov 18:24). Thanks, Dave, Ed, and Brian.

As I indicate in the preface, the impetus to write comes from my association with a new pedagogical method in the academic world called "Reacting." Credit here belongs to Mark Carnes of Barnard College for developing and promoting this style of education, the Reacting Consortium, as well as my colleagues and students in History & Philosophy at Eastern Michigan University.

Preface

WHEN IT COMES TO the Bible, there is a yawning gap between scholarship and practice. This regrettably has caused a parallel gap between institution and public. The little that filters down from the specialists often disillusions those who might pick up the Bible for inspiration and guidance. More broadly, as the Bible loses traction, so do the institutions that the Bible would seem to promote—and thus more and more the public identifies with being "spiritual but not religious," as if one can only find what is true within the subjective world and not in supernatural revelation. What is left behind are groups that are increasingly introverted and isolated from each other and a general skepticism predominating among everyone.

This book attempts to bridge the gap between scholarship and practice, and it hopes to address those who identify with being spiritual but not religious. How? By portraying a world where Jesus lived as witnessed by Luke's artful eye, while inviting the audience to enter into the dramatic action he reports.

How can we imagine this time travel? *Memoirs of How It All Began* and its companion volume *Memoirs of an Unfinished Tale* rely on a concept called "Reacting," where the audience enters into a text as performers. They live and act in the world the text represents, something like a virtual reality. Much like virtual-reality games that attract so many young people today, the outcome for Luke's staging in this book depends on how the various participants respond—and it is different each time the narrative is retold. And with each play of individuals and groups, the situation for everyone involved changes. Certain "facts" the text gives or assumes cannot change, but the reacting of everyone to the story's circumstances does change. Thus, the text springs to life, not only in its original context but in the mind of the performer who has to make new decisions about what to do.

Reacting brings us back to the gap above, especially to the one between institution and public. The institution (say, the Church or the Synagogue) has been involved unawares in this very method of communicating for centuries, restaging and rehearsing stories in front of its members, sometimes effectively and sometimes not, something that can be called "liturgy," where the "word" is the text and the "sacrament" is the virtual-reality game.

So Luke is reteaching his audience about Jesus, starting from scratch, starting with the narrative he wrote but ever trying to draw the reader (Theophilus and us) into its action. How would he communicate his point while livening up the details for someone who either was not present for the actual event or did not pay sufficient attention the first time the Gospel of Luke was performed?

Memoirs of How It All Began is Luke's second chance to tell his story to a younger and still eager Theophilus. This current work focuses on what happened that drew disciples to Jesus. It makes no assumptions about Jesus (though of course no updated narrator can simply detach themselves totally from presuppositions about a past story) and allows Theophilus to make up his own mind about what Luke reports.

Luke realizes that if he is to arouse his younger companion to act on what he remembers about Jesus, he must again perform his stories and replay the events before Theophilus's very eyes. He knows that Theophilus is interested in history not as a dry memorization of facts nor of a metal chain of events, but as a compendium of lessons that guide growth and change. History, thinks Luke, unfolds as episodes, cohering around an intelligible theme with drama and suspense. So, not unlike a play, it requires imaginative performance to both entertain and provoke an audience to react.

What follows therefore is Luke's representation of the Gospel of Luke, but it appears improvisionally here as an emerging and entertaining drama. Think of what follows as a play directed by an experienced playwright who stands with one foot on stage and one foot in real life, a creative project with episodes guided by the original text. This cycle of viewing and reviewing past events to derive current meaning constitutes what ancient Greeks tried to do in narrating history and in staging plays about its heroes—and it is a good principle to facilitate the reading of the Bible for anyone.

The performance below reformulates in modern language what Luke might say to an audience today. At the same time it selects and highlights particular episodes and details instead of repeating the whole story. While it may not cover each verse and reference that a full commentary does, it hopefully will narrate the line of adventures that ties the book together and then can shed light on everything that a more thorough reading of the Gospel of Luke brings out.

The presentation corresponds to the layout of the text Luke wrote, that is, it follows the chapter-by-chapter development of the book. It divides each chapter into episodes that the reader can follow in regular intervals, day by day and week by week. Alternatively, the episodes often stand independently enough that one can consult them for particular interpretations. There are at least six particular applications of this representation that allow for a dramatic *performance* of the Bible as a method of reaching an audience. This method of teaching is particularly useful in today's "virtual reality" world.

Finally, at the end of each episode within this representation are questions geared for an individual reader or (with slight modifications) an audience. The questions are based on the lessons of the episodes as laid out, but are updated for modern and sometimes secular contexts.

FIGURE 1: *The Narrator* (by Jamie Treadwell)

Introduction

Greetings, Reader!

IT'S TIME TO START over, Theophilus and fellow reader, to go back to the sources. What drew me and others to Jesus in the first place? Why him—and not others who made similar claims and had similar followers? To do this, I think I have to start over and reduce what I wrote in my first book to the basics of what we should now review.

You can call it, I suppose, an "orderly account" [1:3] of what you read earlier. Only this time, I'm asking you to start over and meet Jesus as if he were striding onto the stage for the first time—and the stage is your life. Just in case you missed it in my first book [Gospel of Luke] about Jesus or my second book [Acts of the Apostles] about the generation after Jesus, I don't just write history as if to repeat what others have said. Nor do I simply reenact things as if to entertain. No, Theophilus, I write to *perform* these stories. Now, more than ever, I write so that you enter into the drama and react to what I have staged.

Invitation

Tell me, O readers, that my text is a ruse
—that no one can whistle the song of Jesus!
To force his words and his life onto stage,
—to play him like this in lights is obtuse!

And I reply with wicked wink
That all you need do is hear

1

How Jesus piped his tune and danced
For crowds to hiss or to cheer.

Performing his message about a throne—
The audience, provoked, now guessed,
Is Elijah to come, John to judge,
Are you Moses or one of the rest?

A lead, a role, a script, I'll add;
He knew what others rehearsed before;
And he, the best and sum of it all,
Spins salvation out of such lore.

CHAPTER ONE

Preparation for Performance

Part One: Advance Publicity

> Luke 1:1–4 Inasmuch as many have undertaken to compile a narrative of the things which have been accomplished among us, 2 just as they were delivered to us by those who from the beginning were eyewitnesses and ministers of the word, 3 it seemed good to me also, having followed all things closely for some time past, to write an orderly account for you, most excellent Theophilus, 4 that you may know the truth concerning the things of which you have been informed.

MOST EXCELLENT THEOPHILUS, I want to begin a retelling of "the things accomplished"—that have changed both of our lives. I chose a word here to sum up those events: "accomplished." These things achieved their purpose, a purpose for which many had long hoped and waited. I began writing what others "had delivered to us," so I am part of a chain of transmission stretching from the first generation who saw with their own eyes to those who passed it on in the second and third generation. I arose to take my place as the link to you. What is my aim? In a word, formation. When I say, "concerning the things of which you have been informed," the very last Greek word I use (*katēcheō*, κατηχέω) is the basis for the word you may know as "catechesis" or "formation." Take hold of these words, and you will be able to cope with the force of circumstances that sometimes threatens your confession. Be formed by them!

Remember also that I wrote to give you "an orderly account" of all the details. That means that I assembled and organized the story in my own way. As you will see in the pages ahead, there is an overall design to the material I received—it is my way of telling you what is important. Others have put together their versions of the story, yes, but this one is mine; and I want my account to give voice to the Jesus as I understand him.

Now I invite you again to listen and learn. Before Jesus came into the public eye, seven episodes promoted his arrival and promised greatness for his life. I shall now labor to explain these divinely ordained events as "visitations." Now what is a visitation? It is a word we all know as Roman subjects. Caesar claims to visit his people with security and prosperity when he sends out his armies and his decrees. Occasionally he himself travels to inspect lands and peoples. Depending on your loyalty to Caesar, these visitations can be favorable or fearful.

The Almighty did the same: he intervened and communicated in three visits before the birth of Jesus, three after the birth of Jesus—all of these events setting the stage for Jesus in the public eye. Almost as a capstone clue, a prophetic speech came forth in the middle episode that interpreted why God was revealing these preparatory events. All seven episodes were messages of divine publicity alerting us to get ready for someone or something big.

I fear you may have missed the drama of my narrative. So let me review for you the opening seven episodes and suggest at the end a takeaway for you as a follower of Jesus. I shall not now lay out the entire text, but only a résumé of the visitations I tried to bring to your attention. At various points, I will interrupt my account with questions to see how well you are understanding. If something stirs your interest or leaves you puzzled, I urge you to go back to my original text.

Visitation One: Angel (Gabriel) Comes to Zechariah

Luke 1:8–11 Now while he [Zechariah] was serving as priest before God when his division was on duty, 9 according to the custom of the priesthood, it fell to him by lot to enter the temple of the Lord and burn incense. 10 And the whole multitude of the people were praying outside at the hour of incense. 11 And there appeared to him an angel of the Lord standing on the right side of the altar of incense.

The elderly Zechariah and his wife Elizabeth were representatives of Israel's past—they represent the old order. They follow the strictures of their venerable religion as serious consciences and traditions dictate. In this sense, Zechariah fulfills his name, "The LORD remembered," by offering the *Zikkaron* incense[1] at the prescribed hour. Elizabeth, on the other hand, walks uprightly as required by tradition (customs called *halakah* in the Jewish tongue[2]), fulfilling the meaning of her name, "My God is my pledge." She will exhibit an unswerving character as God's partner in the later visitations I will tell. Together they represent Israel's ongoing validity as a people recognized by God.

Yet as these two figures grow old without children, they represent Israel's fading hopes and dreams. In spite of their life together, they have not produced an heir to complete their labors. In this condition, you may compare them to Israel itself—in need of divine intervention to make good on its age-old testimony.

Exactly at the appointed hour of priestly intercession, an angel visits the priest and shows that the Almighty remembers.[3] In this first visitation, we see remembrance of Israel and its ancient traditions, as well as an advance preview for something new from God.

I wish I could say much more about the name of this angel and the message he brought—for as you can already tell, I love the meaning of names—but now is not the time.[4] For now, consider how the promise of a son named John (meaning "The Lord has given" or "The Lord's grace") lays the groundwork for a new age, a Kingdom to come in the mission of Jesus. Meanwhile, Zechariah responds to the angel's news with cold silence—a tacit reminder that Israel's response is often resistance to the visitations of God.

---

1. What is the *Zikkaron*? It is the priestly ritual connected to temple liturgy—in Greek translation, often called the "memorial" or "remembrance." [See Mark F. Whitters, *Memoirs of an Unfinished Tale* (Eugene, OR: Cascade Books, 2017) 56.]

2. *Halakah* represents the principles that guide daily life conduct for an observant Jew.

3. This will happen again when an angel arrives in response to the *Zikkaron* prayers of Peter, triggering the entrance of those outside of the Jews into the Kingdom [Acts 10:1–20].

4. Gabriel means "God is my champion." [Luke's playful use of puns and double meanings come across often: see his discussion of such names as "Eutychus" and "Felix" in *Memoirs of an Unfinished Tale,* 146.]

1. What challenges around me now beg for special interventions to resolve? How do I see the divine hand operating in such circumstances? Do I offer faithful *Zikkaron*-like prayers for such interventions?

2. Have I ever experienced "visitations" (natural or supernatural) that helped me cope? What was my response? What would qualify as a supernatural visitation?

3. What would my response be if God did intervene?

Visitation Two: Gabriel Comes to Mary

> Luke 1:26–28 In the sixth month the angel Gabriel was sent from God to a city of Galilee named Nazareth, 27 to a virgin betrothed to a man whose name was Joseph, of the house of David; and the virgin's name was Mary. 28 And he came to her and said, "Hail, O favored one, the Lord is with you!"

This time the angel visits Mary with the news that she has been chosen for beginning this intervention. Her special commission is to bring Jesus, "son of the Most High, son of God" [1:32] into the world. She humbly receives this task, and this acceptance now reverberates throughout the rest of her life in profound ways.

Mary's answer sets her apart from Zechariah. A door stood before both of them; one willingly opens it to the divine messenger, the other fearfully blocks it. One welcomes the new age, the other clings to the past.

Her yes to Gabriel will only gradually dawn upon her with its consequences. Occasionally in these early episodes, you will learn of her private musings. It was quite a load for a girl on the verge of adulthood to carry, so here and there I allude to her puzzlement about her son and his destiny. Advance publicity (like advertising) entices but rarely explains the details.

Before I take leave of this visitation, note what the angel recognized about this "virgin": "The Lord is with you." Gabriel sums up the whole covenant promise that the Almighty chooses and allies with Israel, and he bequeaths it to Mary. "How can this be," we might echo with Mary, that an entire people (the Jews) is epitomized in one woman? Where previous generations and representative individuals had faltered, this solitary and simple girl by her response would bear the mantle of the covenant partner.

Of course, a deeper matter is the role of the son she was to bear, so take some time to reread what Gabriel says about her child. The mission of Mary will unfold first in my narrative, and then Jesus's will come later—one subtly bearing the responsibilities of Israel on her willing shoulders, the other dominantly executing the responsibilities of God. In my narrative, Mary's would take up less space—for you have the whole of the Jewish Scriptures to ponder her place as the "virgin" daughter of Israel.[5]

1. Think of unlikely heroes that might be similar to Mary. How do such people inspire? How do they give me hope for my own tasks?

2. What is my view of Mary? In other words, how do I describe her role in salvation history? How might she be a source of hope for me?

Visitation Three: "Blessed" Mary Comes to Elizabeth

Luke 1:39–45 In those days Mary arose and went with haste into the hill country, to a city of Judah, 40 and she entered the house of Zechariah and greeted Elizabeth. 41 And when Elizabeth heard the greeting of Mary, the babe leaped in her womb; and Elizabeth was filled with the Holy Spirit 42 and she exclaimed with a loud cry, "Blessed are you among women, and blessed is the fruit of your womb! 43 And why is this granted me, that the mother of my Lord should come to me? 44 For behold, when the voice of your greeting came to my ears, the babe in my womb leaped for joy. 45 And blessed is she who believed that there would be a fulfilment of what was spoken to her from the Lord."

This visitation causes us once again to ponder who this woman Mary is. On one level, the story seems to be unadorned and charmingly human: cousins of widely different ages reach out to each other in their pregnancies. Mary's child is a treasure held furtively in her womb, and she is the much younger one. Her aim in this visit shows support and secret solidarity with her elder relative. Dare she tell Elizabeth what happened?

---

5. For a sense of what I mean by "virgin" daughter of Israel, see such Jewish Scriptures as 2 Kgs 19:21 [Isa 37:22], Ps 9:14, Isa 1:8, 62:11; Zeph 3:14; Zech 2:10, 9:9.

FIGURE 2: *Mary & Elizabeth Meet* (by Jamie Treadwell)

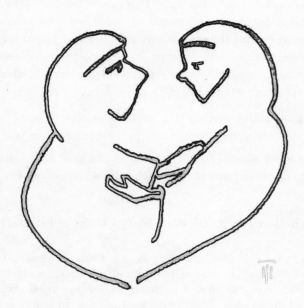

On another level, the story reveals more than meets the eye—unless you mean the gaze of women's intuition. What should we draw out from this feminine encounter? Elizabeth has no need for Mary to say anything, for she already knows. The babe within her has already informed her. Mary's gesture of service and solidarity to her elder abruptly pivots into Elizabeth's veneration of Mary! Twice in her greeting she calls her cousin "blessed," but notice that she uses two different words in my Greek account: The first [1:42] is *eulogēmenē* (εὐλογημένη), a word attributed mainly to God (Jesus?); while the second [1:45] is *makaria* (μακαρία), a word attributed mainly to human beings (Mary?). In between these statements, she recognizes that this pregnancy has transformed Mary, and now her kinswoman Mary represents a status she is unworthy to receive. Even the infant within Elizabeth starts to perform according to the news that this visitation brings. What is Mary's rank now? Who is really visiting—a darling girl or a virgin overshadowed by the divine, "mother of my Lord"? Whatever the case, a divine alert registers with both women that something remarkable is going to happen.

1. Have I ever had an experience of intuition, knowing something without having been told?

2. How does Elizabeth help me to recognize divine prerogatives which do not center on me? How might it guide me in relating to those younger or newer than I?

3. Again, reflect on the identity of Mary. How do I describe her in this episode?

Centerpiece: Zechariah's Prophetic Speech about "Visitation"

Luke 1:68–79 "Blessed be the Lord God of Israel, for he has visited and redeemed his people, 69 and has raised up a horn of salvation for us in the house of his servant David, 70 as he spoke by the mouth of his holy prophets from of old, 71 that we should be saved from our enemies, and from the hand of all who hate us; 72 to perform the mercy promised to our fathers, and to remember his holy covenant, 73 the oath which he swore to our father Abraham, 74 to grant us that we, being delivered from the hand of our enemies, might serve him without fear, 75 in holiness and righteousness before him all the days of our life. 76 And you, child, will be called the prophet of the Most High; for you will go before the Lord to prepare his ways, 77 to give knowledge of salvation to his people in the forgiveness of their sins, 78 through the tender mercy of our God, when the day shall dawn upon us from on high 79 to give light to those who sit in darkness and in the shadow of death, to guide our feet into the way of peace."

This is the fourth episode, not a visitation per se, but the centerpiece for the whole divine publicity campaign. Here you find the central message, the meaning behind all of the interventions before the arrival of Jesus on the public stage. While the rest of the world is oblivious, Zechariah realizes that supernatural forces are at work. God is bringing about the dawning of a new day for Israel and for the whole world.

Zechariah makes his statement here as a prophetic interpretation of the events I have laid out as visitations. We are seeing, according to him, an infusion of God's "tender mercy" (σπλάγχνα ἐλέους, *splanchna eleous* [1:78]) upon those who live by the "holy covenant." The Greek words here reflect a visceral dimension to mercy, for it reflects a native expression tied to deep-seated compassion, often physically associated with a mother's womb.[6] God's mercy, in other words, patterns the pregnancies

6. The Hebrew root is *rakham*.

of these women. If you know Hebrew, Theophilus, you would catch the pun in the prophecy—like a slogan in an advertisement promoting an upcoming Roman circus. I know enough Hebrew at least to identify the code when I see it.

Beware of glossing over the obscure Greek Zechariah uses when he says, "The day shall dawn upon us from on high." In fact, the words might be translated, "when the dawn from the heights shall visit us" (ἐν οἷς ἐπισκέψεται ἡμᾶς ἀνατολὴ ἐξ ὕψους; *en hois episkepsetai hēmas anatolē ex hypsous* [1:78]). Since Zechariah knows that the birth of Jesus is coming, he means that this event is like the rising of the morning star in a darkened sky, or the first light generated out of the utter blackness. Others might translate it "dayspring," as if it is that first glimmer giving full day its beginning. In case you don't recognize it, Theophilus, Zechariah is citing an ancient phrase, which cryptically reads as follows: "Out of the womb of the morning, like dew, your youth will come to you" (Ps 110:3). For many of us, this is a line announcing the arrival of the Messiah of Israel. Thus, we are brought back to the advance publicity—the visitations before the arrival—connected to the child of Mary and the child of Elizabeth, still in the wombs of both women.

Zechariah encourages us to imagine that this glimmer is irreversibly radiating out into the darkened world. So he prophesies about "those who sit in darkness" [1:79], most likely meaning those furthest from enlightenment, the Gentiles. You should consider the ancient prophecies of Israel's prophet Isaiah, for example, for they speak of the bursting forth of divine light to give understanding and hope to the nations.[7]

Then Zechariah says that it will be a dawn for those who sit "in the shadow of death" [1:79]; that is, those who have hateful and hostile forces to contend with, not merely worldly ignorance or human limitations. Death waits for us all, Theophilus. The darkness of all the forces confronting the world reminds us of the chaotic void dispelled by the visitation of light on the first day. We will run into such superhuman opposition in the pages ahead.

In fact, these notions of darkness and death spell out our current crisis. We are well acquainted with governors and generals who pay visits to inspect and scrutinize their lands and peoples. They expect due submission from their subjects. Oh, they promise "salvation," but not through "tender mercy"; rather, they come with martial law and brute force. This

---

7. See Isa 60:13, for example.

is the kind of advance publicity (imperial propaganda) that puts fear into our hearts. Thus Zechariah's prophecy is all the more poignant in its appeal: this visitation will deliver us "from the hands of their enemies" that we can "serve him ['the Lord God of Israel'] *without fear*" [1:74]. This is a new twist on what we know about visitations. Some have proven to be allied with the shadow of death, but this one with tender mercy.

This "dayspring" then will deal with enemies who cause hardship and heartache for "Israel," and this godly force of the "Most High" will "guide our feet into the way of peace" [1:79]. In other words, Zechariah's subtle suggestion is that the coming of Jesus into the world installs an alternative kingdom to the Roman Empire. "Peace" here is analogous to the native word *shalom* and Latin translation *pax*—that is, something like prosperity and the ability to live "in holiness and righteousness before him [the new ruler] all the days of our lives." The Romans tell us about their visitations in the vocabulary of wars, monuments, and propaganda, but God testifies to his through ancient Scriptures and sage interpreters.

The principles of Zechariah's poetics emanate through all the episodes I have arranged in my account. They apply to Gabriel, standing like the morning star that announces dawn. They apply to Mary and Elizabeth, offering their pregnancies like the promise of a new day. You will see they manifestly apply to Jesus, whose humble birth and infancy surreptitiously banish the old order of death and signal a rejuvenated (literally a "re-youthed") order for the world. Who can put a boundary on such prophecy once unleashed? In my arrangement of these events surrounding Jesus, Zechariah's prophecy is the capstone for the entire preface—summing up the first three visitations and foreshadowing three more to come.

1. What darkness am I struggling with which requires the light of God?

2. What might be an example of visitations—either natural or supernatural, human or supernatural—that would betoken severe judgment?

3. Compare the rhetoric of politicians and political systems to the reign of God promised in this passage. What are the similarities and dissimilarities?

4. Who am I more like, Mary or Zechariah, when it comes to accepting God's will? Why?

Visitation Four: Heavenly "Hosts" Come to Shepherds

> Luke 2:9–15 And an angel of the Lord appeared to them, and
> the glory of the Lord shone around them, and they were filled
> with fear. 10 And the angel said to them, "Be not afraid; for be-
> hold, I bring you good news of a great joy which will come to
> all the people; 11 for to you is born this day in the city of David
> a Savior, who is Christ the Lord. 12 And this will be a sign for
> you: you will find a babe wrapped in swaddling cloths and lying
> in a manger." 13 And suddenly there was with the angel a multi-
> tude of the heavenly host praising God and saying, 14 "Glory to
> God in the highest, and on earth peace among men with whom
> he is pleased!" 15 When the angels went away from them into
> heaven, the shepherds said to one another, "Let us go over to
> Bethlehem and see this thing that has happened, which the Lord
> has made known to us."

The dayspring continues, now wondrously shining upon men of the
field tending sheep. Why these rustic souls? Then again, why Mary? The
story I tell can only peel away the layers surrounding the paradoxical
ways that the Almighty chooses. (You will hear this point often in the
early going of these *Memoirs*, Theophilus!) Angels witness such mysteries
firsthand, but only report what their commission allows. I count myself
but a small link in the chain of this divine promotion. Thus, an angel—
was it Gabriel again?—visits them with news of an unheard-of event: a
"Savior" of the kind that monuments and inscriptions publicize has come
as the Jewish Messiah. By worldly standards, a strange Savior—though
in accord with the visitations surrounding him, a Messiah born in lowly
surroundings—who turns the tables yet again. Now he invites the likes of
these rustics to pay *him* a visit.

Yet in a way that appeals to the strange logic of divine communication, these are precisely the guests one would expect for an audience "in
the city of David." Who was David but a shepherd, called to be king, from
whom all the kings of Israel referred to themselves as shepherd kings? If
they did not reign as they ought in biblical history, perhaps the humble
trappings of this babe would be a "sign" [2:12] of something unparalleled
that shepherds in the Judean fields could recognize.

Suddenly the world of death and darkness is transformed by the
presence of a "heavenly host" [2:13] in song and celebration. Who is this
"host"? Look up to the stars, Theophilus, and let your imagination free
to hear the voices of these witnesses, animated lights in the sky, all with

names and roles that we cannot fathom. They are full of good cheer that what Caesar could only dream of—universal and complete peace and prosperity (*shalom*)—now has slipped in unobserved by Roman legions and pompous processions. No royal entourage, no assembled court; just a tumbledown hut and its admiring stockyard animals! How laughable that bumpkins and babblers—what the Scriptures call babes and infants—should be the first to see the day dawn! Only you and I—and the angels—can appreciate their mirth!

1. Describe instances where unlikely characters or situations have disclosed profound answers or solutions unexpectedly.

2. Do I see any parallels of instances today where the humble and lowly are vindicated or victorious? Think of films or sports, for example. How did their triumph make me feel?

Visitation Five: Infant Jesus Comes to Simeon and Anna

Luke 2:22–38 And when the time came for their purification according to the law of Moses, they brought him up to Jerusalem to present him to the Lord 23 (as it is written in the law of the Lord, "Every male that opens the womb shall be called holy to the Lord") 24 and to offer a sacrifice according to what is said in the law of the Lord, "a pair of turtledoves, or two young pigeons." 25 Now there was a man in Jerusalem, whose name was Simeon, and this man was righteous and devout, looking for the consolation of Israel, and the Holy Spirit was upon him. 26 And it had been revealed to him by the Holy Spirit that he should not see death before he had seen the Lord's Christ. 27 And inspired by the Spirit he came into the temple; and when the parents brought in the child Jesus, to do for him according to the custom of the law, 28 he took him up in his arms and blessed God and said, 29 "Lord, now lettest thou thy servant depart in peace, according to thy word; 30 for mine eyes have seen thy salvation 31 which thou hast prepared in the presence of all peoples, 32 a light for revelation to the Gentiles, and for glory to thy people Israel." 33 And his father and his mother marveled at what was said about him; 34 and Simeon blessed them and said to Mary his mother, "Behold, this child is set for the fall and rising of many in Israel, and for a sign that is spoken against 35 (and a sword will pierce through your own soul also), that thoughts out of many hearts may be revealed." 36 And there was a prophetess,

> Anna, the daughter of Phanuel, of the tribe of Asher; she was
> of a great age, having lived with her husband seven years from
> her virginity, 37 and as a widow till she was eighty-four. She did
> not depart from the temple, worshiping with fasting and prayer
> night and day. 38 And coming up at that very hour she gave
> thanks to God, and spoke of him to all who were looking for the
> redemption of Jerusalem.

Visitation comes to Simeon and Anna. Just as Zechariah and Elizabeth tell us about Israel of old, so Simeon and Anna speak something
new about Israel. These two people hang out in the precincts of the
temple and hope for divine intervention to come to Israel. What can I say
about the groups they represent, those who gravitate around Jerusalem?
Both of them seem to have renounced family and life pursuits to focus
on prayer and devotions in the temple. Yet they are not official priests or
institutional functionaries, so far as I know. Rather, they are like seeds,
long dormant, now sprouting in the light of this appointed dawn. Unaware of the timing of their visit, Mary and her husband Joseph travel to
the temple to dispense with the customary "purification" rites to bring
closure to the child-bearing process. Simeon and Anna recognize that
Jesus is a "presentation" to God on behalf of the people of Israel and a
visitation of favor to the garden of Israel. They long have waited for this
change of the spiritual season.

Consider, Theophilus, what Simeon and Anna represent in this visitation. First, neither person owns or claims anything much by worldly
measures or recognized rights. They only arrive on the scene exactly
when the presentation of Jesus occurs. Whatever their former status or
role, now they are mainly recipients. Are they representing God? Israel?
By what right? Yet, Simeon holds the baby easily in his arms as if the presentation were to him. Yes, for one ecstatic moment, whoever this little
one represents is *in his charge*—yet Simeon is neither biological parent,
nor divine agent. In this instant, he realizes the meaning of his name,
"God has heard." Soon thereafter, Anna, whose name means "grace," joins
with this blessed "accident," an intersection of God and Israel.

Secondly, though Simeon and Anna own nothing, they both have
paid everything for this moment. Anna's life, for example, has revolved
around the temple for some sixty years, without husband or natural support, a celibate who has spent herself in prayer and fasting. Simeon has
waited until death approaches for the fulfillment of an oracle he heard
long ago. Both are like many Jewish devotees of that generation, living in

consecration and vigilance, focusing on the Jerusalem and the temple for defining their existence. Renouncing family and possessions, Simeon and Anna receive the presentation of Jesus.

Thirdly, this visitation once again promises consolation to Israel, no matter the oppressive circumstances that bedraggle its plight. How? These two representatives express faithfulness to the covenant and the assurance that happy retribution awaits them both. The garden of Israel is already sprouting blossoms as the dawn brightens. Simeon's and Anna's lives resonate deeply with the ancient proverb that desire fulfilled is sweetness to receiving souls and a tree of life for everyone around them.[8]

Finally, what is the "presentation" but an expression that the child himself is dedicated to the same life that we see here in these seers and saints? Jesus himself will similarly experience how the dispossession of self will result in the payment of everything to fulfill the divine plan.

So I raise the question: who is being presented here? Is it not also Israel and the human race, as summed up in the actors so far: Zechariah and Elizabeth—the past; Simeon and Anna—the present; Jesus—the future who will summon a full response from Israel first and then from all the Gentiles? All are offered up to God who rightly owns all things and calls everyone into submission.

1. Make an inventory of things that are precious to me. How easily can I let them go? How much have I given ground to a sense of ownership and control of things that are valuable to me?

2. Imagine letting everything that matters (job, recognitions, family, social status, possessions) go now. How much do I grieve their loss?

3. Pray for Anna's "grace" to let it all go, for her joy and freedom that she has found in a life of self-abandon. Or perhaps even more to the point: pray for Anna's *self-realization* that fame, wealth, and power are both deceiving and futile.

4. Is it possible to maintain hope when nothing positive seems to be happening? How? How does Simeon ("listening") give us a clue? How much do I listen to the Lord? How much do I listen to other sources?

---

8. I am citing another Jewish Scripture passage here: Prov 13:12, 19.

Ode to Simeon and Anna

Simeon, Simeon, how the world looks at you askance,
You don't catch our ear now, so why pay you a glance?
Our ear is not tuned, our eyes do not observe,
Our mind is not planted, our path is a-swerve.

Anna, Anna, I think only of pity:
How many are like you,
How many in this city?
They beg for what they cannot attain,
They seek for a sojourner's smile,
They stand all alone in the gate,
While strangers gawk and revile.

Come in, come near, O friends of God,
Come in, come here to share your news,
Come in and bolster those drained of hope;
Come in, come near to share your views.

A child is here, a joy is found:
Lift him up in your arms and heart.
A hope for Israel now is known,
For prophets, a fresh new start.

Visitation Six: Child Jesus Comes to the Temple— A Visitation to Us

Luke 2:41–52 Now his parents went to Jerusalem every year at
the feast of the Passover. 42 And when he was twelve years old,
they went up according to custom; 43 and when the feast was
ended, as they were returning, the boy Jesus stayed behind in
Jerusalem. His parents did not know it, 44 but supposing him
to be in the company they went a day's journey, and they sought
him among their kinsfolk and acquaintances; 45 and when they
did not find him, they returned to Jerusalem, seeking him. 46
After three days they found him in the temple, sitting among
the teachers, listening to them and asking them questions; 47

and all who heard him were amazed at his understanding and
his answers. 48 And when they saw him they were astonished;
and his mother said to him, "Son, why have you treated us so?
Behold, your father and I have been looking for you anxiously."
49 And he said to them, "How is it that you sought me? Did you
not know that I must be in my Father's house?" 50 And they did
not understand the saying which he spoke to them. 51 And he
went down with them and came to Nazareth, and was obedient
to them; and his mother kept all these things in her heart. 52
And Jesus increased in wisdom and in stature, and in favor with
God and man.

I gather fragments of evidence for this final visitation from a
mother's perspective. Mary, like most mothers, studied the contours of
her son's behavior and figured she knew Jesus well enough to predict his
steps. In this case, a pilgrimage journey to Jerusalem, she was quite mistaken. For one thing, she missed his appetite for learning. Certainly, her
son had to walk and talk and so on, like every child growing up. But to
seek out sages and scribes at the temple—to learn as a scholar—well, this
was something she did not expect!

Here he was, seated among the learned ones in the temple. Was he
debating? Was he speculating? Clearly the resident teachers viewed him
as a savant, at the very least a precocious lad of bar mitzvah age,[9] but
immensely older by insight and wisdom. His questions and answers were
as good as any past sage, whose wisdom was passed down to those who
were now gathered in the temple precincts.

She also discovered his independence. He seemingly dismissed her
anxieties, almost as if they missed the mark: did he not have to be immersed in things (not "house") of the Father [*tois tou patros*, τοῖς τοῦ
πατρός (2:49)]?

This responsibility was so pressing that it caused him to disregard
his natural urges for food and shelter, his emotional desire to stay close to
his earthly parents. What focus, what alertness of mind and discipline of
body did this boy show! Did he even notice he was without these natural
things? He knew his priorities were to be absorbed in the Scriptures, in
the debates, in the contemplation of the sages. These are the things of his
Father—not the things you or I or his mother could have imagined.

---

9. The time when a Jewish boy starts bearing his share of the adults' duties and
responsibilities. A "bar mitzvah" is the public ceremony marking this occasion.

This visitation to the temple laid down a pattern for us: Do we understand such a preoccupation? Why not? Why would we not be ready to set aside our three days of human dependence to rely totally on our heavenly Father? When will we do our bar mitzvah and pursue our Father's duties and responsibilities? If Jesus was on loan to his earthly parents, are we not on loan as well? Instead, we identify with Mary and Joseph who know so little about Jesus and the Father's business. Yet Jesus will slip out of our control, out of our sight often. Then along with his parents we will have to journey back to Jerusalem, our first and last destination as a follower of Jesus. When will we join Jesus, once and for all, on pilgrimage and focused on the pilgrim's priorities? Add up all these divine visitations, Theophilus, and we should be vigilant for what is ahead in the life and mission of Jesus.

Luke's Pilgrimage

I once started on my journey of life,
And got sidetracked on the way,
Slightly taken off a course that I had charted—
Or someone charted for me, I can't remember why.
And now I find myself absorbed in something
I never anticipated, and even now do not grasp;
Rather it has grasped me, or he has done so!
No one around me has a calling like mine,
So I spend myself on living in between two things:
The journey my life and affections naturally urge,
And the pilgrimage that has captured my soul.

1. Have I ever been so fixated on something that I lost track of time, obligation, and even sleep or meals? Give examples. Were they noble things—or were they a waste of my attention and resources?

2. Does the example of Jesus inspire me to take a risk or do something that defies people's expectations of me?

3. What would be "my Father's things" in my life? What would I give up or set aside right now to be among these things?

4. A pilgrimage is a setting aside of daily routine to figure out what God's "things" are for me to do. How can I take a pilgrimage now to get to the core of my spiritual Father's duties or orders?

5. Describe such a past time of soul-searching when I devoted myself to figuring out my priorities, either personal or spiritual.

Part Two: Jesus Auditions

Prelude, Scene One

Luke 3:1–6 In the fifteenth year of the reign of Tiberius Caesar, Pontius Pilate being governor of Judea, and Herod being tetrarch of Galilee, and his brother Philip tetrarch of the region of Ituraea and Trachonitis, and Lysanias tetrarch of Abilene, 2 in the high-priesthood of Annas and Caiaphas, the word of God came to John the son of Zechariah in the wilderness; 3 and he went into all the region about the Jordan, preaching a baptism of repentance for the forgiveness of sins. 4 As it is written in the book of the words of Isaiah the prophet, "The voice of one crying in the wilderness: Prepare the way of the Lord, make his paths straight. 5 Every valley shall be filled, and every mountain and hill shall be brought low, and the crooked shall be made straight, and the rough ways shall be made smooth; 6 and all flesh shall see the salvation of God."

For a brief moment, Theophilus, let us take a step back to see the worldly panorama with its famous persons and places: Caesar and his henchmen, the temple and its upper-crust custodians, the heady forces that threaten to pull us away from the homespun details that I have compiled so far. Take a hard look at what seems to be our bearing, the coordinates of our location on the map of human history. Focus on what will happen next, for it will build on the rather humble characters and out-of-the-way events sketched so far. Eventually we'll march onto the world stage—though it may require that you pick up my sequel *Memoirs of an Unfinished Tale*, where you take the baton of the mission.

First, a glance at our humble beginning: emerging from the details—almost like a desert shrub out of native soil—is Zechariah's son John. His rhetoric sounds megalomaniacal after you have seen Caesar or his cronies in imperial posts. His speeches warn of invasion, his demands clamor for complete surrender. You would laugh if you had not seen his stern face, for his gaunt profile and his native audience are but as beggars on the world stage. The desert he makes his throne rooms, small-fry and nobodies his subjects, and his rank more of a crank than a conqueror.

Still he soldiers on, as if he were a scout preparing the way for a military onslaught, requisitioning food, building bridges, straightening out highways and the like, so that the arriving army can focus on setting up a new order of government. Each town and each citizen must surrender if the residents are not thought to be the resistance.

Here is my question for you, Theophilus: What is our focus as we evaluate what is going on in the world? The big events that the Roman world pays attention to? Or am I alert to the surprisingly smaller things out of which biblical visitations come? Both make stringent demands, but one (the spiritual order) I can ignore for now because it treads lightly at first; the other (the worldly order) comes with loud boasts and bearing, with its force and fury demanding our attention. Yet here is this son of Zechariah, John, whose unvarnished voice from the wilderness beckons us to a turn-around, to consider the path less traveled. This other path promises astonishing visitations, and the traveler will see its hills leveling out and its valleys rising up. Here is where the Kingdom of God arrives, while the route Caesar takes will only eventually self-destruct, leaving its corpses and battlefield casualties.

1. How would I describe John in this passage? Are there people today that I might compare to him?

2. What might constitute a path I should consider though few take it? What are the fears I have in considering this path?

3. Give examples of a "voice crying out in the wilderness." Have I ever taken a stand that went against the flow of opinions around me? If not, should I have at some point in my life? How did I (or would I) cope when I seem to be so alone and outnumbered?

Prelude: Scene Two

Luke 3:7–18 He said therefore to the multitudes that came out to be baptized by him, "You brood of vipers! Who warned you to flee from the wrath to come? 8 Bear fruits that befit repentance, and do not begin to say to yourselves, 'We have Abraham as our father'; for I tell you, God is able from these stones to raise up children to Abraham. 9 Even now the axe is laid to the root of the trees; every tree therefore that does not bear good fruit is cut down and thrown into the fire."

15 As the people were in expectation, and all men questioned in their hearts concerning John, whether perhaps he were the Christ, 16 John answered them all, "I baptize you with water; but he who is mightier than I is coming, the thong of whose sandals I am not worthy to untie; he will baptize you with the Holy Spirit and with fire. 17 His winnowing fork is in his hand, to clear his threshing floor, and to gather the wheat into his granary, but the chaff he will burn with unquenchable fire."

18 So, with many other exhortations, he preached good news to the people.

John spoke as though he were driven by forces of another world, soon to invade this current one. While you and I might be tempted to take him as a nuisance who camps out in our public spaces to tell everyone about society's follies (think Socrates), for the Jews he represented something like one of their prophets of old—an Elijah or Jeremiah. As I mentioned above, there were more than a few of these vigilant devotees (like Anna and Simeon above), some of whom had attracted attention.

John more than the others struck a nerve among his people. Different ranks of them started flocking out to him to hear his critique of the times. He seemed to compare his contemporaries to the generation of Sodom and Gomorrah [Gen 19:1–29]. You may remember how the fire of God's wrath rained down on those two legendary cities. But unlike the select few who were rescued out of the flames by the pleading of Abraham, the patriarch, John let no one off the hook when he preached: all seemed bound for condemnation. This generation would not escape harm's way, the way John saw it. Connections to Abraham now would be of no help, but only solid proofs of a reformed life.

I originally reported on three groups who came out to John: the general crowd, soldiers, and tax collectors, so have a look at the lines I omitted [3:10–14]. To all of them, John does not issue high-brow philosophies or radical politics. Rather he gives down-to-earth commands that people "in the system" can gain God's approval: For example, the well-to-do listeners are to share from their material resources, like food and clothing.

The soldiers are to avoid abusive behavior, false accusation, and extortion in their use of force. He also tells them to be content, not to give in to the lust for something that they probably could get if they used violence. Note, Theophilus, he does not tell them to cease from their military duties and from force altogether! The third group, the hated tax collectors, are to collect only as much as they are allowed; that is, they are not to gouge. He does not argue that Rome has no right to collect taxes. As you pick up from my original report, John was no political revolutionary.

It was John's raw intensity that led to whispers about whether he might be the Messiah and not simply the messenger (as he claimed). After all, the crowds thought, if the Messiah would lead the invasion John was warning about, who better than John to speak with such authority and charisma?

His answer was simple: No, he could not even measure up to the most menial of duties for this "coming" one. John would be glad to be at the feet of the Messiah. If only he could help his master with his sandals! His role was to initiate his audience to the Messiah's following through a rite of passage involving water ("baptism:" perhaps simulating a new birth, perhaps a cleansing—he did not say), but the "coming" one would bring decisive change with true spirituality and "fire" [3:16].

I wonder what John meant by fire. Was it the wholesale disaster that struck Sodom and Gomorrah with total destruction? Was it flames that only burned the chaff, the dross, of some desired material? Notice the word I use for this fire: *asbestos* (ἄσβεστος). This word should remind you of the fire that Moses encountered in the wilderness of Horeb, the bush that was on fire without being consumed [Exod 3:1–6]. At any rate, the Coming One represents a divine fire, perhaps consuming the impurities but leaving the true stock.

Notice, however, that John's description of this Messiah is not someone who is meek and mild. Rather this figure stands at the door of John's generation with a pitchfork ready for action. The good grain he winnows will go into the storage barn, but the husks and chaff will go into the fire. Let us hope that the fire accomplishes both ends of the images I have just interpreted, destruction and purification.

1. Can I think of anyone who is able to attract a following with viewpoints that depart from the public consensus? Why would or should anyone listen to such a contrarian?

2. Is there anyone like John (the Baptist) in my life? After listening to this person, did I change my ways?

3. How does John challenge my ethics and conduct? How does he challenge my image of Jesus?

Jesus Auditions: Part One

Luke 3:21–22 Now when all the people were baptized, and when Jesus also had been baptized and was praying, the heaven was opened, 22 and the Holy Spirit descended upon him in bodily form, as a dove, and a voice came from heaven, "Thou art my beloved Son; with thee I am well pleased."

The coming attraction the visitations had advertised joined John and Jesus together in a debut of divine performance. You may have noticed how I arranged the episodes so far, something like choreography: first, the introduction of John's mother Elizabeth, then Jesus's mother Mary. Then came the birth of John, followed by the birth of Jesus. First, the description of the activity of John, and now—in this scene—the focus settles on Jesus. I urge you to return to the entire narrative and re-read it as a theatrical script.

See the anonymous crowds melt away as they approach their baptism; but Jesus all of a sudden emerges from among them and steals our attention. Even John melts away, as if he were already locked up in the darkness of Herod's dungeon. And Jesus's baptism happens as if by itself—my Greek, you will notice, slips into the passive voice.[10] Is it all staged? By whom? What are we supposed to see?

Jesus is solitary among the throngs. His baptism is different than the others and changes everything. John and his preaching join the past age alongside Zechariah and his ancestors, and we sense that the baptism of Jesus sums up everything of the past.

Jesus, as if by himself he inaugurates a new order of the ages. And he and new age are the subjects of the rest of my narrative. What happens next is what you and I would call an "epiphany," denoting the arrival of an *imperator* (conqueror) who had sent out advance messengers (like John) to make demands. At epiphanies you and I know, Theophilus, Caesar

10. I am glad that you know Greek, Theophilus. Thus, you can see that I use a genitive absolute, a clause that is subordinate and independent of the previous episode when I describe the event of the baptism.

comes to demand accountability or tribute. I have also heard the coming of Jesus compared to a "theophany" (god-appearance) because of what happens in this episode.

First, note the sanctity of the moment. Jesus, aware of some impending climax, prepares by offering prayer. He is no mere container of divine favor but an active participant. Notice that at all critical moments in the days ahead, prayer is the starting place for any initiative on the part of Jesus.[11] The fact that he prays signals his own commitment to whatever role is required of him.

Second, "the heaven was opened" upon him. That beam of light shining on the first day, that dayspring that Zechariah had prophesied, now dawns on this man. Is it the beginning of a new age?

Third, if we classify this moment as a "theophany," here is why: "the Holy Spirit descended upon him in bodily form, as a dove." A dove—and not a demon (δαίμων, *daimōn*), Theophilus. For you and I both have seen other "spirit-possessions," where the one invaded must endure violence and bizarre behaviors like self-gashing, raving, trances, or ecstasies. Yet this Spirit is gentle, and Jesus is in control. With the appearance of Jesus, the Spirit is docile and mild even if its presence seems like a surge of power.[12] This Spirit came in "bodily form," Theophilus, meaning that it really happened—it was no hallucination or vision.

Fourth, the signature for this climactic event comes in the declaration from the heavens—perhaps as divine recognition of the identity of Jesus, perhaps as a response to Jesus's own prayer. What does the voice say but what I have been suggesting poorly all along: Jesus is the divinely commissioned Son, separated and solitary from the rest of mortal beings, recipient of God's care and attention like no other man.

I intentionally sketch things out in roughest of detail, leaving the whole matter for you to ponder. My sources reported the whole thing almost as a flashback, and this baptism begs massive questions for us to consider. That is my immediate next task, to explore the riddles that surround this specially chosen Son.

11. Jesus prays to heal others (5:16), before choosing the apostles (6:12), when he predicts his imminent suffering and death (9:18), at his transfiguration (9:28–29), before teaching his disciples how to pray (11:1–2), and at the end of his public agenda (22:46). All these events are coming up, so keep in mind how important prayer is if I neglect to mention it later.

12. For example, look at what I had to say about the descent of the Holy Spirit on the first generation of disciples, the Twelve, in *Unfinished Tale*, 9–12.

1. How do I approach life transitions? Do I mark them with preparatory prayer and periods of reflection? Should I? Should I take time
   to pause from daily routines and take retreats?

2. How do I live in light of the new age that Jesus brings? How is his
   baptism a model for mine?

3. Consider how the Holy Spirit comes to Jesus. Does Luke's description appeal to me? Why or why not? How do I experience the Spirit
   coming upon me? Where is evidence of the Spirit's activity in my
   life?

4. What do I think the purpose of baptizing Jesus was? How does his
   baptism help me to understand my own identity? What does the
   divine declaration say to me about him? Does it speak to me?

Jesus Auditions: Part Two

> Luke 3:23–38 Jesus, when he began his ministry, was about
> thirty years of age, being the son (as was supposed) of Joseph,
> the son of Heli, . . . 36 the son of Cainan, the son of Arphaxad,
> the son of Shem, the son of Noah, the son of Lamech, 37 the
> son of Methuselah, the son of Enoch, the son of Jared, the son
> of Mahalaleel, the son of Cainan, 38 the son of Enos, the son of
> Seth, the son of Adam, the son of God.

I will only recount a snippet of what I learned about this man's origins, his family line, his pedigree, his heritage. What I learned made me
pause and rehearse the baptism and its theophanic signals in my mind. It
dawned on me that what I described as his baptism was in fact the divine
recognition of Jesus as Adam. The genealogy I list above may seem far-
fetched, but I believe that the claims it makes fit the way I tell the story
of Jesus.

As I say above in "Jesus's Audition: Part One," the man Jesus
emerged from the crowd—from the anonymity of the human race, as it
were—separated and alone as if everyone were witnessing a new model
for the human race, a new Adam. And the Spirit came "bodily" upon
him, as if to re-embody this new model of Adam. The voice from heaven
designated him as a second Adam, a Son that pleased him in contrast
to a son that rebelled. This voice carried with it a deposit of truth that

commissioned—perhaps "ordained?"—Jesus with his identity. He now would live out what Adam was supposed to do all along.

Details before and surrounding his birth were unquestionably auspicious, what I called above divine publicity; but the baptism was revelatory and propitious, effectively inviting Israel and the whole human race to consider Jesus and his mission. Yes, think of the baptism as an audition that promises to sweep us all off our feet at Jesus's upcoming performance. The spotlight will largely rest on Jesus; the show is about to begin.

1. What decisions and events in my life have revealed consequences that only gradually dawn on me? Do I take time to reflect on those consequences? Is it helpful? Why or why not?

2. How do my vocation and career reflect my own background and previous life experiences? Take one significant thing in my life (say a challenge or achievement) and trace it back to its earliest memories. Speculate on even earlier origins than my memories take me. Can I see past generations of my family or ancestors in things I face now?

3. Pray for all the links in the chain of consequences that I have imagined in the first two questions. How do I see the voice or hand of God at every level?

4. How does the image of Jesus as the new Adam give me hope for the new perspectives?

Jesus Auditions: Part Three

Luke 4:1–13 And Jesus, full of the Holy Spirit, returned from the Jordan, and was led by the Spirit 2 for forty days in the wilderness, tempted by the devil. And he ate nothing in those days; and when they were ended, he was hungry. 3 The devil said to him, "If you are the Son of God, command this stone to become bread." 4 And Jesus answered him, "It is written, 'Man shall not live by bread alone.'" 5 And the devil took him up, and showed him all the kingdoms of the world in a moment of time, 6 and said to him, "To you I will give all this authority and their glory; for it has been delivered to me, and I give it to whom I will. 7 If you, then, will worship me, it shall all be yours." 8 And Jesus answered him, "It is written, 'You shall worship the Lord your God, and him only shall you serve.'" 9 And he took him to Jerusalem, and set him on the pinnacle of the temple, and said to him, "If you are the Son of God, throw yourself down from here; 10 for it is written, 'He will give his angels charge of you, to guard you,' 11 and 'On their hands they will bear you up, lest you strike your foot against a stone.'" 12 And Jesus answered him, "It is said, 'You shall not tempt the Lord your God.'" 13 And when the devil had ended every temptation, he departed from him until an opportune time.

From John's covert on the River Jordan, Jesus goes deeper into the wilderness. What does this mean but that he is going deeper into the meaning of his identity now that the baptism has revealed his divine calling?

He is all alone as far as his humanity is concerned. He has no peer or companion with whom he could find home and community—yet not alone in this liminal world of invisible beings and spiritual realities. Jesus had two companions alongside him: the very Spirit that "bodily" came upon him earlier now guides him and consumes his devotion and attention; and the Spirit's nemesis, the devil, accompanies and probes him for weaknesses. It was a forty-day "internship" without any regard for daily life necessities—at least as far as my sources say. Then, afterwards, "he was hungry" [4:2].

It is in this hunger, this concession to the human weakness relegated to Jesus, that the devil issues a series of dares. He will challenge this new Adam, truly a man like any man with flesh, soul, and spirit. The first test plays on the physical, fleshly hunger: bread [4:3–4]. Jesus certainly as Son of God could have done what he wanted with stones. Both stone and bread are quite fleshly objects a physical man deals with. *So,* says the devil, *are you not a new kind of physical man? I dare you to conjure up his powers to take care of your fleshly needs.* The devil might have posed the question about the specimen of a man Jesus represents: *Who are you, after all, if you are not what you do?*

The second dare has to do with soul [4:5–8]: *I dare you to stir up your prestige and power by claiming the kingdoms of the world.* The devil tantalizes him with a vision of worldly power. Jesus was shown the reality of the devil's claim through a flash of revelation, through a "stigma" (στιγμή, *stigmē*). The Greek word points to a tattoo or branding that conveys ownership: once a tattoo is etched, it is permanent and evocative. Yet it is nothing other than an image and a representation, certainly not the whole substance of either the owner or the things possessed. It is a flash that catches the eye and purports to control whatever it marks. The point of this test is clear: the whole extent of what the devil claimed would end up under the control of Jesus. The devil might have posed this question as: *Who are you if you are not what you own and control?*

The third dare seems to pertain to the spirit of Jesus [4:10–11]. *Why not create a spectacle where you throw yourself down from some high point so that everyone could see the angels rescue you?* The fawning public would hail him as "savior" and worship him, and a new religion would be born. This is a reasonable thing to ask Jesus, who in his spirit knows that he is uniquely recognized as Son and worthy of such adulation. Why not make this new appeal to humanity? The devil's final interrogation here seems to be: *Who are you if others do not recognize you?*

Note that each of these dares is an intoxicating mixture of truth and allegation. They would test the mettle of this new Adam by appealing to something that Jesus knew had some basis of fact. Jesus could easily transform the stone into bread; the devil does have some measure of ownership over the world and can display a seductive brand of ownership; Jesus is "the Lord your God," and worthy of worship [4:12].

In addition, he was clearly in his weakest moment as a newly commissioned Adam, hungry. The devil knew this and played upon it. When Jesus finally bests and dismisses the devil, even then the devil did not completely give up. He flies away, but just for the moment. In due time, another critical opportunity (καιρός, *kairos* [4:13]) will arise in the course of Jesus's life. Jesus will be at his low point once again, this time at the end of his life, beginning in the garden of Gethsemane. Another dare will arise from the devil, this time though the spotlight will not be only on Jesus but on his closest disciples—perhaps even on you, Theophilus, as you follow Jesus.

1. What is the time when I am lowest and most susceptible to demonic attack? What is the half-truth that often grabs my attention?

2. What "stigma" of the world is most attractive to me?

3. How do I use (and abuse) Scripture?

4. Can I think of some future "opportune" moment when I will face a severe test? Describe the factors surrounding my vulnerability.

Jesus Auditions: Part Four

> Luke 4:13–15 And when the devil had ended every temptation,
> he departed from him until an opportune time. 14 And Jesus
> returned in the power of the Spirit into Galilee, and a report
> concerning him went out through all the surrounding country.
> 15 And he taught in their synagogues, being glorified by all.

If the devil dared Jesus and failed, these lines report the converse: Jesus now receives recognition for his success at overcoming the devil. The devil is vanquished in his efforts to cast doubt on Jesus's own self-standing as Son of God and to undermine his claim to be accompanied "bodily" by the Spirit. So the devil leaves for now, defeated in these attacks on Jesus's times of vulnerability. The spotlight has revealed no flaw in Jesus's audition, and he is perfectly suited for the drama about to unfold.

What happens next is that Jesus begins to receive the credit he is due. The Spirit is manifestly still with him, causing him to be noticed. In this case, his teaching rouses up recognition. The Greek word for this human praise is telling: "glorified." This word suggests divinity, that the public sees flashes of his supernatural origins on their own terms. That is, the devil asked Jesus to prove himself in a way that satisfied the devil's demands, but here Jesus independently and willingly shows his identity. The people see it and "glorify" him. That is, they participate in the glory of God as it shines out and reflects back to its source. One might imagine it in loftier terms as the procession of the Father toward the Son by the accompaniment of the Holy Spirit.

If we were to consider in the previous passage our moments of weakness and how we might have given in, now I am illustrating the opposite outcome for ourselves. Today, Theophilus, let us pause and meditate on our times of overcoming tests and trials. As one of the Jewish psalms says (Ps 119:63), "Let those who fear you see me rejoice because I have kept your statutes." Let us see the new Adam in his victory and rejoice, and so let us reflect on times when others rejoice at our triumphant moments. When we triumph in this way, it is God who also gets the glory. In our own small way then we participate in the Almighty's life and glow.

1. Recall moments when we know that I have succeeded at some ordeal, either in the natural or supernatural world. How did I show our elation? Did others join me in our triumph? How might such an example model for what Jesus encountered in this passage?

2. How does the passage describe the added power of Jesus due to his success? How might it speak to me when I achieve success in the luminous world of spirituality? What are some examples of victory in my life that allowed me to "return in the power of the Spirit" to my regular life?

CHAPTER TWO

Introduction and Supporting Cast

Introduction

THE WAY FORWARD AFTER such a wondrous beginning is *not* so straightforward, Theophilus. So far you have noticed that divine interventions—no matter how profound or auspicious their meaning—happen
in out-of-the-way places to rather non-glamorous figures. As Jesus now
strides into the world at large, the surprises only continue. We follow
him, Theophilus, ready for a journey with a destination that fellow
travelers could not have imagined. The story, at least the way I tell it,
clings to signposts that are sometimes too high to read, or fascinate like
a mosaic whose artistic design can only be grasped from a distance. The
word to express such interpretations of Jesus's life and deeds is *paradox*
(παραδοξία, *paradoxia*), a word that you encountered in my narrative.
Let us now advance, forewarned, into his hometown of Nazareth and
beyond, ready for twists and turns in the path.

"All Eyes Are Fixed upon Him"

> Luke 4:16 And he came to Nazareth, where he had been brought
> up; and he went to the synagogue, as his custom was, on the
> sabbath day.

Without merely repeating all the details of my original text, let
me recreate the drama of his arrival. Jesus marches into the synagogue

among all his neighbors and acquaintances who are gathering for their village Sabbath observance. By now, he has gained a reputation as a local prodigy, and so his visit stirs up curiosity.

Everyone wants to size him up: "Is Jesus what the reports out of nearby towns claim him to be? Can he really be the same boy that they took for granted all those years? Let's give him a chance to prove himself now by letting him give the public reading for the day (called the "haftarah," the passage from the batch of the writings of the Prophets), and see what he has to say about it."

So at the right time in the service he stands and reads from the scroll of the prophet Isaiah [61:1–2 (Luke 4:18–19)]:

> The Spirit of the Lord is upon me, because he has anointed me
> to preach good news to the poor. He has sent me to proclaim
> release to the captives and recovering of sight to the blind, to set
> at liberty those who are oppressed, to proclaim the acceptable
> year of the Lord.

Then he sits—everyone's eyes glued on him. The reading is over, but his presence lingers. From his seat comes the climax (which I quote again from my narrative): "He began to say, 'Today this scripture has been fulfilled in your hearing'" (4:21).

It was a riveting debut in front of his hometown, a dramatic performance not so much about Isaiah. No, it was in the finale to the reading. Notice I report, "he *began* to say," as if this were the start of his whole public life, his teaching, his mission. The reading is over, but the messianic task begins. *Seated* as a teacher with authority over his subject matter, and *he began to say* something that would not stop until his life was fulfilled.

Let your ears also take in this "*hearing*," Theophilus, because it is not just for his neighbors in Nazareth, but for all of us. The words of the ancient Scriptures come to life in his teaching—not just Isaiah, but all the prophets revered by the Jews. Fix your eyes on him, seated and speaking as if the whole town, the whole country, the whole world had called on him to prophesy, to sit and teach about the divine plan for Israel and for everyone else.

It was a dramatic return to his home, but it did not end well (as I went on to report). Though the expectations for this native son were high, Jesus almost intentionally seemed to dash their hopes for him to be a prodigious benefactor. As his teaching continues, he suggests that God intervenes for the unlikeliest of candidates: Jesus recalls the story of Elijah the prophet helping a Phoenician widow instead of all the other needy "chosen" ones in Israel, then he remembers the prophet Elisha healing a Syrian invader instead of the defeated victims of Judah. I won't quote his words here, but keep both of these stories in mind—the widow and the Gentile soldier—as we follow events in Jesus's life. They will appear again, soon.

Imagine the reaction of his once-captive audience! He has put out any messianic fires earlier stoked: "What, what? How can you tell us this? Do you mean to say you bring no favors to your own home folk?" Adulation turns to adjuration. Quickly the sentiment shifts to rage [4:28–30]. They would have hung him in the Galilean hills if he had not slipped away—almost supernaturally, for as with the encounter with the devil, this was not the moment for the curtain call of Jesus.

A bittersweet overture for the opening scene? We will see this turbulence often in the days ahead, at times his disciples riding a wave of euphoria, at other times crashing against the rocks of rejection. The main theme, again, is that the truths of *paradoxes* are not always recognized or appreciated by the people to whom Jesus came.

1. How would I explain a paradox in my own words? Describe one in my life that teaches reassurance or resilience in spite of its apparent defeat. How does it parallel the experience of Jesus in his homecoming?

2. Reread the chapter that Jesus reads from (Isa 61:1–11). What is the paradox of divine concerns reflected in this passage? Are these concerns *my* concerns? How do I demonstrate it in my life?

3. Imagine myself in the shoes of a resident of Nazareth. What are the grounds that the townspeople might have to be upset? Are they valid? Give some examples of dashed hopes and my reaction to the circumstances surrounding once-promising matters.

A Cycle of Sabbaths (5:17—6:11)

From Nazareth to Capernaum—there are a few details I will leave out in this part of Jesus's debut. Sum it up to say that he moved down the road forty miles or so to the area around Sea of Galilee, where again he showed some miraculous powers. It was here in the lakeside village of Capernaum that he invited some local fishermen (especially Simon Peter, whom you will encounter often both in this work and in *Unfinished Tale*) to accompany him in his wanderings. This area would be his base, from which he would conduct visitations to surrounding synagogues and towns.

His first tour shows the outlines of his general pattern of life. It may sound humdrum to say that Jesus followed regular life routines, but in fact this is critical for you to understand about the man. Jesus spoke "everyman's" language—a simple vocabulary and program to make his points to crowds of common folk. He would keep their schedule, too, meaning attendance at village feasts and weekly events. It was through these popular rhythms and cycles that he would teach about his mission.

You get a sense for this process in this first tour from Capernaum to backcountry settlements in Galilee, the region of his upbringing. Normally his protocol was to speak in a local synagogue, and after the service, he would continue his message about the Kingdom in nearby homes. Then, as night would set in, he would let his hosts go to bed, and he would spend time in the countryside to be alone.

You know that his fellow Jews would follow the weekly cycles that turned on the celebration of the Sabbath, or "Shabbat," the seventh day when the Scriptures speak of rest and reflection on God's word. So you would find that the medium and message of Jesus corresponded to the rubrics of this regular event. Shabbat gave Jesus his pulpit and platform.

We will look at a string of three consecutive Shabbats, the cord that strung together public events, knotted at either end by Jesus in his private world of nighttime meditation.[1] These boundaries of prayer are shrouded in his solitude, but they serve as convenient markers [5:16 and 6:12] for the episodes I will relate below. I begin with "on one of the days" [5:17], which I fancy you may take as "Day One" (after Shabbat One of the cycle ended)—thus Sunday, the first day of the week.

---

1. In these early stages, I have very little idea about what made Jesus "tick," to use the vernacular. His inner musings or private life seemed to fortify something in him, some kind of transaction between him and God. My recollections in these early stages revolve around his participation in festivities and community activities, punctuated by such sessions of prayer. Later you will see indications of his inner state—dare I say, his personal struggles—as it manifested in his outward actions. For these clues and hunches, I rely on the testimony of his closest followers.

Cycle of Sabbaths: Episode One

Luke 5:24–26 "But that you may know that the Son of man has authority on earth to forgive sins"—he said to the man who was paralyzed—"I say to you, rise, take up your bed and go home." 25 And immediately he rose before them, and took up that on which he lay, and went home, glorifying God. And amazement seized them all, and they glorified God and were filled with awe, saying, "We have seen strange things today."

The first episode [5:17–26] is the healing of a man who cannot move himself but depends on others to open up the roof for his placement before Jesus. It is on this occasion that Jesus tells the man that his sins are forgiven, an astounding claim for a mere man to make. The sitting religious experts present, whom you know as the Pharisees, immediately balk at such a notion. For no one has this ability save God—a perfectly reasonable position for any Jew to take. Jesus not only boldly makes his pronouncement, but also takes up a title—"Son of Man" [5:24]—that suits his claim.[2] Then he confirms things: Jesus orders the once paralyzed man to walk away, to go back to his home (mentioned twice)—obviously without the aid of his friends who brought him there.

What is the reaction of the crowd? They are thunderstruck. My vocabulary [5:26] twice uses charged words: "mania" seizes everyone (ἔκστασις ἔλαβεν ἅπαντας, *ekstasis elaben hapantas*); "awe" fills them (ἐπλήσθησαν φόβου, *eplēsthēsan phobou*), and they say that they have just witnessed a "paradox" (εἴδομεν παράδοξα, *eidomen paradoxa*). Thus, the stage is set for breaking categories of conventional expectations and norms. Even the ones who devoutly study the Scriptures and Jewish traditions are overwhelmed by this turn of events. These are not simply prodigies or performances. They require pondering, filled with deeper truths and profound meanings—so, Theophilus, I use that word *paradox* to headline what Jesus represented.

Cycle of Sabbaths: Episode Two

Luke 5:29–32 And Levi made him a great feast in his house; and there was a large company of tax collectors and others sitting at

---

2. I will take up this title gradually as the activities and teachings of Jesus unwind its densely coiled meaning.

table with them. 30 And the Pharisees and their scribes murmured against his disciples, saying, "Why do you eat and drink
with tax collectors and sinners?" 31 And Jesus answered them,
"Those who are well have no need of a physician, but those who
are sick; 32 I have not come to call the righteous, but sinners to
repentance."

The next episode after this story is the calling of Levi,[3] and the
"paradoxes" continue to unfold—this time not in the form of a healed
body but in the form of a changed life. Levi is not one we would expect to
respond to the message of Jesus. He has a high standing in the world of
power and money, for the Romans have deputized him as their client. He
will collect taxes for them; whatever is left over, he can keep. As a political go-between for ruler and ruled, he has carved out for himself a rich
lifestyle and a lot of social contacts. He is exactly the kind of person that
skirted standards of Jewish conduct and could care less about religious
people and their advice.

So another *paradox* begins when Levi responds to Jesus by giving
up his tax-collector status. It continues when he immediately throws a
banquet—maybe something like a going-away party—and invites all his
highly-placed social contacts. And Jesus is in the middle of things as the
guest of honor.

The Pharisees look on aghast: "Why," they say, "would Jesus, if he
were concerned for the Kingdom of God, take this approach in public?
He should really mind who is following his lead. Go to the ones who
are serious about keeping the Law and its traditions. Make your case to
those who have proven themselves religious by their past actions." Jesus
surprises everyone with his answer [5:31–32]: he fancies himself a traveling doctor, so he needs to go to the sick, not the healthy.

Cycle of Sabbaths: Episode Three

Luke 5:33–35 And they said to him, "The disciples of John fast
often and offer prayers, and so do the disciples of the Pharisees,
but yours eat and drink." 34 And Jesus said to them, "Can you
make wedding guests fast while the bridegroom is with them?
35 The days will come, when the bridegroom is taken away from
them, and then they will fast in those days."

---

3. Others might know this fellow as Matthew.

Levi's banquet launches the whole topic of how we ought to celebrate the Kingdom of God. The Pharisees notice now that Jesus and his disciples are not finding occasions to fast. Fasting often represents sorrow, Theophilus, and many Jews have incorporated it into their routine. Any person in their right mind knows that the Kingdom has not arrived and that there are plenty of things to grieve in the present day. For what things would his Jewish peers—not just rivals, but even reformers like John "the Baptist"—fast? I suppose things like the Roman occupation of the homeland, the violation of temple offices and rituals, the disappearance of the ten tribes of Israel, the decline of Jewish commitment to the Mosaic Law, and so on. All these things are cause for anguish and abjection that fasting expresses. Why would *not* Jesus, his followers, and all Israel practice such piety?

Yet Jesus once more makes *paradox* out of their expectations. Who knows but that he even flagrantly defies their traditions by eating on one of their customary fast days? Maybe it is the day after Levi's feast—even worse, maybe Levi held his banquet on one of the fast days that his critics regularly observed each week! My sources do not say, but you can imagine the conundrum the whole context might cause.

Jesus's response is to shift focus from fasting to feasting. His primary reference for what he means is a wedding banquet. So he points to what accompanies such an event that everyone in his audience would have known: the people attending, the clothing, and the wine and the food. Of course these things are raised often in the Jewish Scriptures in the context of a divinely-hosted feast—we might call it a messianic banquet. I will not go into these references here. The *paradox* unfolds further when we consider the implication of Jesus's response: he himself is the center of the celebration, and he does not dispute the occasion for joy, renewal, and even revelry. This *paradox* of celebrating in the midst of objective grief and pain points to the riddle of Jesus himself and thus we are back to where the cycle of Shabbats [5:16] began with his claim to be the "Son of Man." Undoubtedly, the Pharisees' criticism did not reel in Jesus's message as the cycle of Shabbats unfold—and their outrage only intensifies.

Cycle of Sabbaths: Episode Four

Luke 6:1–2 On a sabbath, while he was going through the grainfields, his disciples plucked and ate some heads of grain, rubbing

them in their hands. 2 But some of the Pharisees said, "Why are
you doing what is not lawful to do on the sabbath?"

My sources once again point to a chronology that highlights Shabbat, as you will see if you pay attention to the following words: "the second one after the first [Shabbat]."[4] Here the disciples are "caught" doing
something of which the critics of Jesus do not approve: they are helping
themselves to unharvested food in a field—supposedly violating the Sabbath's rules. This is food that a farmer intends to go to the needy, and he
leaves it behind for the taking; so there is no question here of stealing.
"Rather," say the Pharisees, "you are violating traditional rules by doing
so on the Shabbat. You are supposed to plan things ahead so that you are
not working on the day of rest."

Remember that Jesus has identified himself as the Son of Man, a
title he claimed in the beginning of this cycle of Sabbaths. Since this title
was so significant earlier in introducing what I am calling the theme of
paradox, we should continue to look for clues in this episode when he
voices this title again precisely on a Shabbat.

Second, we should remember that the idea of the feast that he raised
just the day before, when he suggested that the feast he inaugurates in
the face of all the miseries the Jews face, is entirely appropriate. His point
seems to be that it is time to celebrate (because the Messiah is present?),
and one needs to take advantage even of the Sabbath, legislated as it is by
commandments and traditions.

To illustrate his point, he brings the Pharisees back to the biblical
example of David and his band of followers, all regular unordained fellows, eating what was meant only for the priests. In that story, it was the
priest Ahimelech who was at a loss for what to do about David's men. Are
they abstaining from sex? Are they ritually pure? Eventually, Ahimelech
gives in to David's request, though later in the story this deed would cost
him his life. Now, mysteriously, *paradoxically*, again, Jesus leaps into mi-
drashic logic,[5] again declaring that he is Son of Man and has the right to
redefine Sabbath and messianic meal.

---

4. Ed. note: See footnote in a standard translation; or check the Greek New Testament notes.

5. A "midrash" is an explanatory "aside" based on another biblical text that gives
meaning to a word or reading in its current context. In this case, Jesus explains why
his disciples "violate" the rules based on another passage where violations of rules
seem to occur.

The implication here is deeper than first meets the eye. If the disciples are plucking and preparing the grain, can we not say that they are preparing a messianic feast, whether it is Sabbath or not? What if it is a marriage feast, as Jesus hinted a day earlier? What does such a riddle imply about the guests and the groom and bride? It would seem to mean that the audience is the guest, the disciples are the hosts, and Jesus is the groom; the same was true for Ahimelech the priest—though for both disciple of Jesus and priest of David involved in this mysterious messianic banquet, later experience would take them into persecution and martyrdom.

Taken further: if the Son of Man (going back to his claim to forgive sins at the beginning of these Sabbaths) is "bar-nasha" in Aramaic—something like son of Adam in Hebrew—do we not have here a "new Adam," a comparison often invoked if you have read the letters of Paul? Does not the title Son of Man suit what I have said about Jesus as the new Adam as shown in the temptation and the baptism of someone who is tied by genealogy to Adam himself?[6]

Is he not founding a movement that aligns itself with the new wine or the new wedding outfit he spoke about earlier? And who would be the bride, but the Sabbath itself, as Jews very often refer to this day as the "queen" and "jewel" of the week? Who is invited to attend such a feast but the audience, whether priest at Nob or you, Theophilus, the reader of my narrative?

Cycle of Sabbaths: Episode Five

> Luke 6:9–11 And Jesus said to them, "I ask you, is it lawful on the sabbath to do good or to do harm, to save life or to destroy it?" And he looked around on them all, and said to him, "Stretch out your hand." And he did so, and his hand was restored. 11 But they were filled with fury and discussed with one another what they might do to Jesus.

Then we come to the next Sabbath. The meaning of *paradox* continues along the lines begun some two Sabbaths earlier—so I will conclude the cycle with this third weekly observance of Sabbath. In this case, a man is called out by Jesus to stand in the middle of the public space. Notice how I go to great lengths in describing how he stands in the middle of

6. See what I said earlier at the baptism and afterwards [3:21–38].

everyone. Jesus clearly wanted to make the man stand as a test case or a model for the world to see.

The Pharisees offer again the same type of response as at the first Sabbath: they are filled with "fury" (αὐτοὶ δὲ ἐπλήσθησαν ἀνοίας, *autoi de eplēsthēsan anoias* [6:11]), but the word in Greek is not so much anger as "lack of understanding" or "senselessness." That is, they do not grasp the *paradox* and have not learned from the first sign. They are clueless about the meaning of this Sabbath in terms of the messianic banquet.

What would Jesus have you learn from this episode, Theophilus? Listen to the rhetorical tone that he uses: it is clearly disproportionate to the actual condition of the man. Jesus speaks about doing good and saving a life on the Sabbath, but all the man needs is for his hand to be healed! Why such oversized terminology?

Clearly this mildly disabled man stands as a symbol. This final story gives a signal that goes back to the *paradox* at the beginning of the cycle of Sabbaths: the man on display here is also the new man, the new Adam, that Jesus is saving. The first Adam is Luke's old order of time. The second Adam was tempted and baptized in the second order of time, the life-time of Jesus. The third order of Luke's timeframe is this man, restored to health in the messianic banquet. We have a clever dramatic presentation before us, one that serves for a thousand words.

What started out as evil has now symbolically been restored as "good," and a new life has been brought into the world on the Sabbath. The Sabbath is the day when the world shall be restored through the unity of God and the world, the Son of Man and his bride. As readers and disciples, we are guest and host and maybe even beneficiaries. That is, we are invited to witness Jesus, then we are to help him with the feast, and finally we are to stand as representative of the new order.

The cycle of these three Sabbaths have brought us into a world of my meanings and approaches to the message of Jesus. *He is performing!* You could use words like "theology," "story-telling," and maybe even "typology," all very helpful words in a book. But what he is doing is more than sermonizing or wonder-working: he is inviting the audience to join in the mission he is leading, for it trumps sect, politics, and even traditions upon which it depends.

While the Pharisees are antagonistic to the aims of Jesus and never really enter into the mystery of his performance, let us not fail to ponder deeply the *paradox* of these verses and read with insight. Prayer has opened and now closes the round of Sabbaths and all the events contained in my narrative, and prayer and contemplation are the only way to grasp what this chain of stories is about. If nothing else, my arrangement of these episodes teaches that you can't get to the heart of Jesus's message about the Kingdom without stepping back and savoring his performance.

1. How do the natural stages of life and seasons often reflect or fore-shadow the realities of divine intervention? Think of a specific case where something supernatural builds on top of natural events, say, a marriage, holiday, vacation, or even a funeral.

2. Have I ever witnessed a conversion like Levi's, firsthand? What forces were at work?

3. Is there a natural rhythm to my week? Do I take times of rest and reflection regularly? How does this natural cycle fit in with my life of faith? What are my rules for keeping this cycle?

4. Have I ever confronted such sorrow that I lost my appetite and did not wish to eat? Is there something constructive about fasting as a form of prayer? How does Jesus temper this attitude toward self-denial and fasting?

5. How might Sabbath (as Jesus interprets it) stand as an expression of my control of time and access to joy? How might it sum up the Kingdom God?

Supporting Cast

Part One: The Twelve and Those Closest

If *paradox* marks the beginnings and development of Jesus's life and work, how are you and I—indeed anyone who recognizes that he is per-forming—supposed to know how to follow him? Therefore we move into the next phase of my story, how Jesus stirred up others to be his disciples. Yes, individuals joined him, something like an audience who became members of his cast. They were drawn to him, but drawn to what? This is what I want to explore with you now.

There were twelve special ones whom he named "apostles,"[7] the very name of which implies performers with a script and a strategy. As this

---

7. An apostle (*apostolos*, ἀπόστολος) is literally "one sent out," and usually implies a messenger or delegate carrying a message for a public hearing. Messages were usually performed by an apostle because most people in their audience could not read or

Memoirs of How It All Began continues—and in my next installment (*Memoirs of an Unfinished Tale*), you will understand the reason for this designated cast of apostles: they carry on the life and work of Jesus, for the performance of the Kingdom is in their hands. Let's call them the Twelve.

He set these Twelve apart after he had spent a night in prayer up in the hills, as if they were ore that he had carefully excavated on high. Then he brought them down to the flatlands [6:17] for refining them in the fires of everyday life, which would burnish them into shiny metal. Sure enough, they met the same crowds below who had flocked to Jesus earlier, ready to sing the praises of the next miracle as long as it brought them favor and fair weather. The following lines from the mouth of Jesus set an agenda that his disciples found hard to swallow, much less to digest; but this was how he prepared them for the plains of real life.

> Luke 6:20–22 And he lifted up his eyes on his disciples, and said: "Blessed are you poor, for yours is the Kingdom of God. 21 "Blessed are you that hunger now, for you shall be satisfied. Blessed are you that weep now, for you shall laugh. 22 "Blessed are you when men hate you, and when they exclude you and revile you, and cast out your name as evil, on account of the Son of man!"

Note well the impact of this speech, Theophilus, often called the Sermon on the Plain. Why do I say that he spoke it here instead of on high?[8] Because this is where you will find everyone living ordinary life. The *paradoxes* Jesus brings are not just for him or for some rainy day when we can't do anything but wait for divine deliverance or the end of time. It is "*now*," as he tells us several times in his speech; for what we do in a daily way makes the Kingdom happen.

The other thing to hear in these words, Theophilus, often times glossed over: he looks right at the disciples and says, "Blessed are *you* . . . for *yours* . . ." The reason he addresses them (and us) directly is that it draws us into the Kingdom as *we* make it. We have heard enough of those who make the performance of the (select) Twelve and their cohort something like a whimsical tale of the idealistic lessons Jesus taught. This

---

write, and the sender would want the exact message, including all its nuances, to be delivered by an experienced messenger. The apostle really is a participant in a public performance.

8. Some refer to this event as the "Sermon on the Mount" [Matthew 5–7], but I have a different perspective on it, Theophilus!

is one way of spinning the story, Theophilus, but I have something different in mind.

No, Jesus's conditions for summoning the Kingdom—poverty, hunger, weeping, hostility, and everything else a prophet like Jeremiah or Elijah might face—are exactly those *we* should expect to encounter: the Kingdom comes on us all who live on the plain of nitty-gritty conflict and not on some heavenly mountain of bliss. Beware of a life that will not allow for divine *paradoxes* to intervene!

1. Compare this passage to its parallel in the "Sermon on the Mount" (Matt 5:3–10). Make a list of similarities and dissimilarities. How does Luke's version fit in with his story so far? What might the Sermon on the Mount be emphasizing by contrast?

2. How does Luke drive home the immediate difficulties of discipleship? What are they?

3. How do the next lines (6:24–26) make much the same point but from a different perspective?

4. What are the paradoxes of discipleship found in these lines? At first reading, why might the audience be unsettled or unsure about the call of discipleship?

To repeat: our stage is the flatlands of everyday living, and our cast includes the Twelve and perhaps even the prophets of old—that much is clear. But how are *we* to do anything practical with these perplexing teachings of Jesus? All I can do, Theophilus, is plunge more deeply into the logic and language of the Kingdom of God. It is an upside-down world that seems to intervene in this sermon, but it held his audience spellbound.

Even now I am held captive by its ability to speak to the present and to the soul. No, it is not for some far-off time and place, nor for an elite group on the "Mount." We are all on the "plain," and his eyes search out anyone who listens to the following words:

> Luke 6:27–36 "But I say to you that hear, Love your enemies, do good to those who hate you, 28 bless those who curse you, pray for those who abuse you. 29 "To him who strikes you on the cheek, offer the other also; and from him who takes away your coat do not withhold even your shirt. 30 "Give to everyone who begs from you; and of him who takes away your goods do not ask them again. 31 And as you wish that men would do to you,

do so to them. 32 "If you love those who love you, what credit is that to you? For even sinners love those who love them. 33 "And if you do good to those who do good to you, what credit is that to you? For even sinners do the same. 34 "And if you lend to those from whom you hope to receive, what credit is that to you? Even sinners lend to sinners, to receive as much again. 35 But love your enemies, and do good, and lend, expecting nothing in return; and your reward will be great, and you will be sons of the Most High; for he is kind to the ungrateful and the selfish. 36 Be merciful, even as your Father is merciful."

For all its dense clauses, the sermon communicates with a formula, and this will help us to untangle its meaning. For example, in the first half of the passage above [6:28–31], he issues seven positive commands[9] (love, do good, bless, pray, offer, give, do). The conclusion is the "Golden Rule" that I have heard quoted throughout Asia and Rome,[10] but until now failed to make it the anchor of a supernatural reality like the Kingdom. To quote Jesus: "As you wish that men would do to you, do so to them."

For the first four commands, the disciple is to act constructively in the face of those who act destructively. For the latter three, I put together the following poem as a summary:

Offer life selflessly.

Give unconditionally.

Thus, convert universally.

Did you get the way the formula takes hold, Theophilus? Now, let's try again in the second half of the passage [6:32–35]—we'll do the final line separately. Jesus restarts things using his drumbeat of seven statements. Same results, but with a shocking—dare I say it, *paradoxical?*—implication. He summarizes the just-mentioned duties of a disciple with three conditional phrases [6:32–34]: *if you love*, *if you do good*, and *if you lend*. In the Kingdom, though, these conditions are for new and strange beneficiaries: *love* for those do not love back, *do good* to those who do not reciprocate, *lend* to those who may not pay back.

What? Why would this be so captivating to the audience? Jesus sums up the disciples' payback with one word, *charis* (χάρις, "credit").

9. Notice, Theophilus, that I use seven simple Greek imperatives for all these words—although I use other ways of expressing negative commands ("do not withhold," "do not ask") as you see in the text.

10. Ed. note: Many ancient ethical traditions appeal to this standard, so it is unlikely that Jesus was the first to make use of it.

However, you well know, Theophilus, that this word allows a broad sweep of meanings. In this context of loving and doing good, *charis* might better be translated as "benefaction" or "grace."

Now we are ready to complete the latter half of the passage by returning to its sevenfold formula. First, Jesus summarizes the three conditions with three simple imperatives: love, do good, and lend without expectation of payback [6:35a]. Then, for the seventh and concluding statement [6:35b], he reveals the climactic comparison that clarifies everything: the disciples who so act will be "sons of the Most High" who is "kind (χρηστός, *chrestos*) to the ungrateful and the selfish."

What does it mean to be "sons of the Most High?" You must understand, Theophilus, that in the Jewish context, "sons of . . . [x]" may mean "disciples of . . . [x]." By saying that they will be "sons of the Most High," Jesus carefully distances the Creator from an organic connection "to the ungrateful and selfish" human race. Anyone therefore who loves, does good, and lends without any return, is a disciple of the Creator by imitating him.

Even though the Most High is wholly responsible for the creation (and I love the line of Greek poetry that speaks of our human dependence on the divine: "in him we live and move and have our being"[11]), how little do his human creatures appreciate and acknowledge him! In fact, might we conclude that our disregard goes beyond ignorance to the point of hostility? Instead he often is the butt of expletives through fits of rage and folly! Yet the Most High patiently sustains the world through unswerving goodness, waiting for humanity to recognize its bounty, repent of its hard heart, and convert to gratitude. By the way, the adjective describing the human race's lack of gratitude (*acharistous*, ἀχαρίστους) is based on the same word *charis*, only it has a prefix that negates the root word.

And this brings us back to the Golden Rule: if disciples do these things to others, their assumption is that hostility against them will end and that enemies will turn favorably toward them. Thus, the climactic seventh statement for both sections echoes back and forth between the Most High and the disciple who lives by this sermon.

For Jesus, Kingdom disciples act in imitation of the Most High. We might offer a parallel speak-out for how the Divine operates in the Kingdom realm:

Respond graciously.

11. See Acts 17:28. For an explanation of the quotation, see *Unfinished Tale*, 98–100.

Pour forth generously.

Forbear considerately.

If this is the economy of the Kingdom that Jesus teaches, then we might imagine the common currency between Divine and disciple is none other than *charis* or, in common parlance for our circles, "grace." It certainly is not something we normally find in the flatlands of human existence, Theophilus!

What do we find here, though, standing right before us, but Jesus himself? Remember that even the most serious of imitators of the Most High, who is so infinitely detached from human context, cannot be disciples on their own. The answer to this dilemma, Theophilus, must be that in Jesus, the *charis* most certainly is found, for he is the point of agreement between the Most High and the disciple.

This is the golden thread in the sermon that keeps leading back to Jesus and draws my attention to the clause, "he [the Most High] is *kind* to the ungrateful and selfish." Let me try to explain this clue by teasing it out in another speak-out jingle:

> *"Kind"*: you think you know its verbal range,
> But I tell you I show another with playful meaning;
> *Chrēstos* it is when I first wrote you in Greek,
> And so its familiar sound should beg for new gleaning.
> Romans had no clue of what was the "Christ,"
> Just that *Chrēstos* was a common name.
> And *Chrēstiani* they hunted relentlessly down,
> And Jesus or *Chrēstos* were all the same.
> Even for me, *Chrēstos* tells of keen tool[12]
> To clear a path to humanity so distant.
> For the Most High is unlike our state,
> But *Chrēstos* the grace for the resistant.

The capstone that ties both formulaic structures together [6:28–31 and 6:32–35] is "Be merciful as your father is merciful" [6:36]. This line expands and explores the climactic seventh members, which are respectively: "And as you wish that men would do to you, do so to them" and "He is kind to the ungrateful and the selfish." I would not capitalize "Father" here so that you can consider on how wonderful is this last claim.

---

12. *Chrēstos* (χρήστος) derives from the Greek verb "I use" (χράομαι) and hence the adjectival form connotes "useful" or "functional."

"Father" applies not only to the parent of natural offspring, but to the master of disciples. The word for "merciful" has its Greek origins in lamentation and grief for victims. How would the Most High express such solidarity except through someone who had actually experienced the miseries of the human condition? As you continue to read these *Memoirs of How It All Began*, Theophilus, you will observe to what extreme Jesus knew grief. So I would merely ask if the "father" here is the Most High or Jesus—or in some undefined unity of both? At any rate, such mercy sums up the previous sevenfold equations of discipleship, and we embrace it as disciples of Jesus and of God, as we listen alongside of the Twelve and the prophets on the flatlands of human existence.

1. Think of times and occasions where all my efforts to give are unappreciated or unnoticed. How do I feel?

2. What kind of personal space, possessions, or resources do I have that I can make more available for the Kingdom of God?

3. How am I invested in those who love me? What are situations where I do good because I am looking for someone to do good for me? Do I ever loan and never check back to get what I loaned?

4. Am I praying for those who might be hoping the worst for me? How hard is it for me to encourage those who are critical of me? Think of some cases for both categories and try again.

5. Think of times when someone spoke critically or ill of me. What was my reaction? Now go back and speak positively about this person.

6. How does God's display of *charis* help me carry out what Jesus is teaching here?

7. How does the association between God and Jesus above help me to understand the relationship between Divine Father and Son?

Hopefully the discussion so far is helping you to grapple with the complexities of the Kingdom as Jesus preached the "Sermon on the Plain," Theophilus. As I said earlier, it is supposed to help us navigate the nitty-grittiness of following Jesus—not just for special disciples or special times when there are awesome vistas of the Kingdom of God on the "Mount." It is a training process, a conversion that initially seems counterintuitive. Once you plunge into the logic of Jesus, and you compute discipleship by his mathematics, you really do begin to understand the perspective of the Most High here and now. The *charis* [6:32, 33, 34] from such discipleship need not wait until the end time, for it is "pressed down, running over, and shaken up" [6:38] as we hold out our lives to be filled with the full measure today.

Further in the sermon, we learn about fruitfulness—an image that suggests natural growth more than understanding as the key building block of discipleship. If we but let a seed of this teaching germinate, something will come up and bear fruit. The whole thing is a process, Theophilus, as the comparisons of Jesus suggest. And so I will skip down to the end of his discourse about Kingdom discipleship and deal with one final image: the building of a house.

> Luke 6:46–49 "And why do you call me, 'Lord, Lord,' and do not do what I say? 47 "Everyone who comes to me, and hears my words, and acts upon them, I will show you whom he is like: 48 he is like a man building a house, who dug deep and laid a foundation upon the rock; and when a flood rose, the torrent burst against that house and could not shake it, because it had been well built. 49 "But the one who has heard, and has not acted *accordingly*, is like a man who built a house upon the ground without any foundation; and the torrent burst against it and immediately it collapsed, and the ruin of that house was great."

A house begins with foundations. So before we launch ourselves into the strange world of the Kingdom, we must go deep into ourselves and start from scratch. After all, if it was true of trees, vines, and plants [6:43–45], it is also true of houses. Most of what we and others see is the outside of any building, but for life we need to go deeper into ourselves to find out what makes us tick. Sum up his words by saying that we ought to put aside distractions and pointless pursuits as we reflect on the Kingdom's *paradoxes*—and the result will be a life that withstands external setbacks and adversities.

Note well the three verbs I quote from Jesus's sermon for digging the foundation—even though your version only gives two actions: "dug deep and laid a foundation." By saying it in three ways, I am trying to point to Jesus's recognition that struggling with these ideas involves some hard work of rethinking priorities and projects in our lives. Since the Kingdom message is so contrary to the outer flow of life, a disciple cannot simply make a superficial substitution of a "Jesus saying" (or two) for a well-established routine. Like a building needs a firm foundation, so a disciple needs a fundamental pattern of life. For following Jesus, we must redirect our normal perspectives, hopes, ambitions, and attractions to get down into Kingdom's foundation—and discipline our minds to stick with the teachings.

Once the house is built, then we can relax safely inside even though the deluge beats on the outside. The opposite picture Jesus envisions is living in a house beset by external forces. This house also looked formidable at one time, but since then the crisis has come with too much force for the structure to stand. Everyone marvels at the collapse of such an impressive building, but now it is too late to do much about it. It is simply a ruin like everything the storm has battered.

1. What would be the things I need to do to start and develop discipleship the way that Jesus speaks about it in the Sermon on the Plain?

2. What kind of depths will I need to descend to make sure later life development is founded firmly?

3. Am I prepared to take on the hard work required?

Part Two: Outsiders—Roman Centurion

Luke 7:1–10 After he had ended all his sayings in the hearing of the people he entered Capernaum. 2 Now a centurion had a slave who was dear to him, who was sick and at the point of death. 3 When he heard of Jesus, he sent to him elders of the Jews, asking him to come and heal his slave. 4 And when they came to Jesus, they besought him earnestly, saying, "He is worthy to have you do this for him, 5 for he loves our nation, and he built us our synagogue." 6 And Jesus went with them. When he was not far from the house, the centurion sent friends to him, saying to him, "Lord, do not trouble yourself, for I am not worthy to have you come under my roof; 7 therefore I did not presume to come to you. But say the word, and let my servant be healed. 8 For I am a man set under authority, with soldiers under me: and I say to one, 'Go,' and he goes; and to another, 'Come,' and he comes; and to my slave, 'Do this,' and he does it." 9 When Jesus heard this he marveled at him, and turned and said to the multitude that followed him, "I tell you, not even in Israel have I found such faith." 10 And when those who had been sent returned to the house, they found the slave well.

We turn the page on the discipleship lessons for now, and I mark the end with this turn of phrase: "After he had ended all his sayings in the hearing of the people." The Greek that I composed really suggests that Jesus knew he had completed what he wanted to say to his audience and was ready to move on.

Now we focus on a couple of examples in Jesus's interactions with residents of Galilee. First, he will have an encounter with a Roman centurion and then he will cross paths with a widow in a funeral procession. What I will do finally is connect these two with the Syrian invader and the widow of Zarephath that Jesus had cited earlier in his public debut at Nazareth [4:26–27]. Should we be surprised that Jesus did exactly what his hometown wanted but in ways that challenged their expectations? Before we get into yet another *paradox*, though, I will largely compare what I see in these examples to things immediately in context.

The first case involves a centurion, a man important in Roman circles. Why, he has dozens of soldiers at his command! At the same time he has enough status and resources to sponsor and fund a nearby synagogue. Quietly, then, he respects the divine calling of the Jewish people, even though he finds himself in the role of the Roman Empire's agent. In fact, he shows this respect toward Jesus by sending Jewish "elders" to negotiate with Jesus. The very fact that he requests a meeting with Jesus shows high regard for him.

He has a vexing problem: his favorite slave is near death, and he thinks that Jesus can do something to keep him alive. Why Jesus? Well, reports of his miraculous acts no doubt reached him. So, at the very least, the centurion thinks of him as a wonderworker or prophet.

Then he thinks better of his initial request and decides not to trouble Jesus by making him go out of his way or bestow on him an undeserved favor [7:6]. In effect, he realizes he is but a subordinate and Jesus the superior—what in Roman circles would qualify as a client working under his patron. Clients are at the disposal of their business and political patrons, not vice-versa, in the imperial world of hierarchies, protocols, and boundaries. Rome has long achieved its results by perfecting its administrative and authoritative system of rule. Subordinates must know their place, and superiors must keep their distance.

The centurion says in effect, "Don't worry about coming to me. I know how things work in our organizational worlds—so give an IOU or send a lackey, and that will be enough." The implication here is that the centurion considers himself in humble partnership with Jesus. Whatever common project this important Roman shares with Jesus, he simply hints at an obligation for Jesus to meet this need, however he sees fit. "I am just checking in to let you know I have a few problems doing my work for you and the Jews. You don't need to come yourself; but if you wouldn't mind taking care of this problem, however you see fit . . ."

Now this is faith! Jesus exclaims [7:9]. In short, it is a bold and presumptuous faith. How many of those from "Israel" come to me begging and really care nothing about the Kingdom of God? Not even among his disciples in training does he see such faith! They simply want him to do something for them. But this centurion presumes he is a partner with Jesus, and it is clear from his life that he knows the meaning of results. We can well imagine Jesus's response: "So your business partnership with me will be diminished unless I help out? Of course I will give you a hand!"

Whom do we see around us, sharing the stage of life with us, Theophilus? There are givers and takers. Most of the people around Jesus are takers, not givers. They just want to borrow a little of Jesus's power to get ahead in life, maybe a healing, maybe an exorcism. But here is a man who stands out as a giver to the Kingdom of God—he shows so much reverence and courtesy that he worries about bothering or disrespecting Jesus!

Where would the Kingdom that Jesus preaches be if everyone were a taker? Part of the lesson I hope you saw in the Sermon on the Plain was that Jesus taught the value of imitating the Most High by loving without expectation, giving generously, and lending unconditionally. *Charis* abounds when a disciple pours out instead of drains in. Oddly enough, that is what God looks for and Jesus calls for, so that the favorable consequences (*charis*) would press down, be shaken to compact its density, and then run over the limits.

For a change, the centurion represented someone who understood the need to give back instead of demanding some miraculous razzle-dazzle from Jesus. I gather that Jesus sensed he could share his mission project with someone like this centurion.

This is true of any endeavor: the more initiative and creativity all the actors offer, the greater the outcome of the production. We all know the difference between someone who is onboard for the thrill but does not invest in the effort. The upside-down world that Jesus has demonstrated in all the previous *paradoxes* seems to have had (so far) little impact on the band of disciples around him.

Instead my writing focuses on this Roman partner: he has helped the Jews and he offers his contribution to help Jesus. Notice what happened, Theophilus: Jesus "marveled" [7:9]! Has Jesus ever "marveled" in my writing before or after? Never. This by itself should make us pause and search for explanations.

Of all things, he is a non-Jew and a highly placed Roman at that! In fact, the centurion shows deep respect for the authority of Jesus here similar to the story where the word *paradox* is used, where Levi respects Jesus by throwing him a banquet that foreshadows the messianic banquet. Jesus commends both men, who are not prophets or miracle workers or popular religious leaders like Pharisees. Both are powerful worldly men, who nevertheless are destined to do great things in the Kingdom.

The marvel of Jesus is something like this: "Unlike the 'Israel' crowd around me who are seeking benefits and bonuses from my power, this man is not a freeloader. He is giving me assets, offering me gain. It is clear that he can be an effective collaborator if I heal his slave. Of course I will help him."

1. Note the commendation that the centurion receives. For what can I hear the Lord commending me, based on this story? How can I be in partnership with God for the Kingdom of God?

2. Who are my partners and benefactors? How do I treat them, and how do they treat me? Would I go out of my way to help them? How much trust is involved in these various relationships? Is there a parallel to the partnership that the centurion and Jesus have in this story?

3. Are there important and capable people involved in worthwhile projects that I know of? How can I support them? Pray for benefactors and clients for the work that I am doing. Pray for benefactors and partners for those who are doing the work of the Kingdom of God.

Part Three: Outsiders—Widow of Nain

Luke 7:11–17 Soon afterward he went to a city called Nain, and his disciples and a great crowd went with him. 12 As he drew near to the gate of the city, behold, a man who had died was being carried out, the only son of his mother, and she was a widow; and a large crowd from the city was with her. 13 And when the Lord saw her, he had compassion on her and said to her, "Do not weep." 14 And he came and touched the bier, and the bearers stood still. And he said, "Young man, I say to you, arise." 15 And the dead man sat up, and began to speak. And he gave him to his mother. 16 Fear seized them all; and they glorified God, saying, "A great prophet has arisen among us!" and "God has visited his people!" 17 And this report concerning him spread through the whole of Judea and all the surrounding country.

Undoubtedly in this second case we have a crowning example of *paradoxes* in the mission of Jesus. It is the companion to the story about the centurion. Together they show how the Lord deals with those who sit in high and low places: on the one hand, the imperial centurion and, on the other hand, the village widow. Together, we start to piece together a divinely arranged rerun of examples Jesus used to confront his hometown audience at his opening debut [4:26–27].

In that earlier episode, the people of the old order (Nazareth) were so infuriated by Jesus's paradoxical teaching that they acted out a sort of reversal of the funeral procession miracle. They would have killed Jesus by hurling him from a cliff upon their city, dashing him upon the roofs of their own houses. It is a classic scene of Israel rejecting the prophet—and it should make us pause just a little before we receive popular acclaim at the end of this episode.

Let us lay out the present scene once more: Jesus comes upon a ceremonial procession, coming out from Nain—a village not so far from Nazareth where he initially returned to public applause. One procession (Jesus's) going in, the other (Nain's) going out. This latter one, though, is a grim admission that no one escapes death's inevitability. What Jesus encounters is a funeral procession, bound by sorrow and grief: a young man had died; his mother, a widow, survives. The woman following knows a particular maternal bitterness, for she bore that son in pain, raised him in toil, and now buries him in tears—alone. There is no rerouting of life to avoid such processions, for all songs of youth end up in the dirges of death. And though choruses of family and community attempt to show solidarity, we all enter and leave the world alone.

Except for when Jesus arrives on stage to meet the grieving woman. Ever since the beginning of these *Memoirs*, you have noticed the unexpected with Jesus. Over and over again, the "visitations" the people of Nain shout out [7:16] testify to my early theme that the Kingdom is unleashed bit by bit. In this case, the weeping of the woman will cease and the funeral procession of Nain—and every city—must stop when Jesus visits. Everyone there stands still and waits. You and I similarly stop in our own funeral processions. The whole old order stops in fact.

Then he touches the bier of this corpse—and every corpse that declares human destiny. Jesus addresses the dead body directly: "Young Man." You realize, of course, that the root of the word he used, *Neaniske* (Νεανίσκε), refers not merely to youthfulness but newness. So perhaps Jesus recognizes in him not a generic youth, but he gives a name here that distinguishes New Man from Old Man Adam.[13] Perhaps he speaks to *every man* within that corpse, for every one of us must die like Old Man Adam. So here I use *Neaniske* as a proper name or title and capitalize it as if Jesus knew this corpse uniquely and personally.

The command he gives is one that you will hear often related to the Kingdom Jesus brings: "Arise!" You recognize, Theophilus, that this word is the standard way of referring to resurrection. Consider that Jesus addresses us: "*Arise, every man and woman* in the procession who must die! Arise, Theophilus, from the tomb that awaits you!"

Something now whistles out a familiar tune, Theophilus. Do you remember? The first speech that Jesus gave in Nazareth! Earlier I hinted at the parallel between these two cases (the Roman centurion and the widow of Nain) and Naaman the invader and the widow of Zarephath. Everyone in Nazareth was incensed because Jesus promised things to strangers and not to his hometown constituents. The paradox lost on the residents of Nazareth, if you think about it now, is that Naaman the Syrian and the widow of Zarephath turn out be allies and friends in their own backyards! Let me draw out my point here with respect to the latter parallel (the widows of Zarephath and Nain), and leave the former (Naaman the Syrian and the Roman centurion) for you to think about later.

In case you don't know the story about the widow of Zarephath, the prophet Elijah raised her dead son by lying on top of the corpse. Elijah offered his body for the son of the widow. Let me now skip to the end of the *Memoirs* and point to the obvious fact that Jesus spread himself out on the cross and offered himself for humanity. In the case of the widow of Nain, he touches the bier as if united with it and offering himself for the corpse. What can we glean from it all, but that Jesus foreshadows here what will be the destiny for all of us in the Kingdom?

Why is it that *Neaniske* "sat up and began to speak?" He could have perhaps started walking or eating, as in the other resuscitation story coming up [8:54–55], but here he sits and speaks. This is my deliberate echo of Jesus, who "sat down . . . and began to speak" to Nazareth's citizens

13. In the other resuscitation soon to happen [8:54–55], the name given is παῖς (*pais*) or "child." In this latter episode, it is surely just a generic noun.

[4:20–21]. If Jesus then begins the new age by declaring, "Today this Scripture is fulfilled in your hearing," so also this man (and everyone who hears) participates in the same performance: both Jesus and the *Neaniske* begin their ministry of proclaiming the visitation of the Kingdom.[14]

The young man also brings us back to the memory of the scene where John's baptism presented Jesus as the new Adam, and then I told you his genealogy going back to Adam. The Kingdom that Jesus and *Neaniske* both affirm now "speaks" to the widow of Nain and the funeral procession powerless to escape the jaws of death. Of course, Theophilus, they also speak to us as we struggle with the same griefs.

Jesus "gave the boy back to his mother," exactly what Elijah does for the widow of Zarephath.[15] In the earlier story the widow first had given her son to Elijah, laying his body on the prophet's bed in grief and despair. Her son's corpse now lies where the holy man would sleep.

Elijah acted intensely as if his fate was bound up with the widow's "calamity" [1 Kgs 17:20]. For his part, Jesus is also gripped with "compassion" [7:13] for the widow, the only time I describe the inner disposition of Jesus this way. This Greek word describes deep pain, practically saying that Jesus closely identifies with the widow. Just as three times Elijah lay upon the boy, now in the prophet's bed, identifying with him in his death, so Jesus "touched the bier" as if to unite with the dead body, and makes the procession of death stop in its tracks [7:14].

The final step was for Elijah to revive the boy and to give him to his mother—exactly corresponding to what Jesus did for the widow of Nain [7:15]. Both Elijah and Jesus demonstrate their power over the dead, restoring sons to their mothers' arms.

So the crowd closes this particular stage scene by stating the obvious: "A great prophet"—think Elijah—"has arisen among us!" and "God has visited his people!" [7:16]. Their statements to the point tell us that Israel is bound up with a new Elijah and a new Adam—and yes, a new calling from God and what Jesus proclaims: a Kingdom. Funny how surprisingly simple statements say so much about the divinely charged meaning of history, the very thing I set out to write.

I'll not elaborate them here, lest I take away from your own meditations. One thing I'll leave you to anticipate, though. Just as the widows bore these griefs—as we all do in life—so Jesus will bear them in the final

14. Keep this "today" of a new age in mind when Jesus tells the man next to him on the cross, "Today, you will be with me in paradise" [23:43].

15. 1 Kgs 17:17–24.

act near the end of these *Memoirs*. But take care that we not over-relate to woes, lest we consider ourselves failures and our life a dead end. Jesus's performance declares that life is not a farce, even later when he dies and the devil seems to control the narrative. At that time, the same reenactment of death's grimness will challenge the audience (you and me) to confront the facts in some more meaningful fashion.

1. What are the "funeral procession" circumstances I am facing that I can do nothing about?

2. What ways can I ask Jesus to stop the procession of these circumstances? Is there peace in my leaving the unavoidable things of my life in his hands?

3. Imagine the Lord stopping all these things from happening and reversing their direction. What would the new situations look like?

4. If time, go back and read the parallels to this story in 1 Kgs 17:8–24 and then Jesus's own commentary on this story earlier in the Gospel of Luke (4:16–26). Do these background stories shed any light on the point of this passage? Also compare the image of Jesus here to what he says about discipleship in the Sermon on the Plain, especially 6:32–36.

5. Try to imagine the implications of the parallel above (Elijah's healing of the widow's son in Zarephath and Jesus's healing of the widow's son in Nain) for the other parallel (Elisha's healing of Naaman the Syrian and Jesus's healing of the Roman centurion's slave). How does Jesus's healing of the centurion's "young man" announce a much bigger meaning of the Kingdom for humanity?

Part Four: Jesus's Mentor

Luke 7:23 "And blessed is he who takes no offense at me."

Luke 7:31–35 "To what then shall I compare the men of this generation, and what are they like? 32 They are like children sitting in the market place and calling to one another, 'We piped to you, and you did not dance; we wailed, and you did not weep.' 33 For John the Baptist has come eating no bread and drinking no wine; and you say, 'He has a demon.' 34 The Son of man has come eating and drinking; and you say, 'Behold, a glutton and a

drunkard, a friend of tax collectors and sinners!' 35 Yet wisdom
is justified by all her children."

The last time I spoke about John, Theophilus, he was fading from
the limelight and for all practical purposes locked up in Herod's dungeon.
You remember he had begun a popular protest movement, and many
demoralized Jews flocked to him in hopes that his challenging preaching
would somehow unleash the Kingdom.

For his part, John seems to have held out hope that his kinsman
Jesus would be the one to fulfill the message he had brought to the stage.
Instead, what Jesus does here—especially in the last two incidents (the
healing of the Roman centurion's slave and the raising of the son in
Nain)—flies in the face of what John the Baptist expected. John had expected a divine visitation against the house of Israel and a day of reckoning for the world powers, but the encounters with an oppressive invader
(the centurion) and Zion's daughter (the widow at Nain) spin the yarn
of a different fabric. Instead of confrontation and judgment, Jesus visits
the centurion and the widow with commendation and compassion. Was
John mistaken in his expectation for the future?

First, let me discuss John the Baptist. He sends from his prison cell
a message asking about clarification [7:18–20]. Who are you, Jesus? My
disciples tell me that you do not fast or practice the devotions that I have
championed. Now I sit in prison, and things have not turned out the way
I envisioned regarding the coming Kingdom. Yes, there have been a few
healings and demonstrations of power. Still, I have preached about the
axe laid against the tree of Israel, and the fire is ready to consume the
chopped wood [3:7–9]. I sit here languishing, waiting for the messianic
mission to unfold. Why has nothing happened?

Jesus's response [7:22–23] seems to question John's interpretation of
what to expect from the mission. Jesus seems to say, "I am precisely about
dealing with the sick and the poor. Don't be offended by what I am doing
even if the whole plan has not unfolded. The mission starts with helping
common people, and it is spreading through my disciples." And then I
add the snippet quoted above, "Blessed is he who takes no offense in me":
In other words: "Listen and pay attention to what I am doing. Don't be
discouraged by how this whole plan is unfolding."

1. Have I ever worked intently and even passionately, yet been disappointed by the results? Think of some examples from my own

experiences or the life experiences of others that I know or learned about.

2. When my expectations are dashed, how did it make me think about the state of my life? Has it ever caused me to doubt my purpose in life or even my belief in God?

3. Consider those times when I have been disillusioned because things have not turned out as I had envisioned. Do I take my concerns to Jesus for answers like John did? Have I been satisfied with his answers?

4. When Jesus uses the word "blessed" here, how might it relate to the same word in the Sermon on the Plain, used four times in 6:20–22? What would it suggest about how Jesus might be offering encouragement to John the Baptist?

Second, Jesus addresses the crowds [7:24–30]. "Tell me, why did you follow John the Baptist? Did you go out to see a show or a celebrity? Was his light in reality a falling star, his standoff with authorities a flash in the pan? Was he but a crank who scorned the Status Quo—or a hopeless dreamer who dared challenge Rome and its clients? Why, if it is a show you want, you already have such a person in Herod Antipas, who puts a picture of a reed on our coinage, and plays the role of a rich man in fine costume.

"No, you were drawn to John the Baptist for something supernatural: to see a divine prophet. In fact the greatest prophet who summed up all of divine revelation up to the time of his appearance. He fulfilled the divine prophecy about being the 'messenger' for a final visitation, a prophet who came to prepare you for the Kingdom long foretold. He summoned you to come out of your home and hearth to walk a different path. The path leads to something so different—even now you don't know what to make of it—that it even perplexes John as he sits in a dungeon. How can such traipsing bring us to our destination? *Paradoxes* are often not without pain as they spring back upon the original expectation!"

FIGURE 3: *A Reed Shaking in the Wind* (by Garrett Shireman)

1. Are there John the Baptist figures around us who know that things are not right and who advance a plan that helps to establish the Kingdom of God? Think about individuals or organizations not connected, who are maybe not even Christian, yet help in building a platform for the Kingdom. Pray for them.

2. Am I convinced that people respond to truth or to "prophets" of truth with a God-given sympathy? Are there movements where such truths are promoted and people respond? Think of some examples and thank God for them.

Third, he speaks to the world around him ("this generation") [7:31–35]. If everyone flocked to John the Baptist out of an instinct that his voice was prophetic, why did they not change? Why did they not listen to his message? Now they are like children in a market, aimlessly at play—children apparently with no home to supervise their activities and no money to be of much use to traders. Are they a gang of thugs, or are they playmates who are ready to join in? So far, they seem to be more of the latter, although Jesus has not ruled them out of the Kingdom.

And who is "wisdom" [7:35]? Is it the famous Wisdom who continually calls in the market place for simpletons to learn from her? Listen to how I portray Wisdom in the pages ahead, as she is the one who Jesus compares himself to as he rounds up disciples.

1. Who are the "children" playing around me? Would they notice anything about my lifestyle or behavior that would cause them to ask about me? How would I typify them—as a gang who mocks or a group who is genuinely open? How can I get them to reconsider the direction they are proceeding?

2. Over the course of my life, how have I responded as a disciple to Wisdom in my life? What changes have I made that makes me different from the other children in the market place? Where have I fallen short?

3. How would I typify the behavior of my life as a disciple, one of dancing or one of wailing? Why or why not? How would I know when to do either?

Part Five: Women

I am sure you understand, Theophilus, that this message of Jesus resonated with folks like the tax collectors, a group of people hated by the more respectable members of Judean society, the ones that Jesus referred to as "the men of this generation." But it wasn't just tax collectors: it was the widow at Nain, the Roman centurion, and many others who felt they did not have a place in society. They flocked to Jesus as if they had finally found their family—to use the image Jesus used, their mother. For example, Jesus had a unique following among women who felt marginalized for various reasons.

Rather than recount what I have already written in these *Memoirs*, let me simply report a poem that one lady composed in honor of her newfound identity arising from what Jesus represented to her. Everyone knew her looks and her ways and thus they thought they knew her. She was one of the children sitting in the marketplace who enjoyed the occasional flings of wine and song, only to have her love thrown away the next day. First, she ran into the haunting truths John preached and was baptized; and then she took up company with Jesus and found a new identity alongside of his disciples. You can go back and read the accounts of Jesus with such women [7:36–8:3]. Here I will only cite the poem this particular woman presented to me:

Prodigal Daughter

At night I sashay to play a role,
Looking for escape and attention.
There in the souk I find flimsy rapport,
Palliative family and faction.

A brightly donned form I make for the eye,
A pose and nod that steal the sense;
A smile to make you think I am right—
A veil for self-doubts so intense.

Until one day a voice calls from afar,
Beckoning a way to return,
From walking the streets, from parlors so bright,
And homeward a path to discern.

Here I am now, and strangely I feel
The garish and selfish ways must change.
Adrift my soul was, but home now I seek,
Long-lost—but newborn?—to arrange.

Strange uncle's advice: "Prepare," he says,
Pointing to Jesus as the parent I lacked.
His presence, strange bonding, gives courage
To claim my identity intact.

My tears flood and burst forth, I know true Wisdom:
My kinfolk, my home, and my worth.
In John as my preacher, and Jesus confessor
A new Eve has come now to birth.

Part Six: Conclusion

One afterthought, Theophilus: After all the excitement surrounding
John the Baptist, you would have thought of him as the model disciple;
but remember the paradox that Jesus could consider him least among his

followers in the Kingdom. It was the widow of Nain, the Roman centurion, and this street woman who made good on the Sermon on the Plain. If one were to stage the life of Jesus as a public performance, they would be the stars.

Reacting Game Excursus: Jesus on the Cusp of Fame (Luke 7:19–35)

Introductory Comments by Group Leader (5–10 minutes)

"My name is Theophilus, and I am a student of Luke, whom you may know through writings that he wrote to me. Now Luke is after me again to reread his writings through these *Memoirs*. I have decided to go back and interview people around Jesus to figure out a few things for myself.

So we are at the time when Jesus is on the cusp of going bigtime and getting a name for himself. He had just worked many miracles and had recently finished his famous Sermon on the Plain.

I have put together a few questions for my interview with three groups of people who were there and knew of Jesus and his activities. Why don't the groups get together for discussion and then I will ask them a few questions when we come back together? Then after I conduct the interview, I will bring us back together for conclusions. I will leave you with a few questions you can think over about what Luke wrote, but in your free time."

Small Group Time (20 minutes)

Group One: You are John the Baptist and his disciples

Luke 7:19–23 The disciples of John told him of all these things [while he was in prison]. 19 And John, calling to him two of his disciples, sent them to the Lord, saying, "Are you he who is to come, or shall we look for another?" 20 And when the men had come to him, they said, "John the Baptist has sent us to you, saying, 'Are you he who is to come, or shall we look for another?'" 21 In that hour he cured many of diseases and plagues and evil spirits, and on many that were blind he bestowed sight. 22 And he answered them, "Go and tell John what you have seen and heard: the blind receive their sight, the lame walk, lepers are cleansed, and the deaf hear, the dead are raised up, the poor have good news preached to them. 23 And blessed is he who takes no offense at me."

1. You and your group identify with John the Baptist. Choose a spokesperson or two for your group.

2. What were your expectations of Jesus? (Quickly skim 3:1–20, especially vv. 9, 16–17, and figure out what John expected would happen.)

3. How did Jesus respond to John's expectations? Look at his statement in 7:22–23 above.

4. What did he mean by it? How is that supposed to help John?

Group Two: You are with the crowds now around Jesus

Luke 7:24–30 When the messengers of John had gone, he began to speak to the crowds concerning John: "What did you go out into the wilderness to behold? A reed shaken by the wind? 25 What then did you go out to see? A man clothed in soft clothing? Behold, those who are gorgeously appareled and live in luxury are in kings' courts. 26 What then did you go out to see? A prophet? Yes, I tell you, and more than a prophet. 27 This is he of whom it is written, 'Behold, I send my messenger before thy face, who shall prepare thy way before thee.' 28 I tell you, among those born of women none is greater than John; yet he who is least in the Kingdom of God is greater than he." 29 (When they heard this all the people and the tax collectors justified God, having been baptized with the baptism of John; 30 but the Pharisees and the lawyers rejected the purpose of God for themselves, not having been baptized by him.)

1. You and your group identify with the "crowds" now around Jesus. Choose a spokesperson or two for your group.

2. What were your expectations of John the Baptist?

3. How did Jesus respond to your expectations?

4. What did he mean by his statement? How is that supposed to help (or hurt) you?

Group Three: You are the "generation" at the time of John the Baptist and Jesus

> Luke 7:31–35 "To what then shall I compare the men of this generation, and what are they like? 32 They are like children sitting in the market place and calling to one another, 'We piped to you, and you did not dance; we wailed, and you did not weep.' 33 For John the Baptist has come eating no bread and drinking no wine; and you say, 'He has a demon.' 34 The Son of man has come eating and drinking; and you say, 'Behold, a glutton and a drunkard, a friend of tax collectors and sinners!' 35 Yet wisdom is justified by all her children."

1. You and your group identify with the new "generation" of John the Baptist and Jesus. Choose a spokesperson or two for your group.

2. What were your expectations of John and Jesus?

3. How did Jesus respond to your expectations?

4. What did he mean by his statement? What does v. 35 mean?

Large Group Time (30 minutes)

a. Conduct the interview, group by group, in front of everyone.

b. Ask for general comments once the three interviews have finished.

c. Summarize what you learned from each group.

d. Thank them for their interviews.

Follow-up handout [below]:

"Put yourself now in the shoes of all three groups and meditate on the following questions:"

If you are John the Baptist and his disciples, then:

1. Have I ever worked hard and even passionately, yet been disappointed by the results? Think of some examples from my own experiences or the life experiences of others that I know or learned about.

2. When my expectations are dashed, how did it make me think about the state of my life? Has it ever caused me to doubt my purpose in life or even my belief in God?

3. Consider those times when I have been disillusioned because things have not turned out as I had envisioned. Do I take my concerns to Jesus for answers like John did? Have I been satisfied with his answers?

4. When Jesus uses the word "blessed" here, how might it relate to the same word in the Sermon on the Plain, used four times in 6:20–22)? What would it suggest about how Jesus might be offering encouragement to John the Baptist?

If you are with the crowds now around Jesus, then:

1. Are there John the Baptist figures around us who know that things are not right and who advance an agenda that helps to establish the Kingdom of God? Think about individuals or organizations not connected, who are maybe not even Christian, yet help in building a platform for the Kingdom. Pray for them.

2. Am I convinced that people respond to truth or to "prophets" of truth with a God-given sympathy? Are there movements where such truths are promoted and people respond? Think of some examples and thank God for them.

If you are with the "generation" at the time of John the Baptist and Jesus, then:

1. Who are the "children" playing around me? Would they notice anything about my lifestyle or behavior that would cause them to ask

about me? How would I typify them—as a gang who mocks or a group who is genuinely open? How can I get them to reconsider the direction they are proceeding?

2. Over the course of my life, how have I responded as a disciple to Wisdom in my life? What changes have I made that make me different from the other children in the market places? Where have I fallen short?

3. How would I describe the behavior of my life as a disciple, one of dancing or one of wailing? Why or why not? How would I know when to do either?

CHAPTER THREE

Taking the Show on the Road

Entertaining with Parables and Mystēria

JESUS TAKES HIS SHOW on the road (so to speak), and the crowds flock to him. Like his cousin John, he is masterful at engaging his audience, drawing them to consider new choices and decisions. Their eyes are fixed on him just like they were when he first debuted in his hometown—though not just on him but on the events that happen around him.

To set their expectations for the tour in the days ahead, he tells them a "parable" [8:4–15]. A parable is a story that is geared to entertain the public, while educating those among them (the disciples) who would put a little effort into the "takeaway" lesson. He would speak to the crowds often in this form of communication, but he wanted his disciples to deal with the parable's core meaning or "mystery" (μυστήριον, mystērion [8:10, there in the plural]).

This particular parable was about a farmer who scattered his seed over the fields with varying levels of success. I won't repeat the details here, but you should have latched on to the keyword that ended Jesus's mystērion: "patience" [8:15]. Patience means persistence in spite of opposition. It is this last word in my account that stands for what the disciples are to carry with them to each of the stops on the road ahead. This is their application for the story based on what they would face.

Before they leave, Jesus will speak a bit about how these mystēria serve as something like an investment placed within his disciples—an investment that requires certain returns from them [8:16–21]. Mystēria often suggest secrets or hidden deposits; yet the Kingdom of God is different. He compares it to light for the darkness of the world around us. If we have a bit of the light, we should not hide it. Others should notice how we live and work and ask us questions about the treasure within us.

Second, Jesus says it is useless to try hiding it anyway. Our privacies eventually come into public scrutiny—at least when it comes to the Kingdom secrets. Thus, if the message of the parable strikes us, we need to be on guard for *how* we hear—that is, like the seed in good soil bearing a hundredfold results—or at least as much as we can. Notice the passive forms of the verbs here suggest that we are responsible for our hearing.

How important is this investment of the word within us? That is the next application that arises naturally. Jesus indicates that it is more important than family relationships, which otherwise are most important in the world. I need not tell you, Theophilus, that our societies depend on families for medical and old-age care. So Jesus strikes at a core value here. The takeaway here is that the Kingdom makes provision (somehow) for a new family concept, or at least relationships that touch upon what families do—not just what we think of as "casual friendship."

Anyway, Theophilus, let us hit the road with Jesus and see why persistence is required for the seed to yield a hundredfold return when the farming conditions often seem bleak.

1. Read over the passage in focus here, Luke 9:4–18, and pray for the *mystērion* that applies to my life. How fruitful has the seed been in my life? Think about ways it could be more fruitful.

2. How public is my faith when it comes to the Kingdom that Jesus preaches?

3. How important are my friends to my intent to live in the Kingdom?

> Luke 8:22–25 One day he got into a boat with his disciples, and he said to them, "Let us go across to the other side of the lake." So they set out, 23 and as they sailed he fell asleep. And a storm of wind came down on the lake, and they were filling with water, and were in danger. 24 And they went and woke him, saying, "Master, Master, we are perishing!" And he awoke and rebuked the wind and the raging waves; and they ceased, and there was a calm. 25 He said to them, "Where is your faith?" And they were afraid, and they marveled, saying to one another, "Who then is this, that he commands even wind and water, and they obey him?"

Interlude: Jesus Asleep in the Boat

Sleep, O Jesus, the sleep of the dead,
For past deeds are now over,
And your conscience stills dread.
The mission of morrow
Lies beyond what you can do.
Rest now in the boat,
Manned by disciples and you.

The boat ever forward,
The boat ever sure,
You at its center
If disciples endure.
Soon, soon you will arise
With power to show,
Soon, soon be aroused
To steady their row.

Soon, soon to arrive
Where you destined they go.
Yonder shore: Skim over
Hushed waves and storm's throe;
Now wake and face crises,
Stand firm despite woe.
But now, be still, you roiling snares.
Be still, be still, O morrow's cares!
Urgent be gone, your ghosts now flee!
Leave us to God what is left to be.

From the story above, you know that the disciples made it to the other side, somewhat queasy about what this man could and would call forth from them. Below I distilled the narrative into a first-person voice, so you could get a better sense both for its intensity and its application to the *mystērion* we began with, "persistence."

Persistence Despite Disasters: A Disciple's Testimony

"You can be sure that our eyes were again fixed on him [4:20] as never before! For while he clearly showed that he had authority, it was a frightening surrender that he was drawing from our souls. No wonder that he warned that the seed, the word that he was sowing so widely, bore such empty results in the places where it landed. Farming sounds so idyllic until you actually have to do it!

"The price for germinating the seed of his word would be very high, and most of us wondered if we could really keep on the course that Jesus set. Yet we knew from the parable's lesson that we would be responsible to both God and the world, like that lamp in the darkness that Jesus had spoken about just before this tour began. Our only solace as we faced such scrutiny was that he chose us to be closer than his own family and that he would always be available to us along the path of discipleship."

1. Recall specific occasions when I passed through "turbulent waters" as I navigated through decision-making. How trustful was I during those times that I was in God's hands? Could I rest peacefully in spite of the uncertainty?

2. How does this passage suggest that the power or authority of Jesus is much bigger than even human circumstances?

3. How does this passage suggest his authority over forces of nature? Give some examples of natural things that seem to conspire against peace and orderly processes.

4. How does this story give me inspiration to pray?

> Luke 8:26–37 Then they arrived at the country of the Gerasenes, which is opposite Galilee. 27 And as he stepped out on land, there met him a man from the city who had demons; for a long time he had worn no clothes, and he lived not in a house but among the tombs. 28 When he saw Jesus, he cried out and fell down before him, and said with a loud voice, "What have you to do with me, Jesus, Son of the Most High God? I beseech you, do not torment me." 29 For he had commanded the unclean spirit to come out of the man. (For many a time it had seized him; he was kept under guard, and bound with chains and fetters, but he broke the bonds and was driven by the demon into the desert.) 30 Jesus then asked him, "What is your name?" And he said, "Legion"; for many demons had entered him. 31 And they begged him not to command them to depart into the abyss. 32

Now a large herd of swine was feeding there on the hillside; and they begged him to let them enter these. So he gave them leave. 33 Then the demons came out of the man and entered the swine, and the herd rushed down the steep bank into the lake and were drowned. 34 When the herdsmen saw what had happened, they fled, and told it in the city and in the country. 35 Then people went out to see what had happened, and they came to Jesus, and found the man from whom the demons had gone, sitting at the feet of Jesus, clothed and in his right mind; and they were afraid. 36 And those who had seen it told them how he who had been possessed with demons was healed. 37 Then all the people of the surrounding country of the Gerasenes asked him to depart from them; for they were seized with great fear; so he got into the boat and returned.

Let me interject an editorial comment before proceeding, Theophilus. As you know, Jesus and the disciples come to the other side safely, and now they are on Gentile land. As I report the firsthand testimony, consider all the ways I tried to illustrate for you how strange was this place and the events they witnessed. Something involving Jewish-Gentile relations is involved here, and I don't think our Greek or Roman audiences are often aware of how separate are these categories in the divine scheme of things. With this in mind, let us proceed to my eyewitness source.

Persistence Despite Demons: A Disciple's Testimony

"Once we arrived, it was like the land itself was on high alert. First, it seemed to have its own bizarre emissary greet us, only it was not a welcome—more like a surrender. He was more brute than man, half-clothed and half-rational, living in a half-world of ghosts and tombs, hounded by hysteria and harassed by demons. One could speculate that the graveyard was the source of this land's strangeness, and it was only fitting that this man lived there. As such, we Jews find such a fixation on the grave not only religiously alienating but downright toxic.

"Somehow he was forewarned about our visitation and literally driven to meet us, as if a sword were pushing him along. He feared that we had come here to torture him, and that this land was now under invasion. Even more strange was the perspective of Jesus. For he was on guard even before the man on the approaching shore was in earshot. From afar

Jesus was declaring his authority, taking charge over an invisible opponent. And then he met the man—as if they both had anticipated this showdown for a long time. This time, though, the other simply groveled. The man knew his time was up, and he simply wanted terms of surrender.

"When Jesus questioned him, we learned that he was not one, but many. He identified himself by the word we had grown up dreading: 'Legion.' Legion to us means only humiliation and scorn for our way of life and our calling as Jews. Legion of course is the term used for the Roman occupiers. Yet there was no army here, only Roman territory and a raving psychopath who posed as a spokesman for this land on the other side of the lake. Did he speak for Rome itself? If so, the man was now cringing before Jesus, like a criminal caught at the scene of a crime.

"'Legion,' not the man, took over and now spoke to Jesus. Legion begged not to be banished from the land, but instead to find refuge in a nearby herd of swine. Again, no accident, for pigs to us are symbolic of the worst imaginable Gentiles. It was fitting for Jesus therefore to accept these terms of surrender—a herd of swine for an army of demons. And the Kingdom of God instead of the Roman Empire.

"But the poor pigs! Even the pigs found Legion intolerable and stampeded over the cliff to escape the oppression of Legion. For them it was a mercy to be drowned rather than to be inhabited by demons.

"Now that the land—its residents are called Gerasenes—was free of Legion, all the inhabitants spread the word. But, as I mentioned, such divinely executed actions often leave us unsure about our own bearings and how much we really want to stay the course of Jesus. Persistence is easy to conceive, harder to practice when it comes to the real world.

"So, the Gerasenes gather and collectively wring their hands, see. Are they better now that they are free of Legion? Did not Legion provide a measure of stability? At least there were pigs in herds and jobs for herdsmen. Was not the possessed man tucked away and out of sight in the graveyard or in the uninhabited places?

"What was this new equation that Jesus brought—one man in his right mind versus a whole herd of pigs now lost? What were they to make of this Jesus, hailing from a land across the water and so alien to their Gentile way of life?

"Jesus represents a whole new currency of value, one that takes getting used to. And like the seed on rocky soil or among thorns, human hearts are still able to chart their own course of acceptance—or rejection. So the people reject Jesus, for the light on his lampstand is too bright and too harsh. The fears aroused by being in the limelight are too much for them.

"Still, there is the man who once served as Legion's host. What of him? He wanted to join us, but Jesus told him to stay among his own people [8:38–39]. I suppose you might call him a missionary to this strange land, a little less strange now that Legion is gone. Jesus commissions him to remain as God's representative instead of Legion's. He played this role perfectly with one adjustment: yes, he would be emissary to this land, but an emissary of Jesus."

1. Imagine what struggle the man went through trying to fight off "Legion." Tell this story from the man's point of view, both "before" and "after" the action of Jesus.

2. Imagine the campaign Legion conducted to conquer both the man and the land. Tell the story from Legion's point of view, both before and after the action of Jesus.

3. Imagine this story from the Gerasenes' point of view for both the herders and the townspeople both before and after the action of Jesus. Why are they resistant to Jesus? Who of the Gerasenes might be sympathetic?

4. Imagine the story from the pig herders' point of view. Did Jesus do what was best by allowing the demonic legion to invade the pigs and their personal "space?"

5. Imagine the territory that Legion inhabited. What kinds of things are associated with exclusion from society that the man's neighbors tried to impose? What kinds of things do we impose on others, even though our efforts are futile? Think of soup kitchens, elderly facilities, mental hospitals, or even "bad" neighborhoods and locations.

6. What are the strange lands that I must visit? How can I prepare spiritually? Is there a "Legion" at the source of its strangeness?

7. Are those that are benefited by my presence often still resistant to divine healing and blessing? What are some ways that Jesus made his peace with such an outcome?

8. How does this passage focus me better on intercession and prayer?

Reacting Game Excursus: Jesus and Legion
(Luke 8:26–37)

Preliminaries (5–10 minutes)

Read the passage above out loud, leaving out 8:38–39. These verses serve as a conclusion to the game.

Organize everyone into three teams. Usually, just counting by 1-2-3 is the easiest way to get three random groups. One will be the "Disciples," one the "Herdsmen," and the final group the town "Council" (βουλή, *boulē*). The moderator will be the *archōn* (the head of the council) who conducts the cross-examination.

Dismiss everyone to their respective groups, asking them to choose a team representative or two who will face questions at an imminent town meeting. The object of the public hearing will be to determine if Jesus should be allowed to stay in town. Each group should discuss the following points.

Group Discussion: (10–15 minutes)

Hand out the following checklist to everyone:

1. Choose one or two members to be representatives for your group. Read the passage out loud.

2. Discuss among yourselves what your roles are at this point in Luke's story, and what your worldview is. Briefly read the passage (Luke 8:22–25) leading up to this episode, for the context.

3. Discuss among yourselves what you saw. Be prepared for questions from the *archōn*. "Disciples" should pay close attention to 8:26–33, "Herdsmen" to vv. 34–37, the "Council" to the whole passage.

For this exercise, the *archōn* will have to brief the Council privately during the discussion period about what the Greco-Roman perspective would be toward this extraordinary event Luke describes. A few of the things the *archōn* would tell the Council is that leading members of the town would be concerned both for the safety and well-being of its citizens—thus paying heed to the evidence of 8:35. Educated elites of the Roman Empire were known for valuing rationality and civic décor among all their citizens.

On the other hand, the Council needs to be concerned about the town's order and prosperity, and the loss of a large herd of swine would have harmful consequences to the city's economy and diet. Moreover, the Council should be concerned that the expulsion of the "Legion" might also reflect on how these visitors regarded Roman order in general. It was, after all, the Romans and their legionaries who protected their city and established it in league with other similar cities in this land. (The Gerasenes are probably a part of the "Decapolis," a league of ten cities that Rome founded for veterans and colonists associated with the legions.)

The image of Jesus driving out the demons by itself neither offends nor wins over the Council to the side of Jesus. There are many stories that circulate about heroes (like demigod Herakles/Hercules) who vanquished monsters and did spectacular deeds. The existence of "demons" (*daimones*) also is not surprising, although the Greco-Roman understanding of them did not involve the same religious and moral qualms that Jews brought to the discussion of their essence. Even "demon" possession was not so strange among them as it might seem to a modern audience.

The Public Hearing (15 minutes)

Gather everyone together after fifteen minutes of discussion. The moderator as *archōn* calls the meeting together and says the Council will make a decision about whether Jesus and his disciples can stay or go. First they must hear from both sides, both groups. The question the *archōn* raises for the whole assembly is whether Jesus should be allowed to stay. He (*archōns* are male in the ancient world) should begin the line of questions and press for relevant details, but he invites the other groups for their comments as well. In other words, the *archōn* should skillfully draw out facts that the whole town should know and are relevant for the Council to make its decision about Jesus.

After the *archōn* feels that the case has been made, he invites the Council to ask any final questions. The Council retires to make its decision as a group. Depending on how well either disputant made its case, the Council can modulate its decision. It does not need to correspond to the outcome of Luke's story. Then the Council reports to the whole assembly the decision, based on what either team, the "Disciples" or the "Herdsmen," said. The decision can reflect whatever case either group made, that is, it does not need to be either full acceptance or rejection. There can be conditions attached to the judgment.

Debriefing (5–10 minutes)

After the game, each participant should "debrief" by saying what his or her impressions were of their temporary identity, what the challenges for playing their character were, and what he or she learned in retrospect. Finally, in order to make sure that the teaching objectives were achieved, the moderator can offer a "takeaway" statement at the end of the exercise; or he or she can hand out the questions like the ones listed at the end of the passage above. The takeaway may simply be a large group discussion about how Jesus and his disciples would have reacted to the Council's judgment.

Persistence Despite Disease

Luke 8:40–56 Now when Jesus returned, the crowd welcomed him, for they were all waiting for him. 41 And there came a man named Jairus, who was a ruler of the synagogue; and falling at Jesus' feet he besought him to come to his house, 42 for he had an only daughter, about twelve years of age, and she was dying. As he went, the people pressed round him. 43 And a woman who had had a flow of blood for twelve years and could not be healed by any one, 44 came up behind him, and touched the fringe of his garment; and immediately her flow of blood ceased. 45 And Jesus said, "Who was it that touched me?" When all denied it, Peter said, "Master, the multitudes surround you and press upon you!" 46 But Jesus said, "Someone touched me; for I perceive that power has gone forth from me." 47 And when the woman saw that she was not hidden, she came trembling, and falling down before him declared in the presence of all the people why she had touched him, and how she had been immediately healed. 48 And he said to her, "Daughter, your faith has made you well; go in peace." 49 While he was still speaking, a man from the ruler's house came and said, "Your daughter is dead; do not trouble the Teacher anymore." 50 But Jesus on hearing this answered him, "Do not fear; only believe, and she shall be well." 51 And when he came to the house, he permitted no one to enter with him, except Peter and John and James, and the father and mother of the child. 52 And all were weeping and bewailing her; but he said, "Do not weep; for she is not dead but sleeping." 53 And they laughed at him, knowing that she was dead. 54 But taking her by the hand he called, saying, "Child, arise." 55 And her spirit returned, and she got up at once; and he directed that something should be given her to eat. 56 And her parents were amazed; but he charged them to tell no one what had happened.

I will now superimpose my voice over what my source told me, simply to organize the evidence and help you to understand as an outsider what happened. I will describe two more incidents showing the power and authority of Jesus and his Kingdom. Earlier we saw the Kingdom that Jesus brings and its authority over nature (the storm [8:22–25]) and nations (the "Legion" of the Gerasene demoniac [8:26–37]). Now it is Jesus over disease and death—and we are right back where we began, the centurion's slave and the widow of Nain [7:1–17]. What we are realizing is that there is no tour that Jesus leads that can completely evade disease and death, for it is a fact of the human condition.

The first case is the woman with a flow of blood: this is not a passing illness Jesus heals. It is an intractable thing, for the woman has had problems for twelve years. This is a problem that has involved consultations with doctors and enormous outlays of her own resources. Her life has revolved around this problem.

Theophilus, remember this about Jewish scruples: when a woman has a flow of blood, she is considered unclean and a social outcast. Her twelve years have largely been ones of loneliness and embarrassment, for she cannot have normal interactions without a twinge of guilt and maybe fear that someone will find out. No wonder then that this Kingdom that Jesus preaches seems to offer a way out. So she sneaks up on him, mindless of her contaminating everyone all around Jesus. It is her desperate effort to get out of her long misery. She reaches out to Jesus. . . . Did she risk touching him physically? No, that is too much—so she snatches the tassels of his robe. Just like that—twelve years of untouchability and embarrassment come to an end in an instant!

Persistence Despite Death

The second case is the dead girl. Theophilus, what I want you to experience in my source's telling is more than a close encounter with death: it is the grief of the parents who have gone to great lengths to save her life. The father Jairus was an important man who had responsibility for the synagogue. He was willing to travel far to fetch someone on the social boundaries of his faith. He was willing to fall down in front of everyone and beg—all for his daughter. Imagine how desperate he became as Jesus delays his arrival, sidetracked by the woman with the flow of blood. Imagine how despairing he became when his servants came to him with the grim news that he was too late—she was dead! All your efforts, Jairus, to save her have come to nothing.

Here we encounter the shallowness of human solace, the emptiness of well-meaning acquaintances, when we wrestle with our family griefs. Theophilus, there is a saying from a Jewish book of wisdom that is worth remembering here for anyone who struggles with such family tragedies: "The human heart knows its own bitterness, and no stranger shares its joys" [Prov 14:10]. Ultimately, death seems to say that there is no escape for the wasted and lost lives of our nearest and dearest.

That is why I included in my story the fact that Jesus takes the parents in with him, for he is near to the broken-hearted, as the psalm says [Ps 34:18]—and the true broken hearts here are the mother and father of the twelve-year-old. I took note in my first account to you to mention that it was the *parents* who then were most astonished—though no doubt everyone was shocked by what Jesus did. Those who know sadness by death are the ones I most want to fix their eyes on Jesus and the Kingdom he brings.

Two other details I want you to dwell on: first, the people around the parents "laugh" at the claims of Jesus to raise the girl up. Too often our comforters cannot snatch hope out of the jaws of death. So contrary is the Kingdom of God that often well-wishers miss its power. Let us not sneer and mock when at the end of our efforts only the Kingdom is available to give hope.

Second, and for the second time, Jesus allows or even condones contravening "religion" and its customs. As I indicated earlier, there are restrictions Jews observe—it was blood with the woman, here it is touching a dead body. Thus, he is now as unclean as death itself. What do I mean except that he identifies with death itself? This reminds us of his encounter, not so long ago, with the widow of Nain. He certainly was the direct contact there between death and the resurrection, between those born of woman and those born of the Kingdom.

1. What are some of the chasms of despair or desperation I have faced? How did I cope with such conditions? Name a few problems which drain my time and energy and resources. How do I cope?

2. Have I ever had experiences in my own life or those close to me with unrelenting illness or an intractable physical condition? How did it affect my attitude about myself? How did it impact my relationships with others? Did I feel like an outcast?

3. How have I been cynical about faith's role in major problems? Do I take such problems to God in prayer? How expectant am I that God will answer such prayers?

Persistence Despite Despotism: Herod's Testimony

> Luke 9:1–9 And he called the twelve together and gave them power and authority over all demons and to cure diseases, 2 and he sent them out to preach the Kingdom of God and to heal. 3 And he said to them, "Take nothing for your journey, no staff, nor bag, nor bread, nor money; and do not have two tunics. 4 And whatever house you enter, stay there, and from there depart. 5 And wherever they do not receive you, when you leave that town shake off the dust from your feet as a testimony against them." 6 And they departed and went through the villages, preaching the gospel and healing everywhere.
>
> 7 Now Herod the tetrarch heard of all that was done, and he was perplexed, because it was said by some that John had been raised from the dead, 8 by some that Elijah had appeared, and by others that one of the old prophets had risen. 9 Herod said, "John I beheaded; but who is this about whom I hear such things?" And he sought to see him.

Now I switch to what an informant in the royal court reports about Herod: He is intrigued. He monitors the reports about this new movement of believers. He doesn't know whether to be threatened or thrilled. Rumor has it that the man Jesus and his group are focused on a kingdom—but how could they threaten anything that Rome represents or any clients that Rome has installed? The followers of this movement do things that show real seriousness, real commitment: granted, they form a very small group of twelve, but something about them catches on and spreads like a brush fire. They go "native" wherever they are sent, and go off at Jesus's word. When they find a receptive crowd, they perform the same feats as Jesus and hope to connect in the same way with their audience.

Reports have it that the public is fascinated when the disciples of Jesus come to town. What are they, a circus? A troupe of entertainers? If they don't win over their audience, well, the Twelve stomp off in a huff, and go on to more receptive locations. They act as if those who reject them are simply village bores, not worthy of their show.

You can review what I said about how Jesus sent off the Twelve [9:1–6], but for now I want you to think about their persistence in the face of despotism. What follows is a statement from Herod about the mission of the Twelve. Though I cannot guarantee its exact accuracy, it is roughly what my sources tell me he was thinking.

"So odd, these fanatics! They claim that they are walking in the steps of their master Jesus. He can't be what many people say about him—for example, I know that John the Baptist is already dead: I killed him! So I am certainly not thrilled about them, for I have had to crush any zeal and idealism to save my skin. Neither am I threatened by them and their master as much as I am curious. I must investigate these people and their leader."

Theophilus, now to you: You have heard me report on how the "word" that Jesus sows would bear fruit beyond our reckoning. His word has power over natural disaster, over demons, over disease, over death, and over despotism. The Twelve tagged along and observed—then they were sent out by Jesus to do the same sowing of the word. I suppose you can think about what happened to them in terms of the *mystērion* that Jesus said they should understand as they prepared for this road trip.

Now you have been a witness to my words. What is the *mystērion* you derive from my *Memoirs* here? Are you also sowing the word I report about Jesus with such purposefulness? Is living with such commitment and resolve something that someone in a high position, say, a despot like Herod, would even notice?

1. Am I part of something that others notice? If people thought of me, would they recognize that I don't seem to be any part of the normal associations of people and organizations?

2. Am I a part of a mission that reaches out to others? How does this mission or membership compare with other social organizations?

3. Am I worried that my Christian identity might stir up attention? If I am not stirring up attention, why not?

4. How seriously do I take my own witness among others? What would it mean to "shake the dust off my feet as a testimony"? Do I worry too much about my testimony not being received or accepted? How does this anxiety compare to the disciples?

The Show Returns Home

Luke 9:10–17 On their return the apostles told him what they had done. And he took them and withdrew apart to a city called Bethsaida. 11 When the crowds learned it, they followed him; and he welcomed them and spoke to them of the Kingdom of God, and cured those who had need of healing.

12 Now the day began to wear away; and the twelve came and said to him, "Send the crowd away, to go into the villages and country round about, to lodge and get provisions; for we are here in a lonely place." 13 But he said to them, "You give them something to eat." They said, "We have no more than five loaves and two fish—unless we are to go and buy food for all these people." 14 For there were about five thousand men. And he said to his disciples, "Make them sit down in companies, about fifty each." 15 And they did so, and made them all sit down. 16 And taking the five loaves and the two fish he looked up to heaven, and blessed and broke them, and gave them to the disciples to set before the crowd. 17 And all ate and were satisfied. And they took up what was left over, twelve baskets of broken pieces.

You may have noticed in the last section of my material that the Twelve were increasingly in the spotlight. In fact, Jesus sent them off for their own short-term training. Now they return to Jesus after their time on the road, expecting to rest (I suppose) on their laurels to Jesus's acclaim. They hope to learn more about stopping storms, delivering demons, healing diseases, and raising the dead. After all, aren't they "apostles," duly commissioned delegates of the Kingdom? Instead there is simply more toil, more long hours, more problems with people. This, a kingdom? So, they reason, why not send the people away so that they go back to their daily lives, or at least enough time to attend to their basic needs?

Jesus stuns them with a vision of never-ending performances and demands: "*You* do something for them out of your resources!" "Excuse me," the disciples must have protested. "Our resources? We never had much to begin with, and our time on the road certainly did not enrich us! All we have now are a meager five loaves and two fish."

Fancy that: the crowds have journeyed all the way out to Bethsaida on the far side of the Sea of Galilee, doing exactly what Jesus earlier told the Twelve to do, that is, take nothing with them! They dropped what they were doing and came, just like the apostles did when they were on mission. If the shoe fit for them, certainly it is no fault of the crowd to try it on for size! Still, how to feed everyone now with such meager resources?

First, Jesus tells the Twelve to organize. Play along with the image of Jesus as "director." Imagine him saying, "If yesterday you 'apostles' were my performing troupe for the coming Kingdom, today the rehearsals do not end. Now you are to be organizers, handlers, and agents for the same cause—encouraging the audience you attract to participate." Jesus effectively says, "Take charge of the multitudes, put them in companies together, and provide direction and care for the working groups. They are a part of the whole performance."

Second, "take those meager resources you have on hand and distribute them!" Well, this is an act of a whole different magnitude! Apparently the Kingdom allows their meager resources to multiply beyond their needs. "The fact that all were 'satisfied' by what they had as resources points back to the parable of the sower and its *mystērion*: the Kingdom does not emerge from impressive raw materials or origins, yet it has authority to heal, deliver, and restore—beyond anything Caesar or Herod can offer. Few among the Kingdom's agents are wealthy, but everyone is satisfied!"

And what of the last detail, the leftovers [9:17]? The twelve baskets of broken pieces points to the role of the apostles, supplying and administering what is needed for the whole operation of the "Church" (although I do not use this word here, but later when the Twelve are on their own). Thus, both apostolic organization and Kingdom authority go together. The Kingdom involves a lot of unnoticed and exhausting labor on the part of the Twelve, but without it, certainly the show would not go on.

1. What role would I envision for myself in this story?

2. Which people around me are my "mission?" Am I tired out by what I see? What resources do I have for them? What is my attitude toward what I have as resources?

3. Apply this idea of the apostles as administrators, distributors, organizers to my life or to my church. How can I respect and support the role of organization and even bureaucracy in the Kingdom of God today? What can I do to be a part of this level of spiritual life?

4. According to the Gospel of Luke's narrative, Jesus yesterday invited the disciples to be ambassadors, today administrators. How are both needed in the Kingdom of God? Pray about which aspect I feel more called to.

More Training and Rehearsal

Luke 9:18–26 Now it happened that as he was praying alone the disciples were with him; and he asked them, "Who do the people say that I am?" 19 And they answered, "John the Baptist; but others say, Elijah; and others, that one of the old prophets has risen." 20 And he said to them, "But who do you say that I am?" And Peter answered, "The Christ of God." 21 But he charged and commanded them to tell this to no one, 22 saying, "The Son of man must suffer many things, and be rejected by the elders and chief priests and scribes, and be killed, and on the third day be raised."

23 And he said to all, "If any man would come after me, let him deny himself and take up his cross daily and follow me. 24 For whoever would save his life will lose it; and whoever loses his life for my sake, he will save it. 25 For what does it profit a man if he gains the whole world and loses or forfeits himself? 26 For whoever is ashamed of me and of my words, of him will the Son of man be ashamed when he comes in his glory and the glory of the Father and of the holy angels.

Down Time for Jesus? Phase One

Even though Jesus was available to the masses of needy people who came to him, he also tried to be alone to gather his thoughts and spiritual resources. The apostles were often privy to these times of prayer. Out of these sessions of recollection, he worked out his own understanding of self-identity, mission, and calling. Was his prayer for his own well-being? Was it for his immediate followers or maybe for us? If for him, I do not venture to say, and my *Memoirs* can at best poorly guess what were the core ingredients of his mind and spirit. If for followers that include us, the challenges he faced were daunting—for he had only unprocessed raw materials and limited time to set everyone on the right path. Nonetheless, Jesus seized such opportunities for personal refreshment, what I call "down time."

One occasion after a time in deep prayer, he called those close to him to see if they could figure out what he was about. I sense that he hoped they could fix a seal of assurance on where his thoughts had taken him. Who am I? he asked. The disciples gave him the same candidates Herod and others had proposed—John the Baptist take-two, Elijah returned, Moses re-performed. Still he pressed the question: *You*, who do *you* say I am? Peter stepped up, center stage (as usual), spokesman for all those close to him: "You are more than the sum total of these figures, for you are Messiah."

Once he heard this answer, Jesus apparently appreciated it as confirmation of his own drift of thought since the time of his baptism. Then he revealed what seemed to them as a horror story of where things would end up: rejection, death, and finally some kind of return to life. "Cover up those tracks for now," he advised, "don't let anything out."

This was a bitter medicine for the disciples' regime of training and rehearsal. After all the wonderful things they had seen while traveling with him (storm being stilled, demons being delivered, diseases healed, and the dead restored to life, and so on), now he tells them their mission would culminate in his death. "Moreover," he says, "don't tell others about my identity and this outcome for my life." For some reason he does not want the world to know, perhaps lest they fight on his behalf or force some different path. Perhaps he wants the audience to see his performance in full and make up their minds only after the whole presentation (as I will later suggest).

After this startling announcement to this select group, then he addressed everyone else. Without telling them what he told the disciples privately, he warns them that following after him will require enormous self-commitment and sacrifice. It was as if he addresses his disciples about *his* mission and the rest of the people about *their* mission. The closer you are to Jesus, the more you realize that tragedy more described the outcome of the show. When the curtain comes down, the acclaim for the performance would come only from God. Keep that in mind, Theophilus, *tragedy* and not *farce*! These kinds of endings are often unimaginable even to the prophets who predict them.

1. If Jesus is a figure of John the Baptist or Elijah or one of the prophets, what kinds of things would be expected of him?

2. If he is the Christ, as Peter says, how does that figure sum up the other examples that have been put forward to compare to Jesus?

3. What are the conditions for initiation to the "troupe" of Jesus?

4. Speculate on what the next verse (Luke 9:27) could mean to "not taste death before they see the Kingdom of God." Some possible interpretations of seeing the Kingdom include the transfiguration (the next event seen by Peter, James, and John), the death of Jesus (seen by the apostles), and the Pentecost experience (seen by the apostles).

> Luke 9:28–36 Now about eight days after these sayings he took with him Peter and John and James, and went up on the mountain to pray. 29 And as he was praying, the appearance of his countenance was altered, and his raiment became dazzling white. 30 And behold, two men talked with him, Moses and Elijah, 31 who appeared in glory and spoke of his departure, which he was to accomplish at Jerusalem.

> 32 Now Peter and those who were with him were heavy with sleep, and when they wakened they saw his glory and the two men who stood with him. 33 And as the men were parting from him, Peter said to Jesus, "Master, it is well that we are here; let us make three booths, one for you and one for Moses and one for Elijah"—not knowing what he said. 34 As he said this, a cloud came and overshadowed them; and they were afraid as they entered the cloud. 35 And a voice came out of the cloud, saying, "This is my Son, my Chosen; listen to him!" 36 And when the voice had spoken, Jesus was found alone. And they kept silence and told no one in those days anything of what they had seen.

Down Time for Jesus? Phase Two

One other period of "down time" came eight days later. This session turned to be the climactic one that would define his whole mission for the rest of his life. This time he exposed his closest comrades to his experience: this small group consisted of Peter, James, and John. To escape the attention of the public, he took them on a pilgrimage to the top of a nearby mountain.

I suppose it was like a hands-on experiment for the trio. They came up to the mountaintop tired, and were quite groggy as Jesus began to pray. Suddenly as if in a dream, they saw their whole perception of Jesus shift into something brilliant, other-worldly. And then two of the very ones to whom Jesus was earlier compared, Moses and Elijah, appeared and spoke with him.

Did Jesus call them for consultation? They speak with him about "departure" [ἔξοδος, exodos (9:31)], a topic that both would have known a lot about. After all, Moses led an "exodus" out of Egypt; and Elijah took leave of this world and mortal life in a "fiery chariot," his own exodus. Moses's end is uncertain, for all we can say for sure is that he went up a mountain and his burial place was never found. Was his body taken up like Elijah's? What did their experience signal to Jesus about his coming departure?

Peter and his companions snapped out of their drowsiness and fatigue. Since it was Exodus that was on their minds, he suggests that three tents serve as "booths" for the occasion—just like the Jews to this day observe the Feast of Booths (Sukkot) in remembrance of their wandering after the exodus from Egypt. Though the suggestion sounds reasonable, it is out of sync with what unfolds afterwards. Instead of festivity the way Peter thinks, it is darkness and awe that now fall upon the whole group. Rather than pay attention to the figures of Elijah and Moses, an unseen voice in the mountain fog commands them to focus on Jesus. Then just as suddenly as it began, now it is over, as if nothing happened—and the three decide not to say anything about it publicly until their preaching about Jesus much later.

You will see, Theophilus, that the "exodus" of Jesus is the main plot of the overall drama for the rest of the Memoirs. You will also see that Jesus was trying to expose this small group of the apostles to something that could not be captured by wooden comparisons to Moses and Elijah. Their educated guesses about Jesus's identity were accurate, but they had no idea of where the truth would lead. Jesus summed up predecessors like Moses and Elijah, but he also transcended them. And now they were in the throes of the drama involving some kind of exodus for Jesus—an end that was already unimaginable from their previous conversation with Jesus [9:18–21]. Clues might come from Moses or Elijah, but they would listen to Jesus and still struggle to understand what was happening. It is mainly in retrospect that we understand divine oracles, Theophilus.

1. How does Jesus rely on a "screenplay" in this story? In light of what happens ahead, what is the significance of Moses and Elijah? What is the story of their lives that sheds light on the life of Jesus?

2. Compare this experience of Jesus to his "theophany" (appearance of God) experience in 3:21–22. How does the Gospel of Luke earlier rely on Elijah examples (for example, Luke 4:24–27)?

3. Speculate on why Peter's plan might not be the right response to this experience.

4. What are the mountaintop spiritual experiences I have had? How did I sense the presence of God in those times?

5. Have I been mistaken about how these experiences should be interpreted or integrated for life direction? Explain.

> Luke 9:51–56 When the days drew near for him to be received up, he set his face to go to Jerusalem. 52 And he sent messengers ahead of him, who went and entered a village of the Samaritans, to make ready for him; 53 but the people would not receive him, because his face was set toward Jerusalem. 54 And when his disciples James and John saw it, they said, "Lord, do you want us to bid fire come down from heaven and consume them?" 55 But he turned and rebuked them. 56 And they went on to another village.

Whatever Peter, James, and John made of the mountain-top experience, Jesus saw it as his cue to take his mission to a new level. Jerusalem was the place of exodus. He would be on a stage where ancestral heroes had played out their often unappreciated but holy desires for endless generations. While Jerusalem was the destination for the most celebrated of Israel's prophets, priests, and kings, it also brought back grim scenarios of violent fates.

Jesus seemed to interpret his consultation with Moses and Elijah in a different light: they gave him firsthand testimony that he was not alone in the pilgrimage that lay ahead. They had given him advice about upcoming events in the script he was fulfilling. "Drew near" [9:51] is a somewhat shallow way to deal with the word I use for συμπληρόω [symplēroō]; the word suggests that time and intersections have been orchestrated. In the course of what I consider salvation history, the "exodus" story has played out in the exploits and expectations of Moses, Elijah, Isaiah, and many others you will eventually pick up from my writing. All this background steeled Jesus for the days ahead—for they would be difficult times.

They also seemed to give him assurance that he would be divinely approved (literally, ἀνάληψις [analēpsis (9:51)]), which means "received on high"). No matter what happened, no matter how mocked and scorned the gallery received his performance, the critic that mattered—God—would give his acclamation.

So Jesus "set his face to go to Jerusalem." There he would finish his mission. It would fulfill all the prophecies and visions you have encountered so far, Theophilus. Even if the story has so far been tucked away in obscure places and events, you have seen how it whispered the language of *paradoxia* through all of its lowly characters. The pilgrimage would however cascade eventually into Jerusalem, a stage that would make clear to everyone how it fulfilled everything as a crowning visitation.

What does this decision mean for the disciples of Jesus? I will leave out my exact account here, but point you to the outline of what I think is useful now. The pilgrimage to Jerusalem is a fearful fork in the road for everyone concerned. Jesus lets go of his familiar surroundings and braces for crossing into outsiders' lands. His first encounter is with the Samaritans, a group we will meet later when one of its members helps a beaten-up pilgrim. In this case, though, the village rejects Jesus because he projects a Jerusalem-centered visitation—and this violates their sympathies for Shechem as capital and center of the promises of God.

The response of James and John [9:54] shows that they know the ancient script, but still don't understand their director: they urge Jesus to do what Elijah had done when he was approaching his "exodus." (Those who threatened the prophet were consumed in fire, right?) Try to find the story in the Jewish Scriptures [2 Kgs 1:9–16] and compare it to how Jesus and the disciples interpret it here.

Throughout my narrative I have shown that Jesus knows Elijah's story quite well. We must remember that heavenly voice which Peter, James, and John heard on the mountain-top: listen to Jesus rather than to Moses or Elijah! After all, Jesus has already consulted with Elijah, so he has learned how to take an earlier performance to a whole different level. No, Jesus says, there will be no fire from the sky to destroy these outsiders!

Remember from past examples that we must be careful when we say that anyone is an "outsider." For the Kingdom, the outsider just might be the one who is your comrade-at-arms, as the following examples in my narrative tell. Now that Jesus is making a break from Galilee, his supposed followers have to decide if they are serious enough to take this path. What about home, family, and land? Just how real is the support that Jesus and his (invisible) Kingdom can provide to those who have been tagging along, but keeping at arm's length? The fundamental matters of one's identity come into question at this fork in the road. For sure, it will not be easy for us as we venture across strangers' lands, and it might even be harder when we finally arrive at our pilgrimage destination. We have so far survived this life of discipleship, but many others may not be able to endure. If we are to make it to the "exodus," we must endure what awaits us in Jerusalem.

1. Think of a hard decision I had to make, one that implied radical changes in my life. How hard was it for me to keep to the course of my decision? What made me continue or discontinue with the decision?

2. Give some examples of famous people who lost support when they took an unpopular decision.

3. Read Luke 9:57–62. Put into your own words what excuses these would-be followers expressed as reasons for not following Jesus. Try to think of modern examples for each of the three excuses. What would be your responses to their excuses? What are Jesus's responses to these excuses?

CHAPTER FOUR

Preparations for the Big Show

Mobilization

Luke 10:1–12 After this the Lord appointed seventy others, and sent them on ahead of him, two by two, into every town and place where he himself was about to come. 2 And he said to them, "The harvest is plentiful, but the laborers are few; pray therefore the Lord of the harvest to send out laborers into his harvest. 3 Go your way; behold, I send you out as lambs in the midst of wolves. 4 Carry no purse, no bag, no sandals; and salute no one on the road.

5 "Whatever house you enter, first say, 'Peace be to this house!' 6 And if a son of peace is there, your peace shall rest upon him; but if not, it shall return to you. 7 And remain in the same house, eating and drinking what they provide, for the laborer deserves his wages; do not go from house to house.

8 "Whenever you enter a town and they receive you, eat what is set before you; 9 heal the sick in it and say to them, 'The Kingdom of God has come near to you.' 10 But whenever you enter a town and they do not receive you, go into its streets and say, 11 'Even the dust of your town that clings to our feet, we wipe off against you; nevertheless know this, that the Kingdom of God has come near.' 12 I tell you, it shall be more tolerable on that day for Sodom than for that town."

ONCE THE MARCHING ORDERS of pilgrimage and exodus were revealed on the mountaintop, Jesus turns back to a program of basic training for his followers. He must work with a new cadre of supporters, those who have stuck it out in spite of the mounting sacrifices his mission demands. So we begin this chapter with another tier of the Kingdom's "forces" that Jesus is directing. Imagine, if you will, how an invasion occurs—for that is how the performance is playing out, if you have not already noticed.

First, he sent out the Twelve and gave them nearly ambassadorial status for their roles. Then from a strategic position on the mountain he conferred with three of the Twelve who play the role of key advisers, and they were briefed on the bigger scheme of things for Jesus and his impending visitation. In the account above, one gets the feeling that Jesus is drafting any able-bodied personnel who are close at hand. The fact that he chose seventy (or seventy-two) workers is a symbolic number that in the Jewish traditions stands for the nations of the world. I suppose it means that this mission of Jesus includes everyone—the Gentiles, the Jews, and you in the world that you live in.

One gets the feeling that we are witnessing the mobilization of a Kingdom, as if royal forces are soon to arrive, and now Jesus dispatches the scouts. For the scouts, speed is of the essence. They must reconnoiter the area ahead of the vanguard and draft whatever supplies and volunteers they can muster. Their target is to reach the villages where Jesus will go, perhaps to offer them terms of surrender, so to speak. This message of theirs is urgent and serious: Surrender now and you will escape with your lives! And yet they have no capability for violent action, no army, no cavalry, no one to back them up. In fact, their Kingdom appears to others as meek, like a flock of lambs [10:3], and they face a world of predators, like a pack of wolves.

They rustle up, however, whatever they need. If they are not welcomed, they march to the streets and issue their ultimatum. They cite Sodom as an example, and then they move on. If you remember Sodom, you recognize that judgment can come with sudden and serious intervention.

1. How do I approach my daily routine or discipline in light of the urgency of Jesus's strategy above?

2. How can I envision my daily responsibilities and duties as selected and dispatched by Jesus? How have I been chosen for this "routine" of life?

3. What is my task for today in light of this mission? How can I conclude what is my mission?

4. Read Gen 19:1–29. What application does this story have for the mission that Jesus envisions for the seventy?

> Luke 10:13–20 "Woe to you, Chorazin! woe to you, Bethsaida! for if the mighty works done in you had been done in Tyre and Sidon, they would have repented long ago, sitting in sackcloth and ashes. 14 But it shall be more tolerable in the judgment for Tyre and Sidon than for you.
>
> 15 "And you, Capernaum, will you be exalted to heaven? You shall be brought down to Hades.
>
> 16 "He who hears you hears me, and he who rejects you rejects me, and he who rejects me rejects him who sent me."
>
> 17 The seventy returned with joy, saying, "Lord, even the demons are subject to us in your name!" 18 And he said to them, "I saw Satan fall like lightning from heaven. 19 Behold, I have given you authority to tread upon serpents and scorpions, and over all the power of the enemy; and nothing shall hurt you. 20 Nevertheless do not rejoice in this, that the spirits are subject to you; but rejoice that your names are written in heaven."

How seriously do we take our role in the overall plan? If we are in this mobilization of forces—with numbers much bigger than before—how seriously do we take this commission with its (worldwide?) scope? The call of Jesus enlists the first to respond, the last to respond, the elites and the masses, those originally called (like the Jews), those lately summoned (like you, Theophilus). No one's voice is more valuable than anyone else's.

Whatever confrontation Jesus has in mind, the drama involves life-and-death commands. It is like that line in the sand that the Roman diplomat famously drew to divide those for him and those against him.[1] Doom, doom, doom! We are walking prophets who have nothing but

1. You may or may not know the following story, Theophilus. Antiochus IV Epiphanes of Syria invaded Egypt, an ally of Rome, two hundred years ago. To ward off the Syrians, the Romans dispatched a single legate, invested with the full weight of the Senate. He drew a line in the sand in front of the whole Syrian army, and warned the invaders to withdraw by the time he crossed it. Antiochus immediately pulled out, intimidated and humiliated. That is the kind of ultimatum I am thinking of here.

peace to give and judgment to hand out. Take the two cities in the garbage heap of Israel's collection of nearby cities, Tyre and Sidon. What you represent in your Kingdom message is more authoritative than what a typical prophet like Isaiah[2] expressed in his condemnation of those two cities! Your message is comparable to the fire and brimstone unleashed on Sodom, and the destruction far greater than what Alexander the Great visited on Tyre and Sidon. So, whether you are a Jew who knows your Scripture, or a Greek who knows your epic history, Jesus is speaking stern language! The rhetoric also gauges how great the authority Jesus invests in disciples as his front-line troops, even those recently added. Thus the straightforward connection between the one "who hears you hears me, and the one who rejects you rejects me, and he who rejects me rejects him who sent me" [10:16].

When these fresh troops come back, they have tasted the thrill of battle—unleash them, Jesus did, and they treaded on Satan like they would squish spiders and snakes. Jesus knows it is the undoing of his ancient enemy, the one who once was in the heavens, but now flees to secure things on earth. Now this rival cowers and runs for cover as these new followers draw lines in the sand.

What power you and I have, Theophilus, though we do not count ourselves among the Twelve or the closest trio. We are among the third or fourth generation after them, like the seventy that represent all those besides the first few, but we share in the same battlefield zeal.

And finally, Theophilus, it all begins with the fact that Jesus himself has signed them up—whether you envision them as his supporting cast or his conscripts. Apart from him, they can do nothing. This is the source of their calling and their authority. Lose sight of this fact, and we count for nothing in drama or even give ground on the battlefield. For we then begin to act or fight on Satan's terms. If heaven backs us up, though, we have singular recognition and acclaim, certain rescue when needed, and certain victory when the curtain call or finale comes.

1. How would I classify myself among the ranks of Jesus's followers, a newcomer or a veteran? How do I regard the veterans if a newcomer, or the newcomers if a veteran? What new things do I need to back up with my support—or what old traditions or ways do I need to respect?

2. Isaiah [chap. 23] had a lot to say in condemning Tyre and Sidon.

2. What victories have I seen in my discipleship over the short or long term? How do I experience the "joy" of battle?

3. Do I sense the weightiness of judgment that I carry as a follower of Jesus?

4. How do I exercise "authority" over "serpents and scorpions"? What would I classify as this category of opposition?

> Luke 10:21–24 In that same hour he rejoiced in the Holy Spirit and said, "I thank thee, Father, Lord of heaven and earth, that thou hast hidden these things from the wise and understanding and revealed them to babes; yea, Father, for such was thy gracious will. 22 All things have been delivered to me by my Father; and no one knows who the Son is except the Father, or who the Father is except the Son and any one to whom the Son chooses to reveal him."
>
> 23 Then turning to the disciples he said privately, "Blessed are the eyes which see what you see!
>
> 24 "For I tell you that many prophets and kings desired to see what you see, and did not see it, and to hear what you hear, and did not hear it."

Jesus once again draws his select corps of disciples to him and explains to them privately what is going on. When I spoke of the return of the seventy (or seventy-two) draftees from their mission, Theophilus, I spoke of the thrill of battle. Jesus, however, sees a bigger plan accomplished by the advances of the Kingdom, one that causes him to go beyond this thrill into a sense of triumph. I used the word ἀγαλλιάω (*agalliaō* [10:21]), a word that means to be overjoyed, what we might say is being giddy. Jesus realized that he was already seeing the completion of a grand strategy that was only glimpsed by previous generations. It was a strategy that imposed the Kingdom upon a world that up to this time had been resistant. It was a world that bowed to Caesars and Herods, but was far from the "babes" that he had enlisted in his ranks. Yes, previous generations did have their Kingdom ambassadors, but they did not have the full picture. Even though the epic finale would take Jesus through bitter struggle and tragic pain in the days ahead, for a moment Jesus tasted the good things that were sure to come when his exodus was complete.

1. What are the "prophets and kings" Jesus is referring to here? How does this privileged position that Jesus gives to the disciples compare with what he said earlier (7:28) about the privileged position his followers have over John the Baptist?

2. How does this description of Jesus being giddy with joy fit with my conception of Jesus? What are the things in my life or more broadly in the world that also might bring such joy to Jesus?

Excuses

Luke 10:25–34 And behold, a lawyer stood up to put him to the test, saying, "Teacher, what shall I do to inherit eternal life?" 26 He said to him, "What is written in the law? How do you read?"

27 And he answered, "You shall love the Lord your God with all your heart, and with all your soul, and with all your strength, and with all your mind; and your neighbor as yourself." 28 And he said to him, "You have answered right; do this, and you will live." 29 But he, desiring to justify himself, said to Jesus, "And who is my neighbor?"

30 Jesus replied, "A man was going down from Jerusalem to Jericho, and he fell among robbers, who stripped him and beat him, and departed, leaving him half dead. 31 Now by chance a priest was going down that road; and when he saw him he passed by on the other side. 32 So likewise a Levite, when he came to the place and saw him, passed by on the other side.

33 But a Samaritan, as he journeyed, came to where he was; and when he saw him, he had compassion, 34 and went to him and bound up his wounds, pouring on oil and wine; then he set him on his own beast and brought him to an inn, and took care of him.

Another potential recruit for Jesus walks on stage and wonders why he is not among those who represent the Kingdom. He knows the Jewish Scriptures by heart and probably has tried hard to keep them. He wants to know more about what Jesus says it will take to "do" this written word, to put it into action. Here is where Jesus tells a parable to illustrate the whole point of the Kingdom. Let me rephrase the first part of the parable as if Jesus were retelling it:

"What would happen if you saw a man who was needy to the point of repulsiveness? What would the written law tell you to do if you were a priest, just coming off temple duty? What would it tell you to do if you were a Levite and concerned to teach this word carefully in various places, and had just now also come from your pious service in the temple? What would you do if you were at the lowest rung of Jewish religious status, a Samaritan born of mixed background?"

I will stop the synopsis for now, because I have reached the point of something worth mentioning. What is the parable's *mystērion* for this would-be disciple, that is, what is he supposed to take away from these choices? You have to go back to the Sermon on the Plain to summon a collage that pulls together the various pieces of this parable puzzle. In that sermon Jesus speaks about a mercy that welcomes the humble, the poor, the hated, and the unlikeliest of candidates to the Kingdom. It was a mercy that was shown in the divine visitations: a mercy designed not to pay back the wages of laws correctly memorized and applied, but instead freely given *charis* or favor to the lowliest and most obscure figures. Ultimately, as I tried to point out earlier, the focus is on Jesus himself as the source and center of mercy. That is why even though the Samaritan is the apparent hero in this story, I think the implications go much further—as I will illustrate from Jesus's reframing the story below:

"And what would you do if *I* (yes, you heard it: *me*) were that beaten-up excuse of a pilgrim, one who ventured into the wrong neighborhood and was jumped by robbers and cutthroats, what would you do for me? What kind of *charis* would you offer? What would you want done if you were victim, waylaid because you follow me? Because that is where I send my Kingdom disciples, like lambs among wolves.

"Now you understand better why just knowing the Law does not make you wise for the Kingdom, why I called the 'babes' in the previous passage to go out in my name . . . and not you. If you are willing to show mercy, then you are fit to follow my Kingdom teaching; because I am the one who needs such care. The Law therefore is not only about keeping commands but also about practicing beneficence."

Such is the paradoxical lesson that Jesus leaves us with here, Theophilus. Can you hear echoes of the Golden Rule again?

1. How would I respond to each of Jesus's questions above, imagining that I am priest, Levite, and now Samaritan? Are there persons who might correspond to each of these in today's society?

2. Think about someone similar to Jesus as a beaten-up traveler that I have encountered recently or perhaps some time in the past. How might I have been better suited to respond if I had recognized Jesus in this person?

3. What do I think now is the relationship between the written word (the Law) and the Kingdom directives that Jesus gives his followers in the previous passages about mission? Do they complement one another? Are there tensions? Where are there tensions for me?

FIGURE 4: *The Good Samaritan* (by Garrett Shireman)

Luke 10:38–42 Now as they went on their way, he entered a village; and a woman named Martha received him into her house.
39 And she had a sister called Mary, who sat at the Lord's feet
and listened to his teaching. 40 But Martha was distracted with
much serving; and she went to him and said, "Lord, do you not
care that my sister has left me to serve alone? Tell her then to
help me."

41 But the Lord answered her, "Martha, Martha, you are anxious
and troubled about many things; 42 one thing is needful. Mary
has chosen the good portion, which shall not be taken away
from her."

Here is the second story which I don't think you will find elsewhere
in anything you have heard about Jesus, but you can see how it fits. Jesus
continues on his way—seemingly wandering in my version—but purposefully, if I have it rightly understood. He is on his way to Jerusalem,
yes, everyone sees that. But what is he in the process of accomplishing
along the way? As I just reported, he called seventy trainees as a sign that
he intends discipleship to be a universal call. He began with the Twelve,
he intensifies it with the trio, and then he expands it to everyone (the seventy). Many that he calls have excuses, ones that you have already heard
in my narrative [9:57–62]—"I have to know what the provisions for this
mission are"; "I have too many family obligations"; "I need to sign off on
my previous commitments"; and so on. You may remember that all of a
sudden these things came up when Jesus made his momentous decision
to head for Jerusalem.

Just now I have given you two episodes that I found according to my
own sources, the story of the Samaritan Jesus told to the lawyer and this
one about Martha and Mary. What do these episodes have in common?
They show even more "good" reasons to avoid the call to join the mission.
The good is often the enemy of the best—or to cite a popular saying, "The
road to hell is paved with the best of intentions." You see, the lawyer probably lived a good life according to the commandments, so Jesus set him
straight about religious people so caught up in their "duties" as religious
people that they missed Jesus who was beaten up along the road. Then
we come to these two women who have the choice of the Kingdom or
service, even good service and responsibilities.

People too often mix up things by comparing themselves to Martha
and Mary, which only in part gets at the point of the story. It is not that

everyone is either a Martha or Mary, but that everyone is called to recognize Jesus in the Kingdom. Don't ignore him like the lawyer (or the priest or Levite), and don't get tied up in duties and excuses like the would-be disciples full of excuses why they couldn't (or wouldn't) go to Jerusalem. Similarly, Martha would miss Jesus by staying in the kitchen or serving the food. Don't misunderstand me: she was probably doing helpful service, maybe even following her sense of duty.

But Jesus changes everything: listen to him! Who serves or attends to Jesus? Many of us feel more comfortable paying for the banquet. Too many others feel fine about coming to the banquet, but forget about the *charis* that the woman gave to Jesus when she wept at his feet and wiped them with her hair [7:36–49]. He honored her above the one who threw the party. Mary has the right priorities in view here, and Martha needs to realign hers.

1. Are there times when I feel the burden of responsibilities to the extent of missing its meaning? Have these things ever gotten in the way of following Jesus?

2. Think about good things, even seemingly "necessary" things, that consume a lot of time in my life. Are they ever so consuming that I might worry about them or be distracted by them? What are some ways I can lessen the pressure of the situation?

3. Describe a time when I have turned away from stress and pressure and found "a good portion" as a result.

4. What does it mean to me to "sit at the feet of Jesus?"

Getting Ready through Prayer

Luke 11:1–4 He was praying in a certain place, and when he ceased, one of his disciples said to him, "Lord, teach us to pray, as John taught his disciples."

2 And he said to them, "When you pray, say: 'Father, hallowed be thy name. Thy Kingdom come. 3 Give us each day our daily bread; 4 and forgive us our sins, for we ourselves forgive everyone who is indebted to us; and lead us not into temptation.'"

In my arrangement of events as Jesus marches toward Jerusalem, we take a pause from the rehearsals that the public sees and focus on the private lessons for his disciples. This is a tutorial on prayer and how it sustains us. I have already reported how Jesus's inner compass seemed to come from his times of private reflection. Now the disciples want to know his secret. Let me now go over the core of the lesson he gave.

He stresses that the disciples had an identity that began with naming God as Father apart from all other loyalty claims. Packed into his concise "demonstration" is the understanding that they had the privilege of summoning the Kingdom—perhaps establishing the Kingdom Jesus brought. After recognizing the primacy of "Father" and Kingdom, then he taught them to see their resources coming from God day by day [11:2–3].

Next [11:4] he implies that they would show shortcomings both to God and each other, and thus they would need to be forgiven and to forgive. Finally, "lead us not into temptation" (the translation above) puts a smiley face on a dark reality that many Jews around him knew: there would be some future universal reckoning enveloping everyone—you might retranslate this phrase as "put us not to the [final] test." (And often another phrase from Jesus is quoted here, "But deliver us from the evil one.") He was suggesting this crisis might be averted by prayer. Four short lines he offers as the basics for how one might pray.

However, lest you think that Jesus's prayer was somehow detached from everyday reality, he told us a story that went in a direction we could all picture and laugh about. It was as if the Teacher took us from the lofty to the ridiculous—a winning strategy Jesus was pretty good at.

Let me sketch the outlines of this story in different words—you can go back and examine my original version later. For now, let me paraphrase Jesus [11:5–8]:

"You know that crazy neighbor of yours. Well, he arrives at midnight and pounds at your door. 'Get up,' yells he. 'I have somebody that just arrived, and there's no food left in the house. All I need is a couple of crusts.' Of course you know he wants more than day-old bread. 'No,' says you. 'Everybody's asleep. If I get up, I have to get everyone up to get to the door. Come back tomorrow!'

"But your crazy neighbor doesn't budge. 'C'mon, get up!' he yells louder. 'Open up, *please*!'—forcing his words through the gap between the floor and door.

"So what do you do? He won't take no for an answer. He is whining and weeping. 'Just three crusts.' Well, you feel like boxing his ears; but when you finally get to the door, he leaps up from the ground and blubbers and hugs you for your neighborliness. What can you do for a fellow like this? Well, you give him what he wants and more. You find yourself opening up the whole food pantry to him."

Jesus's conclusion? That is how we ought to pray to God as our Father, according to Jesus! The word I use to describe "your crazy neighbor" is *anaideia* (ἀναίδεια), not simply "persistent," but *embarrassingly persistent*. Remember the woman who wept at the feet of Jesus—at a banquet, in front of everyone! That is *anaideia*. That is how you need to pray, Theophilus. Follow the basics of that master prayer above, of course, but throw yourself wholly into each application of its utterance. Be passionate, be pleading, be pathetic—if need be—when it comes to the nitty-gritty application of that so-called "Lord's Prayer."

1. How would I assess my relationship with God as my father?

2. Take some time to consider the first obligations of the Lord's Prayer. Go through each clause for the following examination of conscience:

   a. How have I sanctified the "name" or reputation and status of God in my life?

   b. Do I call down the Kingdom of God?

   c. How have I prayed for what I need today (not tomorrow or next year)?

   d. What is forgiveness? How does it differ from pardon or exoneration? Is there someone I need to forgive? Do I need to seek forgiveness from someone?

   e. How do I imagine the tribulation that Jesus brings up at the end of the prayer? How do I respond to it in prayer and intercession?

3. Read Luke 11:5–13. How much *anaideia* do I show in my prayer? Call to mind a memory of God answering my complete neediness. How can I be more persistent and emotionally invested in my prayers? What are my feelings about flinging myself at the mercy of God as Father?

4. "My words ascend, but my thoughts remain below, words without thought ne'er to heaven go." How do Shakespeare's words from Hamlet apply to the Lord's Prayer and the story that Jesus offers right after?

Getting Ready for Spiritual Opposition

Luke 11:14–23 14 Now he was casting out a demon that was dumb; when the demon had gone out, the dumb man spoke, and the people marveled. 15 But some of them said, "He casts out demons by Beelzebul, the prince of demons"; 16 while others, to test him, sought from him a sign from heaven.

17 But he, knowing their thoughts, said to them, "Every kingdom divided against itself is laid waste, and a divided household falls. 18 And if Satan also is divided against himself, how will his kingdom stand? For you say that I cast out demons by Beelzebul. 19 And if I cast out demons by Beelzebul, by whom do your sons cast them out? Therefore they shall be your judges. 20 But if it is by the finger of God that I cast out demons, then the Kingdom of God has come upon you. 21 When a strong man, fully armed, guards his own palace, his goods are in peace; 22 but when one stronger than he assails him and overcomes him, he takes away his armor in which he trusted, and divides his spoil. 23 He who is not with me is against me, and he who does not gather with me scatters."

Before you turn away from this short tutorial on prayer, you should notice how I arrange things in my "orderly account." The next incident shows how prayer for the Kingdom is opposed by determined spiritual forces. We have encountered them off and on in this volume *Memoirs of How It All Began* and in its companion book *Memoirs of an Unfinished Tale*, so we should realize that Jesus uses such clashes with spiritual forces as teaching moments. So let us get into the gist of prayer's function (besides recollection and petition), spiritual conflict in the demonic realms.

Let me lay out a few particulars here, but I hope you will go back and review what I wrote [11:14–28]: Jesus expels a demon which had some hold on a man's ability to speak. Now that he speaks, the ever-watchful critics of Jesus allege he did it by an alliance with the supreme demon (whose reputation would malign Jesus and everything about the Kingdom he preached)? Other less harsh voices challenge him to do something more to prove his divine and not demonic power sources.

Jesus's response is insightful [11:17–23]: "The forces I'm fighting are organized and calculating, so why would they fight themselves to establish me? The same applies to you if you all do these kinds of things in your struggle against demons.

"Your asking for more signs reminds me of the story about Moses, the prophet you all cite, in his face-off with Pharaoh. Moses represents the Hebrew nation, Pharaoh the oppressive kingdom. So Moses worked his wonders in the public arena—but so did Pharaoh and his magicians. Moses stood for liberation, Pharaoh for bondage. Since Pharaoh could at least hold his own in the early going, he refused to give in to Moses's demands for liberation. He fought back—and when he could not, he stalled by asking for more and more signs to prove Moses actually was from God. After all, Moses had no visible army and nothing valuable to trade for his enslaved people. The thing is, Moses did in the end prove he was the "finger of God," but Pharaoh did not concede to the prophet until incalculable damages were wrought upon his own realms."

Do you see Jesus's point? He is claiming to be a Moses-like prophet who does wield the finger of God. If Jesus is offering liberation to souls tormented like this voiceless man, he is threatening the whole demonic system—as Jesus already mentioned when "Satan fell like lightning from heaven" [10:18] or when he drove "Legion" into the abyss [8:26-39]. I would dare say that Jesus is showing his disciples by this particular lesson that Kingdom prayer of the type he just taught is displacing "Satan" from his stronghold as well as stripping him of his "armor" and "spoil" [11:22].

1. What are the images of warfare and violent confrontation in this passage?

2. What is the "finger of God?" What does this image imply about the power of God? For example, what is the finger attached to? What powers does a finger have?

3. What does the finger of God imply about the power of Jesus? What does it imply about the power of Satan?

4. Take inventory and see how the "finger of God" would make a difference for the people you pray for.

5. What does the last line imply about the stakes of discipleship in this situation?

> Luke 11:24-28 "When the unclean spirit has gone out of a man, he passes through waterless places seeking rest; and finding none he says, 'I will return to my house from which I came.' 25 And when he comes he finds it swept and put in order.

26 "Then he goes and brings seven other spirits more evil than himself, and they enter and dwell there; and the last state of that man becomes worse than the first."

27 As he said this, a woman in the crowd raised her voice and said to him, "Blessed is the womb that bore you, and the breasts that you sucked!" 28 But he said, "Blessed rather are those who hear the word of God and keep it!"

Now I give you a short closing [11:24–26] to this short tutorial Jesus gave on prayer and spiritual conflict. First, just because you cleanse yourself or others of the influence of demons does not mean you are thereby permanently free from them. No, they keep trying to invade the safe haven you carved out of enemy territory, and they come back stronger and stronger. Even though you have made a place for the Kingdom, sorted out priorities, and steered clear of sin, demons will constantly test and attack. If you (or your comrades) give in, the result will be a worse condition than the first one. Remember this colorful proverb, if you remember any: "As a dog returns to its vomit, so a fool returns to his folly" (Prov 26:11). The soul's inclinations and interests tend toward breakdown, spiritually and physically—like a fool toward folly. So you, too, will find a need to be aware that the demonic world subtly capitalizes on our nature.

Jesus's second point to finish off his advice on prayer [11:27–28]: Be careful, lest you rest in your upbringing and natural skills. It is not in one's background or parents or natural virtue that one holds the ground for the Kingdom; it comes through clinging to the word of God. The woman I cited—obviously caught up in admiration for the powers a parent has over the child—lauds the mother (and the father) of such a wonderfully virtuous man as Jesus. Yet Jesus rejects this picture, for he says that spiritual life is based on an individual's response to the divine call, the word that comes to each one of us—not to our families. How well do you know the core of God's call on your life, Theophilus? Is it purely and finally God your father? Or is it mediated and reduced in the echoes of those around us?

1. What are some examples I have seen of "relapsing" in my own life? What bad habits do I have that I must be careful not to indulge in? Give some examples of "relapsing" I have seen at work among those around me. Is the "last state . . . worse than the first"? How can this condition be avoided?

2. How aware am I of spiritual attack and temptation? Do I write off my failures or my lapsing as falling into my personal weaknesses or problems only? Are there ways of claiming authority over these things in addition to human willpower?

3. How well do I hear the word of God right now? What would I say if someone asked me right now what God is saying to me? How well do I know and pay attention to the Scriptures on a daily basis?

Getting Ready for Public Opposition

> Luke 11:29–32 29 When the crowds were increasing, he began to say, "This generation is an evil generation; it seeks a sign, but no sign shall be given to it except the sign of Jonah. 30 For as Jonah became a sign to the men of Nineveh, so will the Son of man be to this generation. 31 The queen of the South will arise at the judgment with the men of this generation and condemn them; for she came from the ends of the earth to hear the wisdom of Solomon, and behold, something greater than Solomon is here. 32 The men of Nineveh will arise at the judgment with this generation and condemn it; for they repented at the preaching of Jonah, and behold, something greater than Jonah is here."

Let us pretend that some extraordinary natural event is occurring, say, a comet shooting across the sky over many nights. Your neighbors gather regularly to gape at this wonder, and everyone asks what it means. Do you cut the discussion short by insisting on yet another comet before you will pay attention to the skies? I doubt it. I bet you will speculate on its message, whether you are as wise as Solon, wealthy as Maecenas, or poor as Diogenes.[3] It is a visitation, pure and simple. So what am I driving at here?

Consider Jesus. He had seized our attention by some of his startling speeches and outlandish ideas. What did this man have to say to the poor and humble—like the prophet Jonah to the masses of Nineveh [11:30]? What did he have to say to the high and mighty like Solomon to the queen of the South, that exotic land of wealth and sophistication?[4] Did

3. Just in case you don't recognize these names, Theophilus: Solon was one of the Seven Wise Men of Greece; Maecenas bankrolled Augustus Caesar; Diogenes the Cynic philosopher sneered at wealth and lived in a barrel.

4. Do you know these stories? Look up Jonah sometime in the short scroll that bears his name. You can read the whole thing in an hour. I am sure you have heard of

the Ninevites and the queen need more to capture their attention? More signs, more miracles? Was the generation of Jesus simply unwilling to hear his message, just like Pharaoh to admit that the finger of God was working liberation? Once folks have decided to ignore a stranger's face, how can they ever recognize the stranger when they meet again? People in the audience of Jesus need to stop ignoring his presentation on the grounds that they want another performance.

The point is this: Jesus had interrupted everyone's daily routines like a comet with a message about the Kingdom. The Kingdom came into their midst with its *charis!*—not ending with a period, but with an exclamation point.

Why does Jesus compare himself to Jonah in this passage? Because Jonah stands as a riddle for a God who often works outside the box and contradicts our expectations. Why does he compare himself to Solomon? Because Solomon had a keen sense of interpreting riddles and proverbs. Jesus shouts to us in this passage: The Kingdom and its *charis* are available! Is this the moment of visitation? Are you ready? Do you want it?

A comet makes us realize that we are at the mercy of strange powers flashing out all around us. Nineveh and the queen of the South realized that divine answers to life's questions are indeed mysterious and miraculous, that God works outside of our customs, habits, and routines. Nineveh had worked so hard to build its city and the queen her throne! Yet they confessed their inadequacies. What are their examples telling us about Jesus?

Jonah and the queen were astonished at God's ways, yet Jesus tells us that they changed as a result of what they heard. Will I change my ways when Jesus interrupts my life with riddles and reversals? Or will I continue to scoff and ignore? At such moments of clear divine interruptions, we must remember that he who sits in the heavens laughs at us.[5] Our insistence for more signs will not alter divine visitations.

Surely Jonah, the people of Nineveh, and the queen of the South represent a throwback to what Jesus said at his hometown debut: outsiders,

---

Solomon as a fabled king who had authority over demons and whose wisdom was the stuff of fables. For Jews they are as proverbial as Odysseus and Agamemnon for the world of Greeks and Romans.

5. This is one of my main themes in my sequel, *Unfinished Tale*, 26–28, beginning with my interpretation of Psalm 2 [Acts 4:23–32 and elsewhere]. Since I recognize God's sense of drama and performance, I write my books in the same fashion, that is, I try to entertain and teach. This is what distinguishes my "orderly account" [1:3] from what others have written.

like widow of Nain and Naaman the Syrian, are included in the path of the comet's brilliance. This goes back to the same warning he issued to Chorazin, Bethsaida, and Capernaum to repent [10:13–16] because he was on his way to Jerusalem, just like Tyre and Sidon were hearing the Seventy who went out. Thus, Jonah went out and Nineveh repented, the report about Solomon went out, and the queen of the South repented. Now the chickens are coming back to roost: Jesus is himself turning toward Jerusalem after the missions of the Seventy and the Twelve. How will Jerusalem and its generation respond when he arrives in Jerusalem? We shall know soon.

An Afterthought

Our involvement in the Kingdom, as Jesus presents it so far, is not primarily something forced upon the world by spectacular signs and miracles. Certainly such things are a part of the drama, but the plot unfolding depends more on our response. Thus, preaching is a higher priority than the spectacle of superhuman acts. Jesus gives two models for his performance on the public stage: Jonah and Solomon. Sure, both had signs connected with them—Jonah was in the belly of the whale, Solomon had the reputation of being an exorcist. But Jesus purposefully avoids their wonderworking side and focuses on their preaching. While some accounts may focus on Jonah returning to life after being disgorged from a whale, this is not the whole message in my opinion. Jesus chose Jonah as his "sign" mainly because of his preaching not his miracles. In like manner, Solomon's wisdom also qualifies, not his exorcisms.

Again, Theophilus, keep in mind that Jesus has just verbally blasted his own kinfolk: Bethsaida and Chorazin and Capernaum. They will suffer condemnation comparable to Sodom and Tyre and Sidon, the textbook adversaries of the work of God. These villages did not respond to the word of God, and the disciples were told to shake the dust off their feet. In other words, an awful fate awaits those who do not respond with acceptance. That is why Jesus's examples of the queen of Sheba and Ninevites get our attention. Even if the public at hand opposes us, we are to continue the mission farther and farther until we reach the open ears of people like you, Theophilus.

1. Read the four short chapters in the book of Jonah. Then read about the admiration of the queen of South for Solomon (1 Kgs 10:1–13). Why does Jesus use these two stories to describe his work?

2. Have I ever dismissed some new idea or person only to find myself reconsidering my assessment because of what others have told me? How would this experience be something like what Jesus is describing here?

3. What does it take for me to be willing to change my ways? What things that I keep putting off need to change?

Getting Ready for Institutional Opposition

Just a bit ago, I described for you spiritual opposition in the form of demonic forces. Then we ran into the skepticism and apathy of our neighbors. Now we encounter institutional opponents, the Pharisees, a group we met in the earliest days of Jesus's touring around Capernaum. All things considered, they should have been allies for Jesus, but they turn out to be localized and determined religious forces against Jesus. There is much about them I said earlier [see, for example, 11:37–54], but now let me point out a few more tidbits to think about.

When the Kingdom ought to have counted on allies from among those who knew and professed the word of God, Jesus was disappointed and expressed it in no uncertain terms. Here he was, invited by a Pharisee to a banquet—attended by all the elites (the leading lawyers, scholars, and teachers). Now, who are these fellows? As a group, these people knew the laws that defined the Jews—laws on how much to give to the temple service, how much to give to the poor, and so on, but they did not keep them in the context Jesus thought was appropriate. We may wonder if by hosting Jesus at their dinners they are trying to hijack the Kingdom movement of Jesus. Are they trying to tap into its energy and enthusiasm?

Jesus's rebuke might be a bit off-putting according to our more polite norms of discourse. So I will attempt to tidy up things from his speech in my summary below. However, keep in mind that Jesus's style is quite common in his cultural world. For some perspective on the context, though, you should imagine the heat of a Roman judicial hearing where you as a speaker have a number of styles and techniques to persuade your audience.

At the same time, Jesus is giving a performance as usual, and he will use this new setting as a stage for his message. Imagine Jesus in your town's forum, driving home his points like an *archōn* at the podium— only here he is in a large hall of Jewish notables. At hand are materials he seizes as props: there are cups, foods, spices, and the like at the table. Outside the door to this dining hall are beggars and panhandlers who congregate at the markets and fountains where Jesus wanders with the crowds. Farther off, Jesus can beckon to the monuments built by rich people on behalf of their ancestral heroes. Just outside the city gates lies the cemetery. Do you have the picture, Theophilus? Jesus is going to use all these objects to make his points clear.

By now Jesus is an artist in the *carpe diem* ("seize the day/moment") method of teaching. That means he has the knack for capturing lessons that arise on the spot and then capturing listeners with passion and wit. In this particular gathering of elites, however, these skills tend to polarize sides. Keep in mind that there is a decided hostility toward Jesus. He is to them a pariah. He has clashed with them earlier in my account, as you know. His opponents even perceive him as a threat, even if the occasional hardened soul may secretly admire and concede Jesus's case.

How do we describe this group's institutional opposition to Jesus's teachings? They pay up on the tithes (religious taxes), but they do not think twice about depriving their poorer brethren of their resources. In other words, Jesus alleges that they wear a mask of charity in public, but of greed in private. Their greed endows them with priorities that Jesus considers alien to the Kingdom (and here you can imagine Jesus picking up a white cup and holding it up for all to see), that is, devoid of social responsibility [11:39]. For example, recall how Jesus commissions his disciples to take to the road with a minimum of baggage. The Pharisees? They "load men with burdens hard to bear" [11:46]. It is as if Jesus would have his followers leaping for joy, while the Pharisees would tie everyone up like a beast of burden.

Instead of keeping the two great commandments, summed up in the justice and love of God [11:42], they concentrated on the little things or only the noticeable things (here Jesus points to the spices on the table: useless if the plates are empty of food)—like the lawyer who did not know his Samaritan neighbor, having missed Jesus beaten up on the road. Similarly the Pharisees focused on being toasted and celebrated by the other Jews [11:43] instead of being prophetic and courageous; popular they were with the notables, but not in solidarity with the down and out. They are like those who promote public monuments (here he points outside to the public square), but don't know who they commemorate or why their deeds were important [11:42, 47]. The ideals worth dying for escape their attention—unless they reverberate in some way to their own self-preservation.

Their institutions (academies, lectures, dinners) look nice as shiny trophies, but there's one problem: if a trophy's inscription is illegible, you really don't know what it stands for. Of course public memorials command our attention as we walk by, but what they stand for can be out of touch with real life. So the Pharisees build up fancy interpretations of the Law, but skip doing much themselves along the radical lines that Jesus taught about the Kingdom.

Then he attacks the "lawyers"—I suppose we might call them scholars and teachers of fellow Jews. They are the ones who give interpretations to assist what the Pharisees say are religious ideals. Instead of lightening up things by clarifying priorities, they pile on even more burdens—and with such burdens come weariness and worries. Remember, Theophilus, Jesus sent out his disciples with nothing and with an uncomplicated message. Instead of the Kingdom's need for itinerant simplicity, the lawyers "load it on" [11:46, 52].

In the end, Jesus tells them, the mission of the lawyers leads to the graveyard [11:47], the ash heap for all prophetic dreams and dreamers. (Here he may have acted out walking through the city gates to pay some courtesy at a tomb.) Ironically enough, the lawyers help to destroy ideals that the Kingdom stands for—these lawyers are no different from Israel's wicked kings who murdered the divine messengers of an earlier era. In short, they snuff out whatever relief comes from examples of past divine visitations.

I can only imagine, Theophilus, what Jesus sensed for his mission, if martyrdom was the outcome for those earlier prophets. His pilgrimage would lead to the same place many of his forebears had preached, and where often they met cruel ends. No wonder then that his words hung bitingly upon the ears of these largely institutional agents: he was facing age-old adversaries, these prosecutors and prison guards and hatchet men. Yes, the blood of bygone days would cry out for vindication from this current generation. If Jesus had earlier tasted the good things of a completed exodus [10:21], at this banquet there was a serving of gall.

Yet, Theophilus, Jesus could capture souls too. His woes and warnings represent the wise counsel of God for the new era the Kingdom was establishing. There would be accountability, he declares:

> Therefore also the Wisdom of God said, "I will send them prophets and apostles, some of whom they will kill and persecute," that the blood of all the prophets, shed from the foundation of the world, may be required of this generation, from the blood of Abel to the blood of Zechariah, who perished between the altar and the sanctuary. Yes, I tell you, it shall be required of this generation. [11:49–51]

He is the voice of this counsel, that is, he is "Wisdom" incarnate.[6] Imagine what this counsel entailed: prophets, apostles, martyrs all lining up to make his voice heard through them. Now his band of disciples go forth as his prophets, and the Kingdom hangs in the balance for the audience.

And what is the final word about "the key" [11:52]? The key opens up the gate that leads to the final outcome for the Kingdom. (Here Jesus performs the ritual of unlocking a gate and walking through.) The lawyers and the Pharisees represent the institution that keeps things closed, that maintains the status quo, and that supports the interpretations that keep everyone from being included in the new order. (Now he dramatically stamps his way out of the hall, leaving his audience frozen in their place.)

I am sure this audience of Pharisees had the same impression of Jesus as the Nazareth synagogue when they listened to quotations from Isaiah: But who is this man performing in front of us now? Is he the corporate conscience for Israel's past? Is he the fountain for Israel's future?

Left behind at this banquet are the Pharisees and lawyers seemingly uninvited to the banquet Jesus has alluded to often. In one stunning moment it hits them. What irony that Jesus is the honored guest at this banquet that locks out his rag-tag volunteers and newcomers. Needless to add, Theophilus, this is a climactic moment that points to what is ahead on this march. In Jerusalem he would make another departure—an *exodus* of his own—again leaving everyone stunned.

1. How can there be people in "professional" positions who keep the public in the dark or ignorant? How do they otherwise have

---

6. Remember the passage where Jesus cited Wisdom as having children [7:35]. Thus, he again imagines himself as Wisdom.

authority or powers of office? How can I respect the office while critiquing the office-holder?

2. Do these people have "keys" that would help me, at least in theory?

3. How is it possible to build the tombs for heroes, but otherwise contribute to the failure of their mission?

4. Imagine you were in the "Wisdom" council of God. What would you have observed from your position about the groups Luke presents here? Give the testimonies of each of the parties presented—the lawyers and Pharisees, Jesus himself, earlier prophets, current and perhaps earlier apostles, martyrs, and so on. What is the background story of the martyrs Jesus speaks about here (Abel to Zechariah)?

Another Afterthought

Luke 11:53–54 As he went away from there, the scribes and the Pharisees began to press him hard, and to provoke him to speak of many things, 54 lying in wait for him, to catch at something he might say.

Several days have passed since I put down my pen. Now I return to the scroll to register these words before sending you the entire *Memoirs*. As I think over what happened, I confess I have been captured by the power of Jesus's dinner speech. He had turned the tables on his hosts, almost as if he had anticipated their future campaign against him. It makes me wonder if Jesus had an idea already that this performance was in fact his apologia—something like a defense of his mission. Was he signaling by his constant references to tombs, memorials, and martyred prophets that his own pilgrimage and mission would earn him this same fate of death and martyrdom? Did he see in his destination, Jerusalem, the place where ultimate scrutiny was required for any visitation in the name of the Kingdom of God? That was where he was bound, and this "send-off" by the Pharisees served as his anti-Last Supper that would prepare him for the events ahead.

I tried to hint at something like this in these closing words above. Now that the Pharisees "begin" to construct their trap for Jesus, I use the word δεινός, *deinos* ("terrible" or "monstrous")—something terrifying is happening here. They "lie in wait. . . to catch" him in a trap, as a hunted beast deserving its slaughter.

How Ready Are We for the Kingdom?

Luke 12:1–12 In the meantime, when so many thousands of the multitude had gathered together that they trod upon one another, he began to say to his disciples first, "Beware of the leaven of the Pharisees, which is hypocrisy. 2 Nothing is covered up that will not be revealed, or hidden that will not be known. 3 Therefore whatever you have said in the dark shall be heard in the light, and what you have whispered in private rooms shall be proclaimed upon the housetops.

4 "I tell you, my friends, do not fear those who kill the body, and after that have no more that they can do. 5 But I will warn you whom to fear: fear him who, after he has killed, has power to cast into hell; yes, I tell you, fear him! 6 Are not five sparrows sold for two pennies? And not one of them is forgotten before God. 7 Why, even the hairs of your head are all numbered. Fear not; you are of more value than many sparrows.

8 "And I tell you, everyone who acknowledges me before men, the Son of man also will acknowledge before the angels of God; 9 but he who denies me before men will be denied before the angels of God. 10 And everyone who speaks a word against the Son of man will be forgiven; but he who blasphemes against the Holy Spirit will not be forgiven. 11 And when they bring you before the synagogues and the rulers and the authorities, do not be anxious how or what you are to answer or what you are to say; 12 for the Holy Spirit will teach you in that very hour what you ought to say."

Three Tests: Internal, External, and Final

The three tests that Jesus now speaks about come on the heels of the confrontation with the Pharisees. It was, as I speculated, an anti-Last Supper, plotted by his adversaries and overturned by Jesus's performance. As he walks out on the Pharisees, now he turns to his disciples "first" [v. 2], in spite of the crowds pressing on all sides. Is it out of concern for them as they face opposition, as implied by the lines immediately preceding this scene [11:53–54]? Or does he want to prepare them "first" in spite of the fawning crowds around them—so as to be sober for the days ahead?

This is the only time that Jesus calls his disciples "friends" [12:4] that I remember from my sources, so we can say he means these words to them as peers or partners in the barrage of three tests that I delineate below from his speech. They certainly would face similar hostile audiences, and he senses an urgency for training them how to perform in like manner.

Test One: Internal Affairs We Can Control

The first section [12:1–3] has to do with a test that Jesus applies to what is "inside" his disciples, that is, what their internal state is before God. If the Pharisees validly keep the externals the Jewish religious law requires, what ought to be the internal dimension of the faith? Here we should know that just like yeast infiltrates from within, so the disciple must be aware of what the "yeast" is within oneself.

God knows every motive and ambition behind decisions, so he can test our solidity and integrity. As Jesus puts it, all intentions and purposes will come out like shouts from the housetop to everyone in the village. Thus, judgment begins on a disciple's internal affairs, something like judgment begins with Israel as a nation before it proceeds outwardly to the rest of the world. Jesus demands that his disciples show genuineness: what they whisper inside themselves should be what they manifest in their behavior. Our internal constitution may camouflage itself, but sooner or later God will flush things out for our comeuppance.

Test Two: External Pressures to Test Our Response

The next section [12:4–7] is what disciples will encounter externally, things which more or less they have no control over. Here the disciples will need to face up to decisions about fundamental directions they go in life. Life's external circumstances are hard and put us in waters that are hard to navigate; and ultimately we all know that life's pathways and crossroads will usher everyone to death's door. Yet, Jesus says, the real fear for life's outcome is not death, but the threat of Gehenna (hell).[7] We all will die, but how will our decisions about life's challenges determine where we will end up?

---

7. I will not define Gehenna or hell here, Theophilus, but I trust that you can get a sense for it when we go over the third test below.

The images that Jesus uses here [12:4–7] are instructive: birds of the air and the hairs of our head. Our soul's journey through life is analogous to the free-flying and lighter-than-air birds. Don't be so weighed down by our external circumstances that we cannot soar like birds. The Scriptures (and Jesus himself later in his discourses) will compare the birds to souls that have been freed from the hand of the fowlers, that is, they have the potential to transcend their circumstances. These creatures seem so slight, but they are the epitome of a life provided for by God. They seem so worthless, but they are the object of a joyous existence.

The hair of the head provides another analogy that harmonizes with the previous one. How? The Jewish Scriptures say that the hoary head provides a lesson for wisdom: "Gray hair is a crown of glory; it is gained in a righteous life" [Prov 16:31]. Thus, Jesus implies that every circumstance of life is measured and ordered carefully by God. He counts our hairs of every climax and crisis, just as he supports the carefree existence and provision for the birds. Where we are planted, there is fertile ground for us to bear fruit for the Kingdom. Just as the birds of the air and the hairs of our head eventually all perish, they still hint at a lifestyle for us to adopt: surrender to the pathway that the Lord provides the disciple to traverse life's ups and downs. We should live in a carefree way and we should live in gratitude for whatever comes our way. This is the flip side of the first section on life's internal details, those things under our control; for what Jesus means here is the flow of circumstances that ignores our best efforts.

Test Three: The Final Accounting

Still, whether we have all things within us ready for exposure (test one), or whether we fully accept until death the external circumstances of what God has arranged for us (test two), the disciple must be ready for a final scrutiny even in this life (test three). This insight about the disciple facing death only occurred at the end of Jesus's anti-Last Supper performance when he spoke about tombs, prophets, and monuments. Sometimes it will come down to this climactic juncture in the life of discipleship. This final section [12:8–12] involves the possibility of sacrificing our lives for the Kingdom—more familiarly called "martyrdom." Will we confess before the world and "before the angels" our relationship with the "Son of

Man" (Jesus)? In the final test or trial for such a disciple, what will be the outcome of this test?

Even in the dire straits of public testing like this, Jesus implies some consolation for everyone, even those who don't fully accept the "Son of Man." All I can say, Theophilus, is that Jesus acknowledges forgiveness for those who speak against him as long as they do not close themselves off from the Holy Spirit. What I gather from Jesus's words is that the Holy Spirit is the driving force for anyone seeking the Kingdom. While we don't understand the Son of Man and may even find ourselves in doubt about claims of his stature, we can stand on that fateful day if we are receptive to what the Spirit of God is doing within us. This "benefit of the doubt" points to how fearful are the circumstances which force disciples to become martyrs. I am sure it also points to the severity of the test Jesus knew he would soon face. He understands how hard the test really is, no matter how idealistic are our sentiments.

I have no desire for this extreme challenge (martyrdom) to come my way, Theophilus. I don't think that Jesus hopes for such an outcome to a life of discipleship; rather he implies that a "natural" death is the "natural" way of departing this life. Death waits for us all and provides its own difficulties. What is indeterminate is salvation—either Gehenna or life with God and his angels. Still, he must prepare those of his "friends," for whom martyrdom is inevitable. They will face "synagogues and rulers and authorities." He needs to prepare them for facing such ultimate choices without panicking. They need to be ready for their own *apologia*.

1. How well are my "internal" circumstances ordered? Are my thoughts and ambitions and the closed and private things transparent before the Lord? Would I be ashamed if someone were to find out about them?

2. How well have I accepted the trials and circumstances of my daily life? Can I live free and joyously in the midst of the things that seem to be divinely ordained?

3. How would I face up to the test of martyrdom? What would be my strategy if I were called to account for my faith or for godly ideals?

Luke's Soliloquy to Life

No desire have I to face a doom,
No heart right now to test my pluck.
Let me like bird that rides the gales,
Who sucks in air and breathes in luck.

So sure a day looms, so grim it leers;
The end will come, its perks so few.
Meanwhile let me fly high and free,
Soar aloft and love the view.

Such beauty let my eyes behold,
So long as life cooks its banquet.
Don't force on me the foe too cruel,
Don't make me a martyr just yet!

Back to the Crowds

Luke 12:13–21 One of the multitude said to him, "Teacher, bid my brother divide the inheritance with me." 14 But he said to him, "Man, who made me a judge or divider over you?" 15 And he said to them, "Take heed, and beware of all covetousness; for a man's life does not consist in the abundance of his possessions."

16 And he told them a parable, saying, "The land of a rich man brought forth plentifully; 17 and he thought to himself, 'What shall I do, for I have nowhere to store my crops?' 18 And he said, 'I will do this: I will pull down my barns, and build larger ones; and there I will store all my grain and my goods. 19 And I will say to my soul, Soul, you have ample goods laid up for many years; take your ease, eat, drink, be merry.' 20 But God said to him, 'Fool! This night your soul is required of you; and the things you have prepared, whose will they be?' 21 So is he who lays up treasure for himself, and is not rich toward God."

After this semi-private conversation, now someone in the crowd—remember: they were so thick that they were on top of each other [12:1]!—raises concerns about things of this world, interrupting Jesus

teaching about martyrdom. The priorities that this man voices are different from the three-tier concerns that Jesus lists for his disciples. What's
on his mind really is not so different from most of the throng listening
in, whose "day of reckoning" will simply be the deathbed and not the
issues that the previous section prioritizes for disciples. Their mind is on
a different sort of *apologia*.

The man's question would tether Jesus to a flatter world, a world
that would avoid even hints of natural death. Jesus is uncomfortable
with playing the role of a community rabbi.[8] He would rather start with
a disciple who is not investing his life in worldliness and acquisitions. He
would rather deal with someone who is invested in ultimate ends and not
short-sighted means—what, after all, are God's priorities. Nonetheless,
he will address these public and worldly concerns through the lens of a
parable. As you know, this is often the way that Jesus addresses those who
are not his disciples [see 8:10].

Note how Jesus describes the dangers of the worldly man, a wealthy
man who finds "euphoria" (εὐφορέω, *euphoreō*) or productivity in a field
he owns [12:16]. To keep his wealth to himself, he decides on a massive
building project to store all his newfound wealth. We learn how this man
thinks about his life: its meaning *is* in the abundance of possessions. If
he has plenty of resources, he can relax and let go of stress. Thus goes
the fantasy of someone not paying attention to the Kingdom. Perhaps,
Theophilus, this parable describes more than a few people whom you
know, who wonder at how someone like you can support yourself while
pursuing your idiosyncratic—and very invisible—"Kingdom."

Yet there is one inevitable outcome of work and career that has escaped this man's perspective: death. That night he would have to give
over his life. Truly all his hard labor, his investment in the new barn, his
desire for relaxation come to nothing at this crisis moment. Anyone who
works this hard for something that ultimately will be futile earns from
God a verbal jab for his new and eternal name: *Aphrōn* (ἄ + φρων, "no
mind" or "fool" [12:20]) instead of *Euphōn* (εὔ + φρων, "good mind;"
here: "be merry" [12:19]). Such a man has violated the most basic pattern
of intelligent ethical action that even the Roman and Greek philosophers
recognized: *do ut des*, meaning "I give that you might give." God gave the

8. "Rabbi" is a word I use only here and advisedly to convey a sense of respect the
petitioner has for Jesus's arbitration skills. Otherwise, I do not use this title at all in any
of my writing.

man his bounty so that he could spread the blessing—this is the principle of nature that only fools ignore.

So how do we avoid such vanity and mental poverty? We must be always "rich" toward God, perhaps by prayer, perhaps by investment of time in godly plans. In fact, the bottom-line implication of the parable is the advantage of committing oneself to the Kingdom. Better to give up what we can in reckless abandon for the sake of the Kingdom, for that is by far what is best. Our first instinct ought to be generosity rather than acquisition. Again, only the disciple grasps the truths that broadcast through the parables; for the crowd jostling for a show, deeper truths are but whispers they cannot hear.

1. How much of myself is invested in things that really don't matter? Take, for example, sports: How long does euphoria last when my favorite team wins? Does it really matter who wins a game? How many crises does it solve?

2. How much effort does the man exert to conserve his wealth? How much do I show?

3. Jesus says, "Take heed and beware of all covetousness." Why should this vice be so dangerous? In what ways is it dangerous to me?

4. Does the topic of death ever come up for me in my dealings with others? How does this question force one to consider the claims of the Kingdom of God? Should it be in my repertoire of discourse to bring others to the knowledge of the Kingdom?

Possessions

> Luke 12:22–34 And he said to his disciples, "Therefore I tell you, do not be anxious about your life, what you shall eat, nor about your body, what you shall put on. 23 For life is more than food, and the body more than clothing. 24 Consider the ravens: they neither sow nor reap, they have neither storehouse nor barn, and yet God feeds them. Of how much more value are you than the birds! 25 And which of you by being anxious can add a cubit to his span of life? 26 If then you are not able to do as small a thing as that, why are you anxious about the rest?

27 "Consider the lilies, how they grow; they neither toil nor spin; yet I tell you, even Solomon in all his glory was not arrayed like one of these. 28 But if God so clothes the grass which is alive in the field today and tomorrow is thrown into the oven, how much more will he clothe you, O men of little faith!

29 "And do not seek what you are to eat and what you are to drink, nor be of anxious mind. 30 For all the nations of the world seek these things; and your Father knows that you need them. 31 Instead, seek his Kingdom, and these things shall be yours as well.

32 "Fear not, little flock, for it is your Father's good pleasure to give you the Kingdom. 33 Sell your possessions, and give alms; provide yourselves with purses that do not grow old, with a treasure in the heavens that does not fail, where no thief approaches and no moth destroys. 34 For where your treasure is, there will your heart be also."

After the man's interruption, Jesus turns back to his dedicated band, those who have taken a different approach than the "fool" of the parable. He launches into a sermon that ascends to vistas that Greek poets and even Hebrew prophets could not imagine. In my "orderly account" [1:3], I place his speech here, and I quote its elevated prose above to give you a sense of its majesty. Its power speaks for itself, while I offer only chatter about its application to us.

I draw your attention, Theophilus, to several details. First, note the broader context: this is a private lesson for the disciples, not something he shared with everyone. Note also how Jesus was provoked to give this lesson: someone had come to him with a request that he arbitrate a personal dispute over an estate [12:13]. Jesus wants no part of family squabbles except to tell his parable about the rich farmer, a story that hints at the futility of such concerns. Then he goes back to his disciples and gives them his Kingdom perspective on their daily and practical lives [12:22–34]—in effect the reason why they should not be drawn into this realm of business and family matters. The gist of what he says is that the Father will take care of those who are dedicated to the Kingdom.

For me, Theophilus, this speech offers the *apologia* for your choice of discipleship instead of what the rich man chose. Your choice is not *against* the necessities that the rich man pursues, but your life is not consumed with this pursuit. You are able to let up on the acquisitiveness of his efforts, let go of their subsequent priorities. Why, you can take to the road if need be, even if it leads toward Jerusalem and its looming threats! You are able to go on mission—pack up lightly—because you are not as attached to the rich man's ambitions. You trust that there is a "King" behind the Kingdom, so you conduct yourself with as much purpose, and, even more, a measure of lightness of heart.

In fact, I would argue that Jesus tells us to look mirthfully at the folly of the man who is consumed with harvesting fields and building barns and yet who is mindless of how perilous his position really is. He has no time for tasting food or breathing in fresh air. Like Solomon who has a kingdom to run and subjects to tax [12:27], the rich man always has things to do. Meanwhile, the disciple of the Kingdom views himself more as a man of being than as a man of doing, and so identifies with birds [12:24]—who fly free, as I mentioned earlier—and flowers [12:27]— whose beauty and fragrance goes unnoticed by this hoard of go-getters.

Yes, Theophilus, it seems that we as disciples are merely a "little flock" [12:32], but we are a happy few. We are the sheep who benefit from the green pastures and restful waters where the shepherd leads. In this calling we are blessed that Jesus invites us to get rid of what is not needed, to treat what little we have as excess alms to be offered freely to others, to live as if we have no need for building barns on earth but have the whole world around us as our treasure house [12:33]. Such abundance means that we need not be stingy or possessive. If we have a perspective such as Jesus gives in this sermon, we truly are subjects of God as Father, King, and shepherd.

1. How much time and attention do material things take in my life? How much time and money do I devote to food and clothing and possessions? Compare this estimate to what I invest in the Kingdom as Jesus describes it.

2. A good measure of my disinterest in the world's priorities is how much I give in the form of "alms." Look up the definition of this word and consider how freely I dispense it. How can I foster a greater sense of almsgiving?

3. Is it possible to have enough distance on daily life requirements that I can escape fear of losing them?

4. How does the beauty and the tranquility of a disciple enter into my self-concept as I follow Jesus? How can I imagine myself as free as a

bird of the air or as fair as a flower of the field in the circumstances
that surround me right now?

5. What are the "nations of the world" that Jesus refers to here? How
   does the worry that accompanies riches and possessions dominate
   international and national priorities and policies?

6. Where do I have to cut back on my pursuits because they are too
   domineering?

Long-Term Strategy

At this point Jesus begins to shift focus a bit. Whereas some disciples may
end up in Jerusalem and share his fate there, others may have to think
about a long-term strategy. I ask that you go back and review what I wrote
in my narrative [12:35–48], though I will cite a few lines here.

> Luke 12:35–36 "Let your loins be girded and your lamps burn-
> ing, 36 and be like men who are waiting for their master to come
> home from the marriage feast, so that they may open to him at
> once when he comes and knocks.

The disciples are not supposed to build bigger barns and then drop
out into a life of leisure—that much we know. But can they simply live in
a world of ideals and metaphors, as though birds and flowers can provide
workable models? So Jesus counsels them about a lifestyle that is their
fallback position. While the public toils away for an endgame of eating,
drinking, and merry-making, your choices are governed by discipline
and the readiness for something beyond this world, the final visitation
of the Kingdom.

I suppose you might ask why Jesus did not complete things when
he announced the Kingdom. In his typical enigmatic fashion, Jesus simply hinted that he was going away, as if to a banquet, as if to a marriage
feast—perhaps his own. (After all, he was unmarried!) As you know, the
celebration of weddings often lasts several days—and that's when they
start on time! Are you preparing for the homecoming banquet when
the bridegroom returns? Like many feasts in the hot Palestinian desert
which wait for the cooling-down of the day, you will have to wait agoniz-
ingly long hours for the bride to get ready, for the bridegroom to arrive.
And time gives way grudgingly, causing your eyes to droop gently. No,
Theophilus, don't give in! Don't sleep away times of preparation! You

must make yourself ready through a lifestyle of cooking, cleaning, learning protocols and procedures, and so on. As I wrote in my introduction, we are now at the second and third generation after Jesus's exodus from Jerusalem. We need to maintain vigilance!

The other thing I wanted to mention here is that you not be taken by surprise. The image that Jesus used for his homecoming was astonishing: a thief digging through a household wall. Jesus seems to imply by it that his actual arrival will be quite a surprise, his timing not conforming to our schedules, our walls not a barrier to his penetration.

The last part of the dialogue is with Peter [12:41–48]. As you may remember, Peter stands for the leadership and institution of the whole movement, what you and I now call the "Church."[9] What is Peter to do? He is to ration the food, even when it seems to be limited or running low. I guess you could say that Peter and his ilk were invested with a charge or duty—in effect, to run the show after Jesus was gone. I will evaluate him in my later works[10]—and anyone who plays the role of Peter in the Church—by how well such "agents" carry out their duties and responsibilities on behalf of those who are waiting for the bridegroom to return. A sumptuous feast requires diligent preparations!

1. Consider hobbies and skills of mine that require training or practice. What should I do to stay ready for upcoming events or demonstrations of my skill?

2. What would Jesus have in mind for his disciples to be ready and awake for upon his return? What are some ways I can join in this regime?

3. What about the element of surprise that Jesus hints at in the passage: what can I do so that nothing takes me by surprise? For example, what are the signals that "the thief" is coming?

4. If Peter represents the Church, what kinds of things should the Church be doing to "ration" out supplies? What are the supplies? What is the purpose of these things from Jesus's perspective?

5. Do I have any responsibilities for others in this time of waiting? What are they? What I am doing to be alert and ready?

---

9. Jesus does not use this word, but I use it frequently in my next volume.

10. For a résumé of Peter, see *Unfinished Tale*, 11–25, 52–58.

In the Meantime

> Luke 12:49–53 "I came to cast fire upon the earth; and would
> that it were already kindled! 50 I have a baptism to be baptized
> with; and how I am constrained until it is accomplished! 51 Do
> you think that I have come to give peace on earth? No, I tell you,
> but rather division; 52 for henceforth in one house there will be
> five divided, three against two and two against three; 53 they
> will be divided, father against son and son against father, mother
> against daughter and daughter against her mother, mother-in-
> law against her daughter-in-law and daughter-in-law against
> her mother-in-law."

Besides preparing and staying alert, what are we to do in the meantime, Theophilus? What I uniquely did in my writings was give you access
to the inner thoughts of Jesus as guidance for your own performance. A
long time ago in my account, I told you about John the Baptist who offered a baptism of water. Jesus, on the other hand (according to John),
would baptize in fire. Certainly that fire implies divine power for mission;
but it also communicates judgment, just as fire burns out impurities and
destroys substances that are temporary. John was surprised that Jesus did
not seem to do what his fiery preaching predicted would happen: the axe
would be grasped and applied to the root of the tree so that it could be
cast into the fire [3:9].

Here Jesus shows that he is aware of what his cousin had envisioned,
and he is eager for the arrival of the Kingdom's power. Before it can come,
though, Jesus knows he must endure his own slated end, a baptism (a
word which means "immersion") into suffering and death. His own mission must come to its completion before anything of John's (and Jesus's)
longing can be fulfilled. Thus, we see an outward judgment in these reflections of Jesus and an inward anguish over his own choices—think
Jeremiah or any of the suffering prophets in the Jewish Scriptures. We
tend to put such characters on heroes' pedestals, but are they thereby
inoculated from anguish because of the aura around them?

Ultimately the realization that Jesus makes known here is that discipleship—connectedness to him and the Kingdom he brings—will be a
divisive thing. As disciples walk along with him toward Jerusalem—and
as we do the same toward our spiritual destination—they will have to
weigh critical priorities about fellowship and family. Instead of shalom

(peace and unity) in a given community, discipleship should bring clarity and decision, that is, choosing either for him and the Kingdom or not.

In this setting, Jesus knows what is ahead for those who are on the road to Jerusalem with him. It involves a fiery ordeal and immersion in suffering. His earlier words about preparation and alertness [12:35–48] had to do with the long-term perspective, but meanwhile he must address what lies ahead for his budding disciples on their way to Jerusalem. Remember the tombs, the prophets, and their monuments!

His inner thoughts reveal a profound struggle with what his own mission, his exodus, entails. He is our model for how a disciple must act: eager, yet anguished; restless, but pent up. His own example provides a sober perspective on discipleship that not everything will turn out how we expected or hoped for ourselves and our fellows. Moreover, his speech points to the stark realization that one's closest connections may not understand or be supportive. They also illustrate that the disciple's own baptism implies suffering and rejection, perhaps even martyrdom for the Kingdom, a topic that Jesus has already rehearsed in his anti-Last Supper speech and addressed as one of his "three tests."

These are sobering words that close out Jesus's private conversation with his disciples. Mark the familiarity Jesus shares with them as he calls them "friends" and turns to his disciples "first of all." He engages "Peter," his volatile confidant in the interchange. Afterwards he will speak to the crowds—and they too will be urged to pay attention to the times and the need for making choices, but not quite so intimately and personally.

1. Have I ever set up a plan that required a total reevaluation of all my priorities and commitments? What kind of struggle did I go through? How did I get through the conflict and realignments required for this plan to take hold?

2. How does my prayer reflect the restlessness, the anguish, maybe the disappointment that might be glimpsed from Jesus in this "exposé" of Jesus's reflection?

3. How do I currently prioritize my own discipleship in terms of what Jesus speaks of in this passage? How do I weigh my relationship with God and my lifestyle with my family and career? To what extent would I sacrifice these things for the sake of discipleship?

4. Where I have seen such "a division of the house," such as Jesus talks about here in the context of discipleship? Have I seen it in politics or

in society? Think of a few examples and then compare them to what Jesus says here. Are there examples in religion or church history?

Back to the Crowds

> Luke 12:54–59 He also said to the multitudes, "When you see a cloud rising in the west, you say at once, 'A shower is coming'; and so it happens. 55 And when you see the south wind blowing, you say, 'There will be scorching heat'; and it happens. 56 You hypocrites! You know how to interpret the appearance of earth and sky; but why do you not know how to interpret the present time?
>
> 57 "And why do you not judge for yourselves what is right? 58 As you go with your accuser before the magistrate, make an effort to settle with him on the way, lest he drag you to the judge, and the judge hand you over to the officer, and the officer put you in prison. 59 I tell you, you will never get out till you have paid the very last copper."

Now Jesus speaks mostly to the crowds until his arrival in Jerusalem, though I will report occasional snippets where he gives asides to his disciples. He addresses "the multitudes" with familiar images and everyday parables. It is as if he is trying to bridge the gap between their curiosity and serious engagement with his message by relying on common experiences. The bridge rests on the power of his story-telling. He expects you and other earnest seekers to get to the heart of the matter quickly—because you are a disciple and have dedicated your heart, soul, mind, and strength to following him. If you don't understand, in other words, don't let go until you do!

In this instance he uses the weather as the topic of conversation. But you don't just chit-chat with Jesus about the weather! Quickly he turns this everyday topic into a dire scenario and an uncompromising conclusion: the weather is not just a passing topic, but a way of stirring everyone up about his mission. The downside of his method is that he's not going to win many friends with his rapid-fire dismissal of interlocutors and conversation partners as "hypocrites."

Apart from what seems to be Jesus's lack of social grace, what is the underlying message of such strident communication? It is that the audience should pay attention to the "present time" [12:56]—the *kairos* (καιρός). Since you know Greek, you recognize that this word means something like "present opportunity." In other words, Jesus holds even the uncommitted and neutral accountable for some response to the events of the moment. As he told the disciples in the previous passage [12:10], someone does not have to confess him (know him fully), but they have to be in touch with the Holy Spirit and what the Spirit is saying to the world in its universal language. Whether disciples or not, Jesus suggests that all people have some sense of what is going on and need to make a commensurate response to the signs of the times.

The rest of the passage speaks to the consequences of our response, that is, Jesus expects everyone to discern "what is right" [12:57]. Everyone is approaching a reckoning, and each step of this path has opportunities for settling or making peace. Though it looks like everyone is different and every stage has its unique elements, the outcome will be "what is right" or a just settlement. We must figure out how to come to terms with this inexorable process before it is too late. Everyone who does not accept the terms that Jesus is proposing will pay the "ultimate price" (ἔσχατον λεπτόν, *eschaton lepton* [12:59]).

In some ways, these opening words to the "multitudes" are comforting, for they stress the solidarity that a disciple shares with humanity. Whereas the passage [12:53] before suggests that the disciple is the gadfly who brings division even to close social units, this passage suggests that a disciple also must figure out ways to communicate and build bridges across the divide among human beings. Jesus will spend the rest of his journey toward Jerusalem attempting to persuade his audience to make peace with God and the Kingdom.

1. What is the world expected to know about God's reckoning? How can I use stories, figures of speech, and even parables to alert those around me to spiritual priorities?

2. How can I help friends and colleagues to know the signs of the times? What would you say are some of these indicators?

3. Have I made my peace with God, now that I realize how inevitable is the ultimate conclusion of life's journey?

> Luke 13:1–9 There were some present at that very time who told him of the Galileans whose blood Pilate had mingled with their sacrifices. 2 And he answered them, "Do you think that these Galileans were worse sinners than all the other Galileans, because they suffered thus? 3 I tell you, No; but unless you repent

you will all likewise perish. 4 Or those eighteen upon whom the tower in Siloam fell and killed them, do you think that they were worse offenders than all the others who dwelt in Jerusalem? 5 I tell you, No; but unless you repent you will all likewise perish."

6And he told this parable: "A man had a fig tree planted in his vineyard; and he came seeking fruit on it and found none. 7 And he said to the vinedresser, 'Lo, these three years I have come seeking fruit on this fig tree, and I find none. Cut it down; why should it use up the ground?' 8 And he answered him, 'Let it alone, sir, this year also, till I dig about it and put on manure. 9 And if it bears fruit next year, well and good; but if not, you can cut it down.'"

FIGURE 5: *The Barren Fig Tree* (by Yvette Rock)

Jesus turns every topic of conversation into a message with ultimate significance. Earlier it was the weather, and it immediately prompted Jesus to lambast "hypocrites" who do not pay attention to the "present time" (*kairos*). If the topic turns to the future and what will happen tomorrow, Jesus then speaks about the inevitability of judgment and punishment. He shifts the topic toward how life's reckoning will be staged. He says that everyone ought to realize that each moment offers an opportunity for reconciliation with God before the ultimate verdict.

Now Jesus turns a conversation about the latest political intrigues into a platform for judgment. He affirms the same things as the earlier exchange: everyone is complicit in rebellion against God, and "accidents" are neither the ultimate of tragedies, nor are they punishments deserved by one more than another. The real tragedy is not repenting now, today, when we have a chance. True punishment (versus illusory punishment) is destined for all unless people turn away from sin.

"Those poor victims whom Pilate executed and desecrated! Those eighteen innocent souls who perished at Siloam!" That's the way we think. We are swept away by the latest crushing news. But Jesus suggests disasters of this type are only superficially the objects of the real tragedy. Jesus sees them as "props," the same as the weather from his earlier story: we need to read the signs of the times and act accordingly. The actual drama their roles point to is our relationship with God and the present moment to make our peace with him.

While we all want to get along and make time pass with pleasant conversation, be wary that we don't end up missing the chances we have and end up in the crowd of well-meaning "hypocrites" who love to chatter away on fair-weather topics.

The next parable [13:6–9] perhaps softens the blow the audience experiences from Jesus's words. It involves a three-year period when an owner has the right to expect some payback for his investment in a fig tree. He says that it is not doing what it is supposed to do in the vineyard, so it is better to cut it down and make space for a new tree. The owner apparently has plans for recouping his investment.

The vineyard worker—who is he? Is he not Jesus or the disciple— you, Theophilus—who volunteers to put in more time laboring? Is he not the one who will tend it and fertilize it—carefully and intensively—for one more year in hopes that it will produce fruit?

Thus, the time is limited for the tree and for the vineyard worker and for the owner of the vineyard. They are living in that final year, waiting for the fruit to come. This is the *kairos* that Jesus had spoken of earlier, the present moment charged with meaning and decisiveness. It is this moment that Jesus and his disciples are living within.

Why did Jesus choose the fig tree in the vineyard as his illustration? You may not realize, Theophilus, that there is a long history of the tree's fruit and leaves being symbolic of Israel's grace and favor, culminating in the coming messiah. The vineyard also harks back to the establishment of Israel as a people. We will later see this same image in Jesus's last encounter before he arrives in Jerusalem.

The grammar I employ in the last image, the tree, suggests that Jesus's expectation for the tree to produce fruit is low. The person going through the court process [12:57–59] will end up in prison. Herod's slaughter of the Galileans and the tower of Siloam crushing the eighteen are indication of what is ahead. I get the feeling from these three illustrations that Jesus is saying that not many are saved . . .

1. What are my priorities in conversation? How do I evaluate what seem to be disasters and tragedies in the world? How am I influenced by what I hear about major events or the way others tell me the news?

2. For my areas of responsibility or concerns, what year of the three-year cycle Jesus mentions here might they be in? How do I participate in the "digging" and "manuring" of the projects I am part of?

3. Think about my own hypocrisy. How might I be one of the hypocrites that Jesus is addressing here?

> Luke 13:18–21 He said therefore, "What is the Kingdom of God like? And to what shall I compare it? 19 It is like a grain of mustard seed which a man took and sowed in his garden; and it grew and became a tree, and the birds of the air made nests in its branches." 20 And again he said, "To what shall I compare the Kingdom of God? 21 It is like leaven which a woman took and hid in three measures of flour, till it was all leavened."

After another confrontation with the institutional opposition [see 13:10–17], Jesus rallies the audience to consider the alternative he offers, the Kingdom of God. I place these vignettes about seed and yeast here to conclude this stage of Jesus's journey to Jerusalem. Don't be too quick to run obliviously past these images. But beware! As with many rhetorical tidbits that Jesus offers, one sentence summons a thousand vistas, and one riddle launches an endless quest. As you have perhaps already discovered, Jesus has a knack for throwing together deceptively simple sketches before his audience, drawing them in like captivated flies before a spider spinning a web of meaning.

Look at the Kingdom, he implies, as two different types of operation: one, the mustard seed, is short-term labor that yields a single powerful effect, the tree; the other, the leaven permeating the dough, is a long-term process that makes bread. Once planted and sprouted, the seed has done its job. Once leavened, the yeast continues its inexorable presence and influence. Think about it in terms of one-time encounters versus constancy of presence. Neither is mutually exclusive; rather they seem to be symbiotic.

Another perspective, he suggests, is in terms of results: one, the mustard tree brings satisfaction to the birds of the air; the other, the yeast, brings nourishment to the eaters of the bread. Consider therefore how bountiful is the fruitfulness of the Kingdom providing home (the tree) and feasting (the bread)—this in contrast to the lifelessness of fallow earth without seed or inert flour without yeast. Going back to the beginning of these *Memoirs*, you may also want to consider how empty are the promises of this world (the earth and flour) without divine visitations (seed and yeast).

Paradoxically, the converse is also true: the earth is bursting forth with nature and the flour is fertile for the yeast. So much promise! So great the potential! Both images from this perspective push back at the pessimism that my earlier interpretations imparted. No, as Jesus looks at what lays before him, he does not see a hopeless cause. Even though the reality is that we as human beings are lurching toward a day of reckoning, either death or judgement, Jesus has come to turn everything upside down.

Another way is to focus on the seed that is so small and so secretly sown or the invisible and seemingly miniscule yeast: both have powerful effects and trigger purposefulness to the overall process. In other words, Jesus implies that the Kingdom he announces is not so low or futile that it is lost, but a calculated and prolific project.

Finally, Theophilus, consider this: is it possible that both seed and leaven are symbols of Jesus himself? He has had his crash encounters with people along the way since he turned resolutely toward Jerusalem (like seed). And, meanwhile, he has been training his disciples every step (like leaven). No word or deed is lost—he is seed to the crowds who receive the benefits of healing and deliverance, and he is leaven to his disciples who receive his teaching—though it is not the wily leaven of the Pharisees [12:1] or those who represent hypocritical institutionalism [13:11–17].

Arguably, Jesus would point to himself obliquely in these lines and say: "I am seed and leaven. Don't be put off by my apparent lowliness or futility. Don't shrug off my words glibly, Theophilus, for the danger is that you will miss me." Into the stuff of this world—the fallow ground or the inert flour of our lives depending on whether we are disciple or distant listener—comes the opportunity for the Kingdom to burst forth and overturn every expectation. Accordingly, the purpose for our existence becomes clear and creative. Life in the Kingdom means that nothing is too small or humble for attention and wonder.

1. How am I that seed, that yeast, of the parables? How am I the man who sows, the woman who kneads?

2. Identify real-life contexts for both images.

3. Give an example of fruitfulness of seed that has been planted and now surprisingly is evident. Give examples of good taste or nourishment from dough leavened—again surprisingly discovered.

4. How would I envision the Kingdom in the form of the picture Jesus gives to the mustard tree? How would I envision the Kingdom in terms of the leavened dough? Pray along these lines for the Kingdom to be manifest.

CHAPTER FIVE

Almost on the Big Stage

The Perils of Traveling

Luke 13:22–30 He went on his way through towns and villages, teaching, and journeying toward Jerusalem. 23 And someone said to him, "Lord, will those who are saved be few?" And he said to them, 24 "Strive to enter by the narrow door; for many, I tell you, will seek to enter and will not be able. 25 When once the householder has risen up and shut the door, you will begin to stand outside and to knock at the door, saying, 'Lord, open to us.' He will answer you, 'I do not know where you come from.' 26 Then you will begin to say, 'We ate and drank in your presence, and you taught in our streets.' 27 But he will say, 'I tell you, I do not know where you come from; depart from me, all you workers of iniquity!' 28 There you will weep and gnash your teeth, when you see Abraham and Isaac and Jacob and all the prophets in the Kingdom of God and you yourselves thrust out. 29 And men will come from east and west, and from north and south, and sit at table in the Kingdom of God. 30 And behold, some are last who will be first, and some are first who will be last."

JESUS RESOLUTELY ADVANCES TOWARD Jerusalem and undoubtedly epitomizes the message of the images contained in this passage. Jesus has already spoken about the need for his disciples to face up to the prospect of a time of reckoning within the life [12:1–3], a time of reckoning at the end of life [12:4–7], and a time of reckoning before men (involving martyrdom [12:8–12]). He has already spoken of chance encounters (the

133

mustard seed sowing) and more regular commitments (the kneading of flour with leaven [13:19–22]), and I have given examples of both since the time of his consultation with Moses and Elijah on the mountain [9:28–36]. You might even say Jesus himself is on the way to Jerusalem from his childhood when he says (in the temple) that he must be about his Father's business [2:49]—the outcome of which we will soon see!

He has addressed crowds of curiosity-seekers with his parables and images, warning about the coming judgment. A "fire" is coming that will divide humanity and is as inevitable as the weather [12:49–56], a fire that will result in ultimate judgment and punishment for everyone [12:57–59]. The perilous condition facing humanity is epitomized by the tower that fell on the hapless eighteen victims or the slaughter Pilate inflicted on the Galileans or the fruitless fig tree about to be chopped down [13:1–9]. Yet at the same time, Jesus's visitation instills its own *kairos* for anyone who responds.

In all of these warnings, both to disciples and audience, he epitomizes the crisis that will come for all. His own soul is in anguish as it proceeds toward Jerusalem, for he knows his likely end [9:43–45; 12:49–50] as he sets his face resolutely toward his destination [9:51]. Certainly he already knows the division he causes with his nearest kin [8:19–21].

Thus, when he speaks about the narrow gate and the locked door [13:24–25], he is not only speaking about what others face. He means that the road ahead of him will bring its own obstacles. He must tread a path that no one else is taking—or at least very few since the days of Moses and Elijah. His destination is Jerusalem and the temple, and its "householder" is God. His decisiveness serves as a model for those around him who are spending time with him, who "eat and drink in your presence" [13:26] and who listen to his teachings. His audience includes both those who have chance encounters (as the seed image above) and those who have long-standing ties to Jesus (the yeast image).

Still, there is a consolation to his message that addresses the question of whether many or few are saved. Consider, for example, Jesus's frequent citation of the Psalms. In the lines above, he alludes to two psalms: "Depart from me, you evildoers" [Ps 6:8], and "Men will come from east and west, and from north and south" [Ps 107:3]. If you go back and check these psalms in their entirety, you will find they teach that the Lord will save in unexpected and diverse ways, even if his disciples and the crowds following him might squander the opportunity he offers them.

Moreover the final line [13:30] contains a hint about who are the pilgrims, the ones who sit down at table with Abraham, Isaac, and Jacob and the prophets. They are the ones who normally would be thought last to be there. What are *these* people doing here, when they don't seem to be related to the patriarchs? Undoubtedly they are the ones "from east and west and from north and south" [Ps 107:3] and the one who is weary with moaning and wasted away because of grief [Ps 6:6–7]. About them we will hear more as the pilgrimage toward Jerusalem continues.

1. What is the city, the household, the Jerusalem that is the object of my pilgrimage? How do I sometimes view Jesus favorably because it is simply easier or convenient rather than out of conviction or passion?

2. How do I give in to an easy path or wide door or a delay in setting off in my current life circumstances?

3. What are my current difficulties in following Jesus or doing his will?

Will Arrival Bring Blessing or Curse?

> Luke 13:31–35 31 At that very hour some Pharisees came, and said to him, "Get away from here, for Herod wants to kill you." 32 And he said to them, "Go and tell that fox, 'Behold, I cast out demons and perform cures today and tomorrow, and the third day I finish my course. 33 Nevertheless I must go on my way today and tomorrow and the day following; for it cannot be that a prophet should perish away from Jerusalem.'
>
> 34 "O Jerusalem, Jerusalem, killing the prophets and stoning those who are sent to you! How often would I have gathered your children together as a hen gathers her brood under her wings, and you would not! 35 Behold, your house is forsaken. And I tell you, you will not see me until you say, 'Blessed is he who comes in the name of the Lord!'"

Jesus again offers himself as the example for taking the narrow gate, the road less traveled. Even now he runs into all sorts of reasons to quit or tone down his fervor for Jerusalem. "Leave," say the Pharisees, "because Herod is laying a trap for you!"

Here Jesus's response is twofold. First, he must finish his journey, his personal call [8:32]. He says in effect, "I will stay the course. I started off exorcising evil spirits and healing the sick, and I will finish my life doing so." One can imagine him recalling those lines that he recited in the synagogue of Nazareth [4:16–30]: "The Spirit of the Lord is upon me . . . to preach good news to the poor, . . . release to the captives . . . recovery of sight to the blind, to set at liberty those who are oppressed, to proclaim the acceptable year of the Lord."

Second, he follows a script that is laid out before him [13:33]. Thus we hear him say here something like, "I walk the steps of a prophet with a message for Jerusalem." He is not just a traveler meandering and causing controversy, but he is called by God to fulfill an appointed mission. We sense this reality already because he has consulted with Moses and Elijah—and he has implied all along that the outcome of his mission would involve martyrdom for himself and his disciples [11:49–51; 12:8–12].

Jesus seems to be well aware of his timing and itinerary, twice mentioning the three-day cycle of activity. In this first instance the three days refers to his own mission, the tasks he must do, and the events ahead [13:32]. The three-day cycle in the next statement [13:33] seems to point to the way his course fulfills the course of a prophet's mission. For sure he means the prophet must preach and warn and confront—leading to his demise.

Then he explains how the three days apply to himself. Like any good prophet, he addresses Jerusalem itself. "Jerusalem, Jerusalem" [13:34]. From his debut in his hometown we see that he is playing the role of a prophet, a rejected one at that. Besides the litany of prophets he has so far invoked over the course of his mission, now he sounds (to me, at least) like Jeremiah. He knows that if he is anything like Israel's prophets, pitfalls and persecution await him. Thus, he role-models what he has just spoken about, namely, that the way into the city (Jerusalem) or into the house (the temple) is torturous—for the door is "narrow" and will surely end up in martyrdom. Yet, he is resolute—as he has been all along.

He is convinced that his role is to provide Israel protection from some upcoming catastrophe. He would gather "Jerusalem" under his "wings." Its unruly citizens are still his people, and he longs to help them as a mother hen her chicks. Because of their opposition to him, now he cites another line from his treasury of psalms, "Blessed is he who comes in the name of the Lord!" [Ps 118:26a (13:35)].

Why this line and this psalm? When you look over the whole passage, you discover it reads like a progressive drama. The speaker is moving toward Jerusalem, engaging enemies [118:12–13], camping along the way [15], marching through the city gates [19–20], arriving just on time [24]. Then comes the line that Jesus quotes, a triumphant acclamation of arrival in the temple. The whole thing is strangely reassuring, like it is the guidebook for Jesus's tour.

Though what I am saying now is certainly more than what I recounted in my original narrative, I do think he was trying to say the following: "I am the culmination of the prophets, their voice—the voice of Jeremiah and Zechariah and the rest—speaking over the ages to all of you. And if I am the voice of them, then my life captures what God is saying to the whole house of Israel." Do you hear this voice speaking to you, Theophilus, as Jesus makes his way to Jerusalem?

Let me return to that line, "Blessed is he who comes in the name of the Lord!" Once the speaker in the psalm has made it into the temple, this is his blessing. This greeting points to the special status ("blessed") of the pilgrim, but the phrase is ambiguous too. It could refer to the way that such a speaker communicates blessing to others. Is Jesus then predicting to his audience that they will eventually understand him as the Kingdom's emissary?

Or does he intend it as a curse? The word in the Hebrew tongue carries a sense of both strands of meaning. A prophet like Jeremiah can announce the impending doom of such things that are held near and dear, like Jerusalem and its temple [Jer 7:11–15]. Thus: "Behold, your house is forsaken." Even for the mythical world you inhabit, Theophilus, Cassandra's prophecy against Troy is nothing but a summons for the resident gods to annul their protection of the city, and to vacate their temple sanctuary. If so, Jesus's citation possibly connotes two things at once: a blessing for those who believe in Jesus as the key for re-fitted temple ("the [cap-]stone which the builders rejected has become the head of the corner" [Ps 118:22]) and who now offer their public blessing [Ps 118:22], and an implicit curse upon those who miss out on this opportunity. This topic I will leave to you and others to think about.

1. How does Jesus's example here serve as a role model for someone trying to stay the course in spite of threats and dangers?

2. What are my work and mission? How do I pursue them?

3. What are some of life's circumstances that discourage me from continuing my pilgrimage? How difficult is it for me to stay the course that God wants me to follow?

4. Are there those whom I am responsible for that I would gather up and try to help get through danger? Who are they? Pray for them.

5. How do I use blessing and curses as a disciple? Is there a role for "curses"? What is it?

Rest Stop: Sabbath (Again)

Luke 14:1–6 One sabbath when he went to dine at the house of a ruler who belonged to the Pharisees, they were watching him. 2 And behold, there was a man before him who had dropsy. 3 And Jesus spoke to the lawyers and Pharisees, saying, "Is it lawful to heal on the sabbath, or not?" 4 But they were silent. Then he took him and healed him, and let him go. 5 And he said to them, "Which of you, having a son or an ox that has fallen into a well, will not immediately pull him out on a sabbath day?" 6 And they could not reply to this.

It should be obvious that I have written my account of Jesus and the Kingdom the way I see it. It is no mere repetition of what has been written elsewhere. I have crafted it at times to be direct and straightforward, while at other times I speak with a muted voice and allusive language. True, sometimes I merely repeat something; but at other times I uniquely declare something else. Many other accounts attempt to convey the pith of Jesus's teaching, but I often give you its punch—meaning its clever presentation by Jesus. For the episode today, it is an attempt at the latter, so bear with me as I display the art of my description. When all is said and done, I may have missed the mark, but let me give my pitch anyway.

Is this episode simply another dispute about the Sabbath? Twice earlier I used the Sabbath as the occasion and perhaps the map for a wider context of controversy regarding the paradox of the Kingdom of God [5:1–6:11; 13:10–17]. Today's episode is the third attempt, and like the prophet who marches to Jerusalem today, tomorrow, and arrives on the third day, or the gardener who has come for three years looking for figs in his vineyard, so this third explanation of Sabbath is meant to bring fulfillment.

The Sabbath brings up a banquet context,[1] and this theme fits exactly the passage about entering the city by the narrow gate, knocking at

1. Go back and look how I arranged events surrounding the public performances of Jesus after Nazareth. Everything was organized around the weekly Sabbath. See

the door of the house, and then sitting at the banquet where Abraham, Isaac, and Jacob are guests [13:22–29]. Who are the invited guests and hosts of this banquet? Who are the ones left outside of the gate and the door, knocking?

The short answer here is the man with the dropsy case is the invited guest, at least as far as Jesus and the Kingdom are concerned. The ones left outside knocking at the door, who are they? This passage gives us the idea: they are the ones who are silent when they see the man with the affliction right in front of them. They are willing to associate with Jesus in the streets and in their meals, but they want none of his challenges for a reassessment of priorities.

In the other two accounts of Sabbath dispute I told, Jesus is quick to call to mind comparisons to what these people allow to save their livestock. Altogether they show that Jesus agrees that the Sabbath should not prevent animal rescue. So far, so good—fairly straightforward.

But how do we communicate a lesson the episode might teach? Let us imagine ourselves on stage, perhaps inside the ruler's house in his expansive dining room. "Behold!" [14:2] Jesus suddenly grabs our attention—and now we focus on Exhibit A, the man at the center of the controversy. Who is he? How did this man get in? Moreover, the Greek I wrote [14:3] actually says, "Jesus answered" (not "spoke")—but who asked a question? So whom is he answering? I propose he is answering all the previous questions about Sabbath in the other parallel incidents. So he addresses the audience right in front—not just the Pharisees and lawyers, but even us: What are you going to do about the man? The man got in, he is in your way. Now what?

Here the tragic part of this act unfolds: the supporting actors (Pharisees and lawyers, the ostensible hosts) are "silent," but the props (the dropsy victim) in their mute witness give testimony to Kingdom priorities! This word, "silent," is not a word I use lightly or frequently. It normally describes the futility of human dialogue.[2] Theophilus, do you feel the frustration and the outrage boiling up in our "silent" witness of this event?

Why don't these Pharisees and lawyers know their lines like Jesus's antagonists did in previous Sabbath arguments? Why don't they do

chap. 2 for details.

2. It is never mere quiescence. I use this word only four times that I remember, Theophilus, and three of those times describes people's reactions to speeches—like a "pregnant pause" to signal the listeners' complicity or responsibility.

something—even fomenting plots against him? The answer is that they are mute and paralyzed like the animals that have fallen into the pit: the Pharisees and lawyers have failed to welcome the Kingdom, so that they are like the very animals that have fallen into the pit that Jesus described two other times—and there they will likewise perish unless someone comes to their rescue. Indeed, they are unable to speak at the end of the episode [14:6], for a dumb animal trapped in the pit has no such ability! Now they are more like props instead of supporting actors.

As you know, I like my puns. The Greek word for "son" is close to the word for "pig." What if the Pharisees and lawyers need to be rescued like livestock—and what if they are as unclean as pigs? Either way, they can't get themselves out. The Jewish Scriptures often describe the helpless and voiceless fate of animals in comparison to human beings.[3] Remember that the symbol that we Jews have for the nations is pigs—the very nations that are coming into the banquet in the Kingdom [13:29]. Are my musings on Jesus's words too exaggerated?

So let's get back to Jesus who himself expands on the implications of this little lesson. If you don't take care of this one who is apparently present at the banquet of Abraham, Isaac, and Jacob, what would you do if your own son had dropsy or some valuable piece of your own property was lost? If you rightfully care for the mute animals—for the shock value before Jews, even pigs?—does this voiceless example not speak volubly (whoops, another pun) about what God intends for his people? And if this is how you take care of your concerns, how would you take care of God's? Are your business and activities more important than God's and his banquet? So many questions emerge as I reconsider this incident!

From here, the importance of the banquet will continue. This prop and little skit allows Jesus to press onward in his dramatic presentation. He will now apply its lesson to bigger things in terms of the Kingdom of God and its priorities.

1. How does God arrange the circumstances of my life so that I run into such a situation as described above? For me, who is the man who has a case of dropsy that inconveniences or irritates me?

2. What are the lines that I am supposed to say when such situations arise? How have I been "silent"?

3. Consider, for example, Ps 49:12, 20 or Isa 53:7.

3. Where is the grace present in such an "accident"? If God has arranged the "banquet," how has he designed the people invited, the
   room, the table, and the food? How can I be a healer?

4. What causes me to overlook the "behold" situations I run into?

Rest Stop (Continued)

Luke 14:7–11 Now he told a parable to those who were invited,
when he marked how they chose the places of honor, saying to
them, 8 "When you are invited by anyone to a marriage feast,
do not sit down in a place of honor, lest a more eminent man
than you be invited by him; 9 and he who invited you both will
come and say to you, 'Give place to this man,' and then you will
begin with shame to take the lowest place. 10 But when you are
invited, go and sit in the lowest place, so that when your host
comes he may say to you, 'Friend, go up higher'; then you will
be honored in the presence of all who sit at table with you. 11
For every one who exalts himself will be humbled, and he who
humbles himself will be exalted."

Another "prop" appears in addition to the dropsy victim when he
is at the Sabbath meal. Jesus notices a jostling for the best place at the
dinner. Everyone wants to be noticed. He applies this tussle to seating at
a wedding feast, probably because the image of the messianic banquet is
still fresh from his last Sabbath meal lesson. A wedding feast, the messianic banquet, and the Sabbath meal apparently all are parallels. Everyone
wants in and everyone wants the best seat possible.

What is Jesus hoping from his audience now? This weekly routine
(the Sabbath meal) serves as a way for the audience to discern bigger
things about how they live and make choices. If they are this way today,
Jesus hints, we have a clue about how they will choose at a wedding feast.
By extension, this tells us how things will turn out at the messianic banquet. Thankfully, in this new application, at least we all have accepted the
invitation to the banquet.

If we vaunt ourselves as deserving the "prime" chair so that everyone will notice us, we have lost sight of the fact that we are all allowed
at table only by gracious invitation of the host. We also might reflect on
the fact that no matter how good we think we are, there is always someone who is better than us or more important. In such a scenario, what is

highlighted is our weaknesses—and thus we are shamed [14:9] in addition to demoted. Then we proceed to where our status should have set us in the first place: the lowest seat.

1. Recall times when I have been snubbed on a public occasion. How did I deal with it? How will I deal with similar snubs in the future?

2. Have I tried to promote myself in public settings? Have I ever been embarrassed when I was "put in my place?"

3. Have I ever noticed how others promote themselves in public? How did I feel? How should I deal with it?

Rest Stop (Conclusion)

In case you have not guessed, Theophilus, the best way to view what is going on is to envision an occasion Greeks would call a *symposium* (toasting over drinks). A topic is selected for all the dinner participants, and the main guest gets to speak first—or even choose the topic for everyone to engage. Other *symposium* participants then publicly respond. So Jesus decides to tell a story about the *symposium* itself. Ingeniously he finds another interesting prop for his speech, right within the dining hall: the host himself! His next teaching is as follows:

> Luke 14:12–24 He said also to the man who had invited him, "When you give a dinner or a banquet, do not invite your friends or your brothers or your kinsmen or rich neighbors, lest they also invite you in return, and you be repaid. 13 But when you give a feast, invite the poor, the maimed, the lame, the blind, 14 and you will be blessed, because they cannot repay you. You will be repaid at the resurrection of the just."

> 15 When one of those who sat at table with him heard this, he said to him, "Blessed is he who shall eat bread in the Kingdom of God!" 16 But he said to him, "A man once gave a great banquet, and invited many; 17 and at the time for the banquet he sent his servant to say to those who had been invited, 'Come; for all is now ready.' 18 But they all alike began to make excuses. The first said to him, 'I have bought a field, and I must go out and see it; I pray you, have me excused.' 19 And another said, 'I have bought five yoke of oxen, and I go to examine them; I pray you, have me excused.' 20 And another said, 'I have married a wife, and

therefore I cannot come.' 21 So the servant came and reported this to his master.

"Then the householder in anger said to his servant, 'Go out quickly to the streets and lanes of the city, and bring in the poor and maimed and blind and lame.' 22 And the servant said, 'Sir, what you commanded has been done, and still there is room.' 23 And the master said to the servant, 'Go out to the highways and hedges, and compel people to come in, that my house may be filled. 24 For I tell you, none of those men who were invited shall taste my banquet.'"

Hosts, Jesus observes, are "blessed" (μακάριος, *makarios* [14:14]) when they are able to accommodate many guests and important outsiders. Such hospitality shows influence and solidarity. So Jesus extends his point by asserting that they are "blessed" when the guests cannot pay back, for such is the nature of what Jesus calls elsewhere [see 6:27–36] *charis* ("grace"). Again, the host shows beneficence and sheer extravagance by such an act. The payback will come in the reward of the resurrection. How? Jesus implies that God will play host on that occasion.

Now someone at table takes his turn to speak: he tries to endear himself to Jesus by appearing to congratulate Jesus for his deft answer [14:15]. He postures himself as one who knows the realities to which Jesus points, as well as the host's responsibilities at the *symposium*. Why not ingratiate himself to all parties?

The dialogue takes a surprising turn, though. Jesus distances himself from his erstwhile friend by asserting that he is the host at the messianic banquet! Twisting the parable just a bit, the host has not just issued an invitation ahead of time [14:16], but he now has everything ready to go. The banquet is ready, the time for the RSVPs has come [14:17]. Now the host is urgent for follow-up to his invitation issued well beforehand.

Jesus presents three examples of invitees who show that they do not value their invited status. They had not made requisite arrangements when they received the invitation notice: one scheduled a field inspection, another a livestock testing, another a wedding. In other words, they had blithely ignored the invitation and now begged off the summons [14:18–20].

At this news, the host loses his temper [14:21–24]. They had all this time to make arrangements and get ready, but they stuck with their priorities and plans! Now the banquet-giver directs his servants to find blatantly undeserving guests (and worse): the deformed and grotesque, the ones without wealth and manners, and the ones without homes and living hand-to-mouth. "Find them anywhere and everywhere," he tells them. "Bring them in even if they are unqualified, unstable, and uncouth. The original ones have written themselves off my list!"

1. Have I ever thrown a party and been disappointed by some of my guests not showing up? What kind of excuses did they give?

2. How did I feel if everything was purchased and prepared when I realized they were not coming? Did I then feel an urge to find others to come to experience my hospitality?

3. Who are the poor, maimed, lame, blind guests that God wants me to include in my hospitality? Think over how generous I can be with them. Who are the ones in this category that I may have overlooked?

4. Have I ever turned down invitations because of other priorities? What if these invitations contained an urgent request for my attendance? What would I have to change or ignore to attend?

5. What are parallel things that stand in the way of whole-heartedly responding to God's immediate request for attention? What are the things I can do to minimize the hold that priorities have on me that keep me from responding to God?

Traveling Again: A Hard-Sell Pitch to the Public

Luke 14:25–35 Now great multitudes accompanied him; and he turned and said to them, 26 "If any one comes to me and does not hate his own father and mother and wife and children and brothers and sisters, yes, and even his own life, he cannot be my disciple. 27 Whoever does not bear his own cross and come after me, cannot be my disciple.

28 "For which of you, desiring to build a tower, does not first sit down and count the cost, whether he has enough to complete it? 29 Otherwise, when he has laid a foundation, and is not able to finish, all who see it begin to mock him, 30 saying, 'This man began to build, and was not able to finish.'

31"Or what king, going to encounter another king in war, will not sit down first and take counsel whether he is able with ten thousand to meet him who comes against him with twenty thousand? 32 And if not, while the other is yet a great way off, he sends an embassy and asks terms of peace. 33 So therefore, whoever of you does not renounce all that he has cannot be my disciple.

34 "Salt is good; but if salt has lost its taste, how shall its saltness be restored? 35 It is fit neither for the land nor for the dunghill; men throw it away. He who has ears to hear, let him hear."

Outside the banquet hall, Jesus once again "turns" toward the crowd. What is in it for them? They have been marching on with Jesus toward Jerusalem, sensing some kind of climax. The banquet stories and the props now swing back to Jesus's message about the Kingdom. Three conditions [14:25–27] arise for the crowd to continue in their focus on Jesus:

1. Will they give up their family attachments? This includes a lot, for a man's livelihood depends on his connection to family land and estate. His mark in life depends on a prolific wife and future children. Will a man consider the Kingdom to be more important?

2. Will they pick up the cross, the emblem of humiliation, and surrender to forces beyond control?

3. Will they give up these things up in the long run, or will it be a short-term fling or fad?

The concept of the short-termers' attitude comes across in the two vignettes [14:28–33] that compare serious versus frivolous pursuits. The one is the builder of a monument, obviously a man of means, who wants to impress—but not enough to sacrifice. The other is the commander of an army, who has an initial surge of adrenaline to prove his manliness, but when the reality of the hard and bloody price that is to be paid for victory sinks in, he does not have the heart to continue.

Both of them then become the fodder of the latest news and gossip because they are sensational examples of failure and thus a comfort to the complacent or lazy bystanders who never got involved in the first place. If anything the Kingdom has been set back, at least in public relations—and the result is that the cynical public never takes it seriously. It is just passing fad, another temporary pastime. The urgency of a response to the Kingdom is diminished.

The final paragraph [14:34–35] shows how worthless the quitter is to Jesus. He or she is like the Dead Sea salt, mixed with so much impurity that it can't be used for food nor thrown out as fertilizer. It will in effect ruin the whole batch of food with its sand mixed in, and add such salinity to the garden that nothing will grow. You might have carted it from the Dead Sea Valley with sweaty effort, but now you realize that your batch of salt is worthless. The only thing to do is throw it out into the street where men heedlessly trample on it. Disciples of this ilk make no difference at all in the course of men's lives.

1. Which category of disciple do I fit in—one of the Twelve, one of the Seventy, or one of the crowd now summoned to follow?

2. What about the people I care about, which group are they in? Or are they in the next batch, the onlookers who find fault with the coarse and uncouth that Jesus now spends his time with (see 15:1–2)?

3. Do I have priorities of "disciples" around me that require different levels of attention or care by Jesus?

4. Do I know of "quitters" of the Gospel? How would I characterize their contributions now to the Kingdom? How apt is Jesus's description of them as salt that men trample on in the street? Does Jesus think that their saltiness can be restored?

Traveling Again: A Soft-Sell Pitch in Three Parts

Luke 15:1–10 Now the tax collectors and sinners were all drawing near to hear him. 2 And the Pharisees and the scribes murmured, saying, "This man receives sinners and eats with them." 3 So he told them this parable: 4 "What man of you, having a hundred sheep, if he has lost one of them, does not leave the ninety-nine in the wilderness, and go after the one which is lost, until he finds it? 5 And when he has found it, he lays it on his shoulders, rejoicing. 6 And when he comes home, he calls together his friends and his neighbors, saying to them, 'Rejoice with me, for I have found my sheep which was lost.' 7 Just so, I tell you, there will be more joy in heaven over one sinner who repents than over ninety-nine righteous persons who need no repentance.

8 "Or what woman, having ten silver coins, if she loses one coin, does not light a lamp and sweep the house and seek diligently until she finds it? 9 And when she has found it, she calls together her friends and neighbors, saying, 'Rejoice with me, for I have found the coin which I had lost.' 10 Just so, I tell you, there is joy before the angels of God over one sinner who repents."

Remember that the context is the high cost of discipleship: Jesus asks for a lot. It cannot just be for cosmetic effect (a monument that we fantasize we will build one day) or a fling we try out (war rhetoric that falls flat before the foe). But if a person really does want to step out, commit, and invest without reserve, then Jesus is prepared to speak about how discipleship looks from the other side of the relationship. It turns out that the commitment of Jesus (or God) vastly overwhelms the disciple's pledge, and it once again reveals the paradox of the Kingdom and its divine visitation.

So Jesus tries to describe how incongruous things are in the form of a three-part skit, so ridiculous in its imaginary staging as to be laughable. One man, a rich owner of one hundred sheep, is featured along with another woman, poor with only ten silver coins. The third character is a father with two rival sons, but that one deserves its own platform; so I will save it till the end. One parable, three parts, with one overarching meaning—that's what I am getting at in these *Memoirs*.

What makes the first two characters comical is the fact that both show an eccentric fixation (almost an obsessive-compulsive focus) on their possessions. In both cases, their driving ambition is to find what they have lost. They express in overblown fashion how much the missing object means to them.

Maybe you recognize the man: rich and a bit eccentric in his tastes. When he fixates on something, he is insanely riveted, forsaking what others see as due responsibilities. In this case, the man leaves his thriving herd—apparently without a shepherd—and goes after his prized possession, a little lamb!

Who can predict what tickles the fancies of the filthy rich? The man goes off to find his little lamb, maybe lost in the briars, and cuddles the little thing around his shoulders in a way he could never do with one of his (more valuable) sheep. Is it his pet? Is it his problem? Does Jesus say? All we can do is chuckle as we contemplate the story's incongruity.

And the woman, well, you know her: maybe a bit batty in her compulsiveness. She lights up the house and maddeningly sweeps until she finds her darling possession, a coin, an earring, a souvenir of some precious memory.

In both cases there is not a hint of blame attached to the objects for their being lost. Who can blame a dumb little lamb? What is the culpability of a coin for being lost? No, our eyes on the possessors, the actors clownishly wearing themselves out for their petty prizes.

To accentuate the comedy of the whole thing: when the owners find what they are hopelessly attached to, their glee knows no bounds. One throws a party so that their associates, laughingly aware of the protagonist's foibles, can join in his merriment.

The other seemingly can't wait for the next day's shopping with neighbors and friends and simply is bursting to tell them at midnight if possible. How ridiculous their lavish attention to such possessions, and how outlandish their response to what they have found! I'm sure you know the kind of people Jesus is referring to, eh, Theophilus? Every village has at least one of both types. Unforgettable characters—even lovable from a distance.

In either case, the rich man with his sheep and the poor woman with her coin, I have visions of myself—or of certain family members. Their fixation on things of particular and peculiar attraction is what others would call a disproportionate focus on the small and obscure. Aren't there more important things to life? Like what? One man's foolishness is another man's fantasy.

Here we have God's attentiveness to what many—especially the Pharisees!—would see as lost causes or hopeless quests. So is the tower that the previous parable addresses really just a pipedream? And is the war that the king began simply a lost cause? No, if we decide to join up as disciples of Jesus, we can expect an incongruous return in the form of attention and help. Heaven looks down with outlandish fondness and favor on those who are its representatives.

Jesus is aware that he has an audience here whom he is trying to entice to join in the revelry. The Kingdom he preaches is lost on the stingy and the resentful (the Pharisees, the scholars, and the scribes); but joy and exuberance await the object of the Kingdom's eccentric tastes. So far the slapstick antics entertained everyone (even the kill-joy scholars), but everyone sensed that the performer was now ready to dispatch part three of the parable toward its final target.

1. What are some of the "lost causes" of my life? How do they still have their hooks in me, even though others would shrug them off?

2. How do these parables speak of what I gain by discipleship? How do they convince me to let go of stinginess and half-heartedness when it comes to how I regard others? How do they console me about divine attentiveness and solicitude for my efforts to be a disciple?

3. How do these tales speak to me about divine love in general? Do they show the madness of God's economy and divine passions?

A Soft-Sell Pitch: Finale

Luke 15:15–32 "So he [the 'prodigal son'] went and joined himself to one of the citizens of that country, who sent him into his fields to feed swine. 16 And he would gladly have fed on the pods that the swine ate; and no one gave him anything. 17 But when he came to himself he said, 'How many of my father's hired servants have bread enough and to spare, but I perish here with hunger! 18 I will arise and go to my father, and I will say to him, "Father, I have sinned against heaven and before you; 19 I am no longer worthy to be called your son; treat me as one of your hired servants."'

20 "And he arose and came to his father. But while he was yet at a distance, his father saw him and had compassion, and ran and embraced him and kissed him. 21 And the son said to him, 'Father, I have sinned against heaven and before you; I am no longer worthy to be called your son.' 22 But the father said to his servants, 'Bring quickly the best robe, and put it on him; and put a ring on his hand, and shoes on his feet; 23 and bring the fatted calf and kill it, and let us eat and make merry; 24 for this my son was dead, and is alive again; he was lost, and is found.' And they began to make merry.

25 "Now his elder son was in the field; and as he came and drew near to the house, he heard music and dancing. 26 And he called one of the servants and asked what this meant. 27 And he said to him, 'Your brother has come, and your father has killed the fatted calf, because he has received him safe and sound.' 28 But he was angry and refused to go in. His father came out and entreated him, 29 but he answered his father, 'Lo, these many

years I have served you, and I never disobeyed your command; yet you never gave me a kid, that I might make merry with my friends. 30 But when this son of yours came, who has devoured your living with harlots, you killed for him the fatted calf!' 31 And he said to him, 'Son, you are always with me, and all that is mine is yours. 32 It was fitting to make merry and be glad, for this your brother was dead, and is alive; he was lost, and is found.'"

So now we have a father longing for his two rival sons—both of whom are also lost in their own ways. What is apparent here is that the father's love for his errant boys is "prodigal," that is, extravagant. It is easy to accept the fact that there are individuals around who show lavish affections for strange things: the worried man who leaves behind his ninety-nine sheep to hunt down a wandering lamb, the compulsive woman who is so obsessed about her possessions that she will burn the midnight oil to find that one lost thing. We say to ourselves, "There are good reasons why people act this way, the one man who carefully accounts for his considerable resources, the other woman who needs this coin for her limited resources." These are cases we understand and define in categories that do not impact us much. After all, what does a dumb animal or lifeless coin have anything to do with me?

But here we have a father who does not seem to know much about raising sons. He seems to reward the one son for his demanding and foolish character, while neglecting to affirm his other son for his faithful discharge of responsibilities. We all agree that the father has been "prodigal" in his attention and generosity toward the errant son. Thus, we instinctively understand the homebody son for his decided distance from the family. It seems that Jesus here is giving us a decidedly more complicated case!

How has the father shown his prodigality toward his younger son? He runs toward his son at his advanced age, he gives him the best robe—the robe he would have worn at family celebrations. He puts a ring on his son's finger, perhaps his own signet ring that validates all family business dealings by sealing all agreements. Then he gives his son a pair of shoes, perhaps himself stooping down in slave-like position to put them on his son's feet—replacing the very shoes that had allowed his son to walk away in repudiation of the family. Finally, he goes over the top by calling for a family reunion to celebrate with the best food and drink, live music and singing. What kind of father is this man?

Now compare him to the older son: How does he distance himself from his wayward brother and foolish father? First, he stays outside the party [15:28]. He refuses to come in—meaning that he probably refuses to change his clothes and put on a "happy face" with the guests who may not even know half the facts of the inside story.

Second, he lodges his complaint that he never was rewarded for his service (δουλεύω, *douleuō*, "slavish work" [15:29]). I mean, he had worked in the open field, perhaps doing the very same grimy and exhaustive job that the brother complained about when he was forced to be a swineherd in a faraway place [15:15–17]. Where was his party and what about his friends?

Third, note his language. He separates himself from the father and his brother by referring to "that son of yours" rather than "my brother, our family." His bitterness is close to breaking the family. It is true that the younger son has wasted the family resources [15:30] on the wrong priorities, but in this case the older son threatens an estrangement in the family that would end its cohesiveness.

What is the father's response? First, he leaves the party to try to reconcile with his son. He patiently hears his son out. Second, he tells him the truth about his inheritance: he will get it all because he never had left his father [15:31]. His love for the resentful son is total (and as incongruous as his love toward the rival brother). Third, he needs to put the unity in the family above personal pettiness: he needs to come in and welcome his brother [15:32].

The implied question here is, Will the kill-joys—the Pharisees and their ilk—do the same? We know that the son was prodigal in his wasting the father's resources, and we know that the father was prodigal in his lavishing resources to welcome his repentant son. But the question the story leaves us with is whether the other son will be prodigal in his response to the homecoming of his brother. If we are family, how can we maintain our distance and not join in the celebration? God is prodigal in his love toward the lost; will we act in the same way?

1. Have I ever had to reverse myself to reconcile myself to another person? Which current relationships do I have where it would be difficult for me?

2. In what ways does my life mirror the younger brother's? In what ways does my life echo the older brother's concerns?

3. How does this story about a prodigal father change my thinking about God? In what ways do I see the lavish show of divine love toward me?

4. How do I think both sons are now called to be disciples? What do they have to do? How does their call to discipleship now change the way I think about my call to discipleship?

5. Whom do you think that this older brother in the parable represents among the people around Jesus? How do you think he responded?

Reacting Game Excursus for Large Group (100 people): The Eccentric God (15:3–10)

Preliminaries

This game is suited for larger groups. It requires only a skilled narrator and depends on everyone pairing up for "interrogation" by the narrator who is playing "Luke" on ship-leave as his ship is in port. He is visiting "Theophilus" to make sure that his correspondent fully understands how reckless or disproportionate is the love of God for someone who is a disciple. The narrator eventually goes over both stories, embellishing the details with humorous examples; but first someone in the audience ("Theophilus") reads the story to everyone else, and then "Luke" (the moderator) goes over details to make sure Theophilus and his friends understand. Then he asks the audience to pair up and answer questions for both stories.

Finally the narrator alludes to the third part on the "Prodigal Son," going into as much detail as there is time. Mostly the third part is simply to emphasize and summarize the points of the first two parts. If time, the third part also lends itself easily to the lesson of the first two parts, though it is not as humorous. It takes more time to unravel the relationship between the two rival sons and then to draw an application out of it.

Introduction (5 minutes)

[Moderator scans audience and then fixes his eyes on one couple.] "Theophilus, Theophilus, where are you? Oh, there you are! I only have shore time for less than an hour, so I am glad to spend it with you. And who are all these people with you? Well, good, I am glad to share this time with them as well. I'd like to think that twenty minutes sharing my memories with you is close to spending time with Jesus, since my task is to represent him to you.

"As long as everyone is with you, I want to go back to a time when Jesus was similarly addressing a big crowd of people about the high cost of discipleship. At first, he made it sound like a big deal for all the members of his audience. It involved a thorough turning over of one's life, a willingness to leave behind friends, family, resources. He compared the demands of discipleship to a commander going on a war campaign or builder constructing a monument. You can't do either project half-way, that was his point. Neither can you turn half-way to the Kingdom of God.

"True enough. But then he poked fun at the notion that it all depended on the disciple. He spoke about the other side of the equation: What does the Kingdom (or Jesus or God) pledge in response? So let me give you two illustrations of the disproportionality of the divine resources or engagement with the disciples."

[Here have a "Theophilus" among the paired-up audience read Luke 15:3–7. Have everyone else follow along in their own Bible.]

The Man and One Lost Sheep (Luke 15:3–7) [5–10 minutes]

[Moderator:] "Let me summarize the details of Jesus's story. The man Jesus refers to must be pretty well off to have one hundred sheep, no? In this case, though, when one wanders off, all of a sudden, the others really don't matter to the owner. He leaves them in the open field and searches the highland pastures. At last he finds it, and is so happy that he cuddles the little thing around his shoulders and then calls everyone together for a village celebration. Why such a big deal when he already has ninety-nine other sheep? The answer can only be that this little one is more like his pet. He simply can't manage without it. You can't fuss around such things with someone who has such fixations. He simply has fondness for this one thing.

"So now let me ask you, Theophilus, and your friend to answer a couple questions about this little story."

[Moderator either has questions written in a public place or passes out lists with the following questions:]

1. Do you know someone who has such fixations, big or small? Name at least one thing that person would make a fuss about. How about for yourself? What do I make a fuss over?

2. To what length of effort would I or anyone else go to do fulfill this urge? In others words, what do you do to get your "fix?"

[After a few minutes of the Theophilus-friend meeting, the Moderator calls everyone back to order and asks a couple participants to stand up and share their answers to the questions.]

[Now have another "Theophilus" among the pairs read Luke 15:8–10. Have everyone else follow along in their own Bible.]

The Woman and the Lost Coin (Luke 15:8–10) [5–10 minutes]

[Moderator:] "Now let me tell you about another case of disproportionality, an obsessive old woman and her lost trinket. We have here an eccentric woman in the village. You probably know who I'm talking about. She loses something—maybe a button, a ring, or a coin. All of a sudden, it is her favorite thing in life—it has sentimental value. It bothers her day and night, so much so that she is up at midnight frantically sweeping and searching all over. At some ungodly hour—say, two in the morning—she finds it! Now she has to go out and tell everyone about her good fortune—it's time for a party.

"Again, a couple questions [below] for you and your friend."

1. Give an example of some lost cause or pet project that you spend time and money on. Maybe a sports team? Maybe a hobby?

2. Give an example of discovering success or recovery for the cause or project. Did you celebrate? How?

[After a few minutes of the Theophilus-friend meeting, the moderator calls everyone back to order and asks a couple participants to stand up and share their answers to the questions.]

The Prodigal God? (Luke 15:15–32) [2 minutes?]

[Moderator:] "Before we end and I have to board my ship again, let me ask you to read the next story in the parchment, Theophilus, the one you call "the Prodigal Son." But is it a story about the son? Rather in light of the eccentric wealthy man, the obsessive old woman, should we not call this story "The Prodigal God"? Is not the message of Jesus that God is disproportionately ready to engage in our relationship with him or commitment as disciples? Such spectacular lengths God will go to recover what is rightfully his!

The Hook in the Soft-Sell Pitch

Luke 16:1–13 He also said to the disciples, "There was a rich man who had a steward, and charges were brought to him that this man was wasting his goods. 2 And he called him and said to him, 'What is this that I hear about you? Turn in the account of your stewardship, for you can no longer be steward.'

3 "And the steward said to himself, 'What shall I do, since my master is taking the stewardship away from me? I am not strong enough to dig, and I am ashamed to beg. 4 I have decided what to do, so that people may receive me into their houses when I am put out of the stewardship.' 5 So, summoning his master's debtors one by one, he said to the first, 'How much do you owe my master?' 6 He said, 'A hundred measures of oil.' And he said to him, 'Take your bill, and sit down quickly and write fifty.' 7 Then he said to another, 'And how much do you owe?' He said, 'A hundred measures of wheat.' He said to him, 'Take your bill, and write eighty.' 8 The master commended the dishonest steward for his shrewdness; for the sons of this world are more shrewd in dealing with their own generation than the sons of light.

9 "And I tell you, make friends for yourselves by means of unrighteous mammon, so that when it fails they may receive you into the eternal habitations. 10 "He who is faithful in a very little is faithful also in much; and he who is dishonest in a very little is dishonest also in much. 11 If then you have not been faithful in the unrighteous mammon, who will entrust to you the true riches? 12 And if you have not been faithful in that which is another's, who will give you that which is your own?

13 "No servant can serve two masters; for either he will hate the one and love the other, or he will be devoted to the one and despise the other. You cannot serve God and mammon."

Just when you think you have things figured out, Jesus changes the game. So in this story, he pops up again like a jack-in-the-box. He insists that even with lavish attention from God that the three stories show, the disciples are still held in scrutiny—they are not let off the hook for accountability. He compares the Kingdom to an absent and demanding owner who comes back to check on his manager. In this story, the Kingdom is run by a bunch of clients and middle men, with one man accountable as manager.

To understand what Jesus means, let's go back to that topic of "prodigality." Let's talk about how Jesus wanted us to respond to such a disproportionate—prodigal—display of divine attention on lost causes. Let's say now that the older brother did tow the line, that is, he did cooperate with his father's plans. What would be expected of him when it came to the extravagance of his life and service to his father?

Well, here is where things change. Jesus tells a parable where the one missing is not the sheep, not the coin, not the son, but the owner or superior of them all. In this case, it is a rich lord who apparently has been absent and now returns to demand an account of his steward's responsibilities.

I will call my story, "The Devious Business Agent"—though I admit I tell this story with arguable shades of meaning. (Apologies, but you must admit it is fun to put together all the pieces of the puzzle Jesus lays out in this story!) The steward knows that he has not been flawless and that there always is something that someone can drum up against his tenure. It is like an imperial visitation, Theophilus: there is always somebody who doesn't like you or wants your job, so your survival depends on whatever political capital you can muster. It is a cause for much hand-wringing and sleepless nights.

So what does this steward do to prove his usefulness? He goes rogue. He starts negotiating his own deals with the clients of his master. The bottom line is that a steward is able to come up with a tidy sum of money, bound to please any inspector or accountant. His strategy is to fight fire with fire: what the imperial inquisitor looks for from him, he will get from his clients. In this world of business dealing, this devious representative knows how to play hard ball!

The moral of the story comes later [16:8–9]: be as reckless with God's resources as this devious steward was with his connections. You see how much the Roman patron—or Caesar—demands of their subordinates, so how much more does God expect a return on discipleship. See how this parable comes at you in reverse? You have already been found and welcomed into the Kingdom from this (new) perspective. You are never completely sure you have pleased your superior, so you take inspiration from this devious business agent.

How does this message fit in with the three stories Jesus just told? I would sum things up in the following sentence. Be prodigal in our investments toward the Kingdom of God. This injunction is in line with what the older brother was expected to do, even though his younger brother frittered away the family estate. God will forgive both sons for their wrongdoing, but he wants everyone to realize that he will demand an account of their lives. The three-pronged parable gives the divine perspective of the Kingdom's disciple, while this parable gives the disciple's perspective of the Kingdom's priorities.

Then Jesus quotes the common proverb: "He who is faithful in a very little is faithful also in much; and he who is dishonest in a very little is dishonest also in much" [16:10]. Here's how I think it applies to the story of the two sons with an indulgent father: the younger son was entrusted with little [15:10] because he had so little cognizance of the family welfare. What little he was allowed, he returned later in his life through repentance.

And the older son? He was entrusted with much—like the devious steward, maybe he had too many jobs, duties, and responsibilities. Unlike the uncertain response of the older brother, this steward returned what he had with his desperate actions at the end of his tenure. If someone does well in rendering an account to a demanding superior, then he or she will obtain true and unimaginable inheritance [16:11–12] granted to resourceful clients of a lord and devoted heirs of the father.

In either case of younger or older brother, clueless or resourceful servant, it is mammon who (Jesus says) calls the shots for the characters [16:13]. It is up to the listener to learn, not to be controlled by such a force, but to be committed to the lord or the family—for both stories, the master is God and the Kingdom.

All of us, Theophilus, are presented with the opportunity to respond to an unbelievable proposition: God is offering us the Kingdom. What is our response to such prodigal generosity? Will we hold back? Or will we be relentless and resourceful in handing ourselves over to God? I know that I really deserve condemnation for my paltry availability and wasteful commitment to the call I received, but I aim to be as earnest as the "prodigal" son and as shrewd as the devious servant in my discipleship. My hope is the same for you.

1. If God were to come to me to make an account of my life, what would I show?

2. If it is deficient, how can I make amends? What more can I do to promote the Kingdom? How would I characterize my investment in the Kingdom: niggardly or extravagant?

3. How does the world teach about investments and expected returns? How does this serve as parallel to Jesus's teaching?

A Story to Interpret the Hard-Sell and Soft-Sell Pitches to the Public

Luke 16:19–31 "There was a rich man, who was clothed in purple and fine linen and who feasted sumptuously every day. 20 And at his gate lay a poor man named Lazarus, full of sores, 21 who desired to be fed with what fell from the rich man's table; moreover the dogs came and licked his sores. 22 The poor man died and was carried by the angels to Abraham's bosom. The rich man also died and was buried; 23 and in Hades, being in torment, he lifted up his eyes, and saw Abraham far off and Lazarus in his bosom.

24 "And he called out, 'Father Abraham, have mercy upon me, and send Lazarus to dip the end of his finger in water and cool my tongue; for I am in anguish in this flame.' 25 But Abraham said, 'Son, remember that you in your lifetime received your good things, and Lazarus in like manner evil things; but now he is comforted here, and you are in anguish. 26 And besides all this, between us and you a great chasm has been fixed, in order that those who would pass from here to you may not be able, and none may cross from there to us.'

27 "And he said, 'Then I beg you, father, to send him to my father's house, 28 for I have five brothers, so that he may warn them, lest they also come into this place of torment.' 29 But Abraham said, 'They have Moses and the prophets; let them hear them.'

30 "And he said, 'No, father Abraham; but if someone goes to them from the dead, they will repent.' 31 He said to him, 'If they do not hear Moses and the prophets, neither will they be convinced if someone should rise from the dead.'"

FIGURE 6: *Lazarus and Dives* (by Jamie Treadwell)

Here is another parable my sources gave me—which I doubt you'll find elsewhere. This story repeats some of the same elements as the story of the rich fool building his barn [12:13–21]. There the message was the foolishness of building when judgment or death was imminent. But Jesus performs this analogue story with great affect for a different lesson. Here the story follows the teachings on how to respond to God's prodigal generosity [chap. 15] and his fierce rigor of accountability [chap. 16]. The lesson seems to be that once one has ignored the need for "shrewdness" in living up to the standards of divine visitation, there may be no recourse for later changes of heart.

In this case, "Dives" (the name Latin-speakers give him because it means "rich man") has paid no attention the needs of poor around him

[16:19]. He knows Lazarus's name [16:20], probably has seen him sitting outside his door, maybe even noticed that the dogs (the street life) left him with no dignity or private space. He was totally at the mercy of "what fell from the . . . table" [16:21] instead of what he had produced by his own efforts. Dives may have wondered, "Why had he not done something with his life?" He was riddled with "sores," constitutional afflictions that held him back—but is it cause or effect? Did his weaknesses keep him in a condition of poverty, or did his poverty hold him hostage to all the miseries he experienced?

Even in passing away from this mortal life [16:22], we see two very different scenarios. Lazarus dies unceremoniously. Just as he lived and had to be carried to his place of begging, so now he is carried to his final destination by the angels. Dives gets a decent burial—and one would suppose funereal honors.

Yet both men face the same ultimate fate: death. When Jesus told the earlier parable, the rich fool had to account for his life suddenly, when he really should have been prepared. Here there is no reason to believe that the rich man or the poor man was unaware of their fate. If there is a surprising thing, it is that "Dives" is in Hades and Lazarus is in "the bosom of Abraham" [16:23]. Given the way the world works, the consensus would have endorsed Dives's assumptions, yet the reverse obtains.

What does it mean to be in the bosom of Abraham? As you know, Theophilus, we dine formally by reclining leisurely on couches instead of sitting stiffly at chairs. So here, he is Abraham's personal guest, reclining so close to him that their lives seem to be interconnected. Whatever Abraham has at his disposal, so now does Lazarus. The rich man is experiencing the deficits of the poor man, while the poor man is feasting away among the heroes.

The rich man, then, was like the Pharisees in thinking: wealth and success would ensure one's salvation. He had ignored what Moses (the Law) and the Prophets had been warning all along about the scrutiny of God [16:29]. He had failed to be shrewd with his resources and thus failed to be welcomed in the "eternal habitations" of potential benefactors like Lazarus [16:9]. In fact, he had failed to do anything, good or bad, for the man at his gate [16:19].

Even in death Dives carries on imperiously as if he can dispatch the poor man to do his bidding [16:24–30]. "Father Abraham, just send the beggar servant to do a service for me." When this request fails for lack of means, then rich man has yet another order for Lazarus: "Send him out to give admonition to my five brothers." When this order comes to naught, now he tries to order Abraham himself to carry out yet another plan: "Rise from the dead, and then they will listen." Always ordering, full of entitlement, deserving—these are his trademarks.

So back to the context of the father and his two rival sons and to the devious steward: who are the beneficiaries for whom we are to expend ourselves generously? The Lazarus figures we encounter in life, for they are Christ in disguise, sitting at our gates, "covered with sores," and keeping company with dogs who run in our streets. On them we ought to invest our resources and attention so that Lazarus will welcome us into our eternal dwellings in heaven. Once our allotted time is up, no bridge can offer us a second chance—the chasm is "fixed" as too wide.

Dives is fixed in the agonies of Hades, and can only observe (and hope) that his five brothers will learn from the Law and the prophets about investing in the other sons of Abraham (like Lazarus) at the gate. Lazarus, the rich man's unrecognized sibling, goes to Abraham his father for his welcome; while Dives is forever without recourse. Ultimately, one does rise up from the "bosom of Abraham," as Dives had imagined—but it cannot change the outcome for him now.

1. Who is the Lazarus in my life, the one who sits at my gate and has the status of a dog in the street? What can I do practically speaking?

2. Who are my "five brothers" to speak to about the need for changed priorities? How can I support them in changing their priorities?

3. Reflect on the fixed chasm between Hades and the "bosom of Abraham." What do these images suggest about the permanence of hell and heaven?

4. What does the story of "Dives" and Lazarus suggest about Luke's sense for divine values and priorities in this world and the "upside-down" economy of God?

Coaching before Curtain Call

Teaching—Last-Minute Pointers before Curtain Call

Luke 17:1–4 And he said to his disciples, "Temptations to sin are sure to come; but woe to him by whom they come! 2 It would be better for him if a millstone were hung round his neck and he were cast into the sea, than that he should cause one of these little ones to sin. 3 Take heed to yourselves; if your brother sins, rebuke him, and if he repents, forgive him; 4 and if he sins against you seven times in the day, and turns to you seven times, and says, 'I repent,' you must forgive him."

At this point in my account, Theophilus, I turn back to the disciples to see what they have gleaned from Jesus's parables to the crowds. Apart from that meta-parable about the devious steward, he had not spent much time addressing his closest disciples as they move toward the exodus in Jerusalem.

What I tell here are Jesus's last words before they arrive at their destination. Rather than a sustained sermon, the narrative will feature an interlude of ten lepers—which has its own meaning along the road. Still, these are words that speak directly to the disciples after they have witnessed a stretch of Jesus's performances and preaching.

If we dare name this discourse "coaching before curtain call," what shall we say is its object? I'd say it is the daily life that eventually the disciples must embrace after they reach their destination and after they have settled back into rituals and routines. Sometimes scandals and controversies, sometimes temptations and adversities—the end of the journey will not exempt them from life's stiff challenges. How will they react to what they will undoubtedly face? Will they fall apart? Will they hang together and work as a unit? My account suggests—I believe—that Jesus was preparing them for how they would relate together as a group after he had left them. I suppose you could call this continuing organization the "Church," but this is a word I use only sparingly in these *Memoirs*, while it is more applicable in my sequel *An Unfinished Tale* when I focus on later generations of disciples.

In retrospect, the discourse resonates with "institutional" themes we have encountered before. For example, the word "temptations" probably refers to teachings that make new believers stumble. Jesus says that such obstacles (misleading teachers and leaders) are impossible to avoid: they are a part of establishing any human organization. Expect them—don't bury your head in the sand and say that our group, the local church, is impervious to errors and problems. Just make sure that you are not the cause of things going wrong. If people around you pick up the wrong signal, you have failed as a leader or teacher. Jesus says that you are responsible as a disciple for a better outcome, lest a severe penalty awaits you.

Jesus is speaking about bringing others into discipleship through what I suggest above are rituals and routines. This involves formation throughout the day, a process that seemingly entails correction seven times *in a day*. Painstaking attention to detail, in other words. Patience is required: if it be once, twice, three times of working out daily affairs as a disciple, continue along these lines in a daily way. Work with an errant follower up to seven times—a fullness of times (as Jew think of the number seven)—until they come back.

1. Recall crisis moments in life. How did these times affect my closest relationships? Are there relationships going back to the times that require attention? Have I forgiven everyone involved?

2. What relationships do I have where I am an example or an authority? Have I ever taken advantage of my position in the lives of such people? In what ways have I ever "scandalized" such people by my example?

Obstacles

Luke 17:5–6 The apostles said to the Lord, "Increase our faith!"
6 And the Lord said, "If you had faith as a grain of mustard seed, you could say to this sycamine tree, 'Be rooted up, and be planted in the sea,' and it would obey you."

Here Jesus tells his disciples to be direct about the aforementioned obstacles and ceaseless duties institutional life presents.[4] The "apostles" (the foremost of the followers whom I often earmark as the Twelve) realize that Jesus's words apply especially to them. The tree stands in their path—whether they are going to Jerusalem as now or whether they go to Rome as some of them will later. In the face of such a roadblock, they naturally feel entirely helpless and powerless, as if their only alternative route leads toward a cliff.

So Jesus speaks to them with images he can show them right then and there on the road. No doubt there were mustard bushes and sycamine [often translated, "mulberry"] trees along the way. Maybe even one tree stood in their path requiring them to bushwhack around it. Plus, they had just seen the Sea of Galilee, so it was fresh in their minds.

4. Again, you and I might (now) call this institution the "Church." Jesus does not use this word per se.

Now what about if they only had a tad bit of faith? Just a little something that they could find a glimmer of promise in and dream bigger about? Faith starts there, as with a miniscule fleck of a seed. Then it's easy to see how it grows by itself—no effort really required.

The morphing of all these images allows the disciples to imagine that they could command the tree in front of them to be transplanted in the water of the sea. It is like a psalm I know [Psalm 24]—look it up, Theophilus—where the pilgrims speak to the city gates and command them to "be lifted up . . . that the king of glory may come in."

From that little start, one now commands circumstances themselves—not people or gods or demons—but objects. And they respond! How do gates respond by themselves to bare commands? I don't know, but the psalm I just quoted tells us they should! Address problems and challenges that are in the path, and powerful things happen.

This is not to say that adversities will disappear. After all, what happens to a tree that is planted in water? The water is not hospitable, the tree presumably still needs to bear fruit; the whole thing is incongruous enough to suggest that the mustard seed faith is merely the beginning of making progress in times of trial and controversy, not the end-all. It is definitely not the "name it-claim it" dynamic that guarantees a fairy-tale existence of eternal bliss.

1. What are the sycamine [often translated, "mulberry"] trees that seem to block my path?

2. Look inward and ask if there is a "fleck of a seed" for faith that my obstacles can be overcome?

3. Address these obstacles directly from a platform of "mustard" faith. Tell them to get out of the way.

Service

Luke 17:7–10 "Will any one of you, who has a servant plowing or keeping sheep, say to him when he has come in from the field, 'Come at once and sit down at table'? 8 Will he not rather say to him, 'Prepare supper for me, and gird yourself and serve me, till I eat and drink; and afterward you shall eat and drink'? 9 Does he thank the servant because he did what was commanded? 10 So you also, when you have done all that is commanded you, say, 'We are unworthy servants; we have only done what was our duty.'"

For the disciples, the day never seems to come to an end. What does Jesus imply by this story? Look at the words: plowing and weeding fields, tending the flock, dressing, cooking, the daily table, all of these things involving details, small things. Always more work to do, always more duties to fulfill, and for the most part no recognition. Come in from a long day in the field and now make dinner and now manage the unruly domestic life. Dress up, play the role—even if you don't feel like it.

Performances—often very good performances—often arise almost magically from exhaustion and apathy. The energy for such theater spontaneously spouts up as the dynamic of the drama takes hold. And who is the unnamed master here but Jesus himself? Thus, the whole crew derives its meaning from the master at the center of the story, as well as its energy from the "star" performer. The word "unworthy" is *achreioi* (ἀχρεῖοι [17:10]), meaning "unleveraged" or "undeserving." There is no ground for demanding a different role or higher wages for our performances. How different the disciple's attitude than Dives's! If Jesus is speaking of "Church" here and the disciples' role in it, their performances will be long and grueling, but the acclaim will be great eventually.

1. What things do I groan about doing when I am tired?

2. What are the duties that I have? What attitude do I have in doing duties?

A Choral Interlude: All Are Off-Key but One!

Luke 17:11–19 On the way to Jerusalem he was passing along between Samaria and Galilee. 12 And as he entered a village, he was met by ten lepers, who stood at a distance 13 and lifted up their voices and said, "Jesus, Master, have mercy on us." 14 When he saw them he said to them, "Go and show yourselves to the priests." And as they went they were cleansed.

15 Then one of them, when he saw that he was healed, turned back, praising God with a loud voice; 16 and he fell on his face at Jesus' feet, giving him thanks. Now he was a Samaritan. 17 Then said Jesus, "Were not ten cleansed? Where are the nine? 18 Was no one found to return and give praise to God except this

foreigner?" [19] And he said to him, "Rise and go your way; your faith has made you well."

The map is now reoriented toward Jerusalem, and the focus is back on the people and events the disciples encounter on the pilgrimage route. They run into a leper colony village, an odd hodge-podge of Jews and Samaritans who have found communion together through their adversities. They lift up their voices like a chorus in Greek tragedy, trying to make sense out of the drama of life and of the divine visitation Jesus represents.

Is not this the community forged among diverse souls that we often run into ourselves? People are bound together by their suffering and "hang out" on the edges of the movers and shakers like Dives and the Pharisees and scholars. They flock toward Jesus as someone who can make sense of their common lot, a "master" or "organizer" (ἐπιστάτης, epistatēs) [17:13] to take charge and orchestrate their living together. In your Greek world, Theophilus, it would be a chorus director or music coach whose direction tells the audience what to pay attention to.

Jesus directs the whole chorus of misfits back into mainstream life. He restores them to wholeness, and instructs them to enter through Jerusalem's gates and presumably into fruitful living. Whatever Jesus is, he is no anarchic crank when it comes to the political order or even the Jewish religious structure.[5] But who in "mainstream" society acknowledges that every one of its foundations and assumptions is really the gift of God who allows such wholeness to happen through no effort or deservedness on our part? Who is responsible for such *charis* ("grace")? Only one recognizes what is going on and gives back a fitting return (*eu-charis-tōn* [17:16]).

Such an *epistatēs* is far more than a chorus master or community spokesman like you might see in a play of Sophocles. He has "cleansed" them and brought them back into normal life. Who cannot fail to return to Jesus to acknowledge that he has done inestimable favor to them? Yet ninety percent of the beneficiaries will not return to the source and humble themselves as totally unworthy of such blessing.

Only a Samaritan, called a "foreigner" (ἀλλογενής, *allogenēs*), someone who is neither Gentile nor Jew, an in-betweener, returns. In the end, he is at home in the band of Jesus, because he does not fit either group, Jew or Gentile, but now "made fit" (17:19: "made well") for the

---

5. For a sense of how the Church and Jewish religious institutions (temple, seasons, customs) related, see *Unfinished Tale*.

Kingdom of God. A return to normal life for this Samaritan boils down to his allegiance to the one God—and pilgrimage to Jerusalem. Ultimately notice that his confession of gratitude is toward Jesus.

1. Have there been times in my life where adversity has placed me in the company of "odd fellows"? Are there such communities of suffering around today? And are there those in such communities who are even more out of place than the other group members?

2. How would I classify myself in terms of the characters in this story? What things get in the way of my acknowledgement of divine grace or supernatural intervention?

3. What benefits do I know in my "normal" life that really come from God? Do I deserve them? Have I thanked God for these things? How do these undeserved things bring me into fellowship with people who are not like me? In other words, are there figurative Samaritans around me?

Waiting for the Kingdom

Luke 18:1–8 And he told them a parable, to the effect that they ought always to pray and not lose heart. 2 He said, "In a certain city there was a judge who neither feared God nor regarded man; 3 and there was a widow in that city who kept coming to him and saying, 'Vindicate me against my adversary.' 4 For a while he refused; but afterward he said to himself, 'Though I neither fear God nor regard man, 5 yet because this widow bothers me, I will vindicate her, or she will wear me out by her continual coming.'" 6 And the Lord said, "Hear what the unrighteous judge says. 7 And will not God vindicate his elect, who cry to him day and night? Will he delay long over them? 8 I tell you, he will vindicate them speedily. Nevertheless, when the Son of man comes, will he find faith on earth?"

I will now skip ahead to another "interlude," though now it is a humorous one from the mouth of the choir director himself. Here we have a high-strung lady and a high-handed bureaucrat, and they seem to run into each other all the time—maybe first in city gates, then in the marketplace. "When will this hysterical woman leave me alone?" he moans. Even a hardened judge fears that she might get so worked up that she will start throwing things and "hit me in the eye" (ὑπωπιάζω, *hypōpiazō*, "wear me out" [18:5]).

Now Jesus circles back to his riddle: "What would happen if we put names on these two characters? Why, one we can call 'faithful disciple,' the other 'God,'" Jesus offers perhaps with a smirk.

In light of what Jesus said about the seemingly slow process of his return (the part I skipped [17:20–35]), when they will long to see his day and when they will be tempted to give in—like Lot's wife, this parable is therapeutic. Vindication seems to be the promise of the story. When intercessory prayers seemingly bounce back into the laps of those who seek relief [18:3, 5, 7, 8], God offends our sense of propriety, just like this judge who has no reverence for God nor respect for people. This man is an official who made a career out of dodging his duties—and that's how we often feel about God! To return to the theme of waiting, our question is always, how can we escape or get ready for the final visitation if it's not going to happen right away when we arrive in Jerusalem?

Yet, Jesus counsels his audience—probably mostly disciples, since they are the ones mostly addressed in the previous passage [17:22], don't quit bringing forth your requests for relief [18:7]. "Cry to him day and night!" Be urgent and even indignant. Remember the importunate desperation of the man who came for midnight help from his otherwise sleeping neighbor. Then when the Son of Man returns, as he says [17:22], he hopes to find his elect faithful in spite of long-suffering and letdowns built into the fabric of history.

1. Are there times when it seems that my prayers or my needs for redress are never answered? What is the natural impact of this silence on my faith outlook?

2. What prayer results can I demonstrate that show long-suffering prayer?

3. Can I find times when my "plans" for results were wrong and impatient, while the divine plan was the correct one even though it took time?

4. What does this parable suggest about how hard it is to maintain faith in hard times?

Unlikely Recruits: Tax Collectors

Luke 18:9–14 He also told this parable to some who trusted in themselves that they were righteous and despised others: 10 "Two men went up into the temple to pray, one a Pharisee and the other a tax collector. 11 The Pharisee stood and prayed thus with himself, 'God, I thank thee that I am not like other men, extortioners, unjust, adulterers, or even like this tax collector. 12 I fast twice a week, I give tithes of all that I get.' 13 But the tax collector, standing far off, would not even lift up his eyes to heaven, but beat his breast, saying, 'God, be merciful to me a sinner!' 14 I tell you, this man went down to his house justified rather than the other; for everyone who exalts himself will be humbled, but he who humbles himself will be exalted."

Here's another one to get a rise out of the audience. People that like to flaunt themselves are the worst ones to put up with, aren't they? So Jesus tells this story to mock such self-centered individuals. Now to get this story, you have to remember that by now Jesus has roused up a rag-tag cast of pilgrims—purist and publican, rich and poor, godly and gaudy—all on their way to Jerusalem.

By some stretch of imagination, they imagine that they will proceed to the temple itself where finally everything will come together—what exactly, we don't yet know. But for Jews, things tend to swirl around Jerusalem. The temple is not a place for solitude and asceticism as if its holiness has no correspondence to the real world. For Jews it is a grand and glorious destination, so splendid a place that even Romans rank it as one of the wonders of the world.

Better to think of the Jerusalem temple as a trophy room, testifying to men's highest achievements. Just like the temple to Zeus (or whomever) in your city, Theophilus, our site represents the best we can offer to our God. Temples become boasting grounds for artist and warrior alike—an archive of memorabilia: monuments, statues, and inscriptions. Benefactors and dignitaries get to put up some public reminder of how much they did and what they accomplished. The closer to the center of temple activities, the more devotees will notice them. The show of beneficence may become so ostentatious that visitors may start mistaking the donor for the divine.

Now you begin to understand the scene for Jesus's spoof. Two people are on their way to the Jerusalem temple precincts—and here

Jesus may have appointed a couple fellow pilgrims to act things out. They both notice the displays of grandeur, celebrating both divine and human achievements to the right and to the left. Ultimately, they both arrive and pray at the inner sanctuary. The remarkable thing about this story is that even the scoundrel (a tax collector, often called a "publican") wants to be counted among the saints. He is on his way with the sanctimonious, who consider access to be their deserved right. In this case, Jesus says it is a Pharisee, who feels as entitled as Dives from my earlier story.

We are privy to both men's motivations and reflections. Note what the Pharisee claims: he not only has not violated the hard commandments (concerning marriage, business, and neighbors), but he has gone beyond the call of duty by fasting more than anyone else and giving money beyond the tithe requirements. All exemplary. Yes, this Pharisee did all the right things.

But don't miss this subtlety of the details or my Greek. For one thing, he marches right up to the front where he posts himself so that everyone will see him. Then he begins with his litany of achievements, almost as if he is dictating an inscription for his epitaph. When I say that he "prays thus with himself" [18:11], look at what the Greek actually says: he prays thus *to* himself! Why, up in front with such congratulatory statements about himself, he well could be his own monument and inscription!

Compare him to the tax collector. He stands in the back where no one will notice his commendation. No one will rank him with God or the high and mighty. In contrast to the statuesque posture of the Pharisee, he won't ever look up. Instead of inscribing himself with all sorts of commendations, he beats his breast as if to strike out all claims to worthiness. It all depends on mercy for him.

Which one of these characters would you rather spend time with, Theophilus? People who are full of themselves have hardly any space for anyone else! For God, one can assume the same. Both Pharisee and tax collector stand before the great mercy seat because they both are equal in their unworthiness before the Almighty. While one prays to himself, the other prays to God. In this "calculus" of Jesus, the publican will walk away "justified," for he recognizes his condition.

1. How can I identify with the common denominator of "sinful" man?

2. How do I tend to identify myself with either party above, the Pharisee or the tax collector?

3. How do I sometimes try to position myself as a statue? What things do I want people to know about me? How do I seek to get attention and notice?

4. What is the place of good deeds in the religion Jesus is preaching?

Unlikely Recruits: Children

> Luke 18:15–17 Now they were bringing even infants to him that he might touch them; and when the disciples saw it, they rebuked them. 16 But Jesus called them to him, saying, "Let the children come to me, and do not hinder them; for to such belongs the Kingdom of God. 17 Truly, I say to you, whoever does not receive the Kingdom of God like a child shall not enter it."

Jesus says, more or less, "Now look at you disciples! You do the same thing that the proud Pharisee does in the temple. For there the tax collector would come to God and say, "Have mercy on me a sinner," while the Pharisee would look down on his counterpart's unmerited ("unjustified") presence. After all, he fasted twice per week, he never sinned, and so on—and how could the scoundrel compare? And now you would make these children do the same: "stand far off" so that you can make space for those who love to put up statues! You would limit access to the Kingdom, implying that it belongs to the mature and the responsible and the productive. No, let me touch these children, those who dare not push their way to the front and scarcely can utter any defense for themselves. Let me bless them in my touch that they may find access to the Kingdom."

It is interesting to me, Theophilus, how this episode shows *our* connection to the Kingdom. In the previous parable, Jesus suggests that the temple is access to God; but here *he* is the way that anyone, mature disciple or helpless babe, makes connection to the Kingdom. "For to such belongs the Kingdom of God" [18:16].

As if to drive home the idea of the parable that the Pharisee cannot "justify" his place in the Kingdom, note how I say "even infants" [18:15] and children were invited. In our homes, these members have little role and place until they can produce something by their labors, either in the market or in the fields. My sources for this story are emphatic that babes and not just "children" were carried to him, proving that there is no basis for "justification" to enter the Kingdom of God.

The point I am making is a little different than the mere innocence of "children" [cf. 9:46–48]. If it were innocence that Jesus was demonstrating, justification or admission in the Kingdom would be understandable and rational; but Jesus here points to children and infants because they don't deserve anything. Unlike the Pharisee who keeps commandments or the next story where a "rich ruler" wants to do whatever Jesus says, children and infants are more like the publican who has no case for justification. We are now back to the unmitigated kindness of God, the *charis*, that Jesus declared in his now-famous sermon to the flatlanders [see 6:27 –36]. *Charis* is as natural as the rain that falls on the just and the unjust, the sun that rises to begin things for the evil and the righteous. Thus it is present at the beginning of life (for children), and it continues for the rest of life (for tax collectors).

1. Who are the weakest of the weak around me? How are they prevented from approaching the Kingdom—be it fellowship or church or personal connections? How can I welcome them?

2. How do I impersonate the disciples in their resistance to the infants and children? Does impatience affect my interaction with the weak? What expectations do I have that I need to adjust?

3. Are there people around me whom I can literally or figuratively touch to help them? How do I bless those around me?

Likely Recruits Unlikely!

Luke 18:18–30 And a ruler asked him, "Good Teacher, what shall I do to inherit eternal life?" 19 And Jesus said to him, "Why do you call me good? No one is good but God alone. 20 You know the commandments: 'Do not commit adultery, Do not kill, Do not steal, Do not bear false witness, Honor your father and mother.'" 21 And he said, "All these I have observed from my youth." 22 And when Jesus heard it, he said to him, "One thing you still lack. Sell all that you have and distribute to the poor, and you will have treasure in heaven; and come, follow me."

23 But when he heard this he became sad, for he was very rich. 24 Jesus looking at him said, "How hard it is for those who have riches to enter the Kingdom of God! 25 For it is easier for a camel to go through the eye of a needle than for a rich man to

enter the Kingdom of God." 26 Those who heard it said, "Then who can be saved?" 27 But he said, "What is impossible with men is possible with God." 28 And Peter said, "Lo, we have left our homes and followed you." 29 And he said to them, "Truly, I say to you, there is no man who has left house or wife or brothers or parents or children, for the sake of the Kingdom of God, 30 who will not receive manifold more in this time, and in the age to come eternal life."

Note what my last two stories have implied about trying to find justification or acceptance in the Kingdom. In the parable, Jesus addresses the crowds who are on their way with him to Jerusalem and ultimately to the temple. Some like the Pharisees use this journey as a way to promote themselves, while the others like the tax collector to humble themselves. Then there are the infants and children. Should they be admitted? They have no recourse to pilgrimage or temple, yet Jesus gives them his blessing for the Kingdom.

In this story a man goes directly to Jesus to gain acceptance to the Kingdom. This rich *archōn* (ἄρχων, "ruler" [18:18]) is going in the right direction as opposed to the Pharisee who relies simply on his merit (versus the tax collector) and the disciples wholly on maturity and adulthood (versus the infants being brought to Jesus). He knows that what he is looking for is not ultimately the temple or a simple blessing, but "eternal life."

So far, so good: he is going to Jesus directly. Or is he? Jesus probes the man with deeper questions. "Why do you call *me* good [18:19]? Let's go through the second table of the Law—commandments concerning love of neighbor [18:20]. Okay, good, you have kept these things [18:21]. If you really want to come to me as "good," then what about the first table of the Law—commandments concerning love of God? Is it possible that your attachment to wealth is an obstacle? If so, then deal with it by giving all your possessions away. Then finish what the second table is about by following me like these other disciples—for *I* am the "good" you are seeking" [18:22].

The point of this encounter is not that wealth is bad—much less that observance of the commandments is bad. But Jesus issues a wake-up call to everyone: you must do more than seek him as a teacher of the "good." One cannot earn admission either by good works (the Pharisee in the temple), by being near the Kingdom to obtain a blessing (the infants), or even by coming to Jesus for a primer on "good life" (the *archōn*).

Jesus does not fail to catch our attention to this lesson by going from the sublime to the ridiculous. This ruler has come with good intent, but his aim is so far off target that Jesus seizes on an example at hand: beside him (perhaps) a camel and its owner. "Drive that big beast with its cargo strapped to its side through the smallest opening you can imagine, like the eye of needle. Yes, the same needle that stitches up the humblest cloak of one of my ragtag disciples. Not possible? So it's not possible for any of your boasts to grant you admission into the Kingdom" [18:25–26].

Peter and the disciples, off to the side, try to suppress their laughter. Somehow, Jesus has once again turned the tables on conventional thinking and approaches. Needless to say, they have been thinking about these lessons ever since they reached the point of no return and decided to take to march toward Jerusalem. As spokesman, Peter rises up to sing the praises of the disciples who have left behind what otherwise was precious to them and decided to cast in their lot with Jesus. "Yes," he unabashedly asserts, "to be a disciple means to follow Jesus without encumbrance of family, home, and wealth. This we have done" [18:28].

Jesus assures them that they are on the right track [18:29]. They will find a rich life when they have approached God in the nothingness of their works (the Pharisee), in the lowliness of their station (the infants), and a life wholly committed to Jesus as the "Good," the fulfillment of the first and second table of the Law (the rich man). Yet this response now exposes Peter and the disciples to the same probing inquiry that beset the rich man.

Jesus will next turn to them and teach that discipleship involves much more than just giving up homes and relationships to receive a blessing or new homes or relationships—it involves humiliation and death, even though it does bring its promised reward: "eternal life." The second table involves letting go of dear things, but who can afford the ultimate cost of discipleship, the topic of the first table? This will require a private lecture.

1. What do I have to give up to be totally a disciple of Jesus?

2. How do I rely on even good things to justify myself and my inclusion in the Kingdom?

3. How total and exclusive is my relationship with Jesus? Is it as total as the tax collector's need for mercy in spite of a depraved life? Is it as dependent as an infant who needs help in getting to Jesus? How sold-out am I?

Luke 18:31–34 And taking the twelve, he said to them, "Behold, we are going up to Jerusalem, and everything that is written of the Son of man by the prophets will be accomplished. 32 For he will be delivered to the Gentiles, and will be mocked and shamefully treated and spit upon; 33 they will scourge him and kill him, and on the third day he will rise." 34 But they understood none of these things; this saying was hid from them, and they did not grasp what was said.

Once Peter has staked his claim to the Kingdom based on the disciples' sacrifice, Jesus reveals the full extent of what following him will cost. He gives himself as example. Yes, in this life Peter's hopes for home and family will find fulfillment along with the promise for eternal life afterwards, but who is ready for the cost? Since they are his disciples, their self-respect and dignity will be tested by the reception that awaits their master Jesus in Jerusalem.

This the disciples do not understand, because of their blindness—at least that is how I interpret it. Three times in one sentence alone, I stressed that the disciples are ignorant of what the cost will be [18:34]. The calculus of the Kingdom that Jesus preaches is nonsense unless there is an inner revelation of some sort. Even the reference to the "Son of man" [18:31] enduring these afflictions is lost on the disciples, who presumably are familiar with what the prophet Daniel says about him [Daniel 7]. But if you look there, you will find no mention of suffering for the one who approaches the throne and to whom nations and authorities pay homage.

Thus, the picture Jesus gives us is that one who wants to be a disciple should be ready to let go of every shred of entitlement and self-worth and follow him into a life of shame and abuse. This is predicted by other Jewish prophets, which apparently none of the disciples remembered—or bothered to rehearse for present performance.

CHAPTER SIX

Visitation on Big Stage

As JESUS AND HIS pilgrimage festival arrive at the verge of Jerusalem, events start to heat up. Anticipation surrounding everyone from Jesus to disciple to spectator to antagonist intensifies. The crowds turn out to get a glimpse of him, laugh at his snappy stories, wonder at his prodigious deeds. Jesus and his public acts increasingly come across as the performance of a traveling show. Not like a sit-down production, but more like a Greek theater festival, this performance sweeps up public attention in its wake and gathers increasing intensity as it goes. Most of all, at least in the Jewish context, the participants hope that some big change is about to occur.

All eyes are on what will happen in the finale, when Jesus arrives. Everyone vaguely knows that the blessing of God is predicted for the pilgrim at the festal climax of Jerusalem. That much everyone knows and anticipates.

However, as you have learned, Theophilus, the *charis* blessing that Jesus represents is not dependent on the pilgrim's social status or moral standing. Rather, from the beginning of these *Memoirs*, divine visitations are surprising and often inscrutable—they fall upon the unlikeliest of beneficiaries. I will therefore begin the last phase of Jesus's performance with two such cases in Jericho. When the road brings you to Jericho, you know you are in the home stretch. Only a short—though tortuous and desolate—ascent to the next city, Jerusalem, lies ahead.

Jericho: The Blind Man and Zacchaeus

First, let me recount an episode [18:35–43] involving a blind man at the entrance to the city of Jericho. The blind man faces three obstacles in his desire to meet Jesus: he is blind and a beggar; when he prays he is criticized and not heard; when he is heard, his request for help is not understood. Still, he persists and is healed for his importunity: but more than healed of blindness, he seems to find the spiritual sight to follow after Jesus.

The interesting thing about this blind man is that he does not know what he really needs! He says he wants to see, but he needs far more than physical sight: he needs to become a true follower of the king of Israel, the "Son of David" [18:38]. As a beggar, he would appear most unproductive of men without claims; yet in this account his true value comes forth as he answers the call of discipleship. Does he, though blind, perceive something that the seeing crowd does not recognize? And he persists in his seeking Jesus, unlike both the rich and observant *archōn* and the disciples who did not understand [18:34].

He is physically blind about what is going on around him, yet the passing of Jesus stirs him to take action. All the more he wants to know what is going on, despite the opposition of others, until he receives full vision. Once in the know, he sees spiritually and physically and follows.

1. Read Luke 18:35–43. Are there times when all I can do is cry out because I don't even know what I really need to deal with my problems?

2. Are there people who have "blindness" keeping them from conversion? Do I pray for them or spend time with them to help them understand?

> Luke 19:1–10 He entered Jericho and was passing through. 2 And there was a man named Zacchaeus; he was a chief tax collector, and rich. 3 And he sought to see who Jesus was, but could not, on account of the crowd, because he was small of stature. 4 So he ran on ahead and climbed up into a sycamore tree to see him, for he was to pass that way.
>
> 5 And when Jesus came to the place, he looked up and said to him, "Zacchaeus, make haste and come down; for I must stay at your house today." 6 So he made haste and came down, and received him joyfully. 7 And when they saw it they all murmured, "He has gone in to be the guest of a man who is a sinner."

8 And Zacchaeus stood and said to the Lord, "Behold, Lord, the
half of my goods I give to the poor; and if I have defrauded any
one of anything, I restore it fourfold." 9 And Jesus said to him,
"Today salvation has come to this house, since he also is a son
of Abraham. 10 For the Son of man came to seek and to save
the lost."

The second case I quote in its entirety if only because it is somewhat amusing—so at least I am told. It concerns a tax collector in Jericho
named Zacchaeus. He has a number of "shortcomings" (I love puns!) in
his desire to have a relationship with God: he is by profession an unclean
tax collector and by status a "rich" man (and seemingly far from Kingdom priorities). He is prevented from getting close to Jesus because of his
shortness. So Jesus looks for Zacchaeus even as Zacchaeus climbs a tree
to look at Jesus. There they meet in the shade of a sycamore tree—Jesus,
seeker of souls, Zacchaeus, consummate sycophant [sycophantēs (see
19:8 for the verbal form)].[1]

They retire for a banquet together. It is not clear what the occasion is
for this feast. Is it for Jesus, who invited himself over? Is it for Zacchaeus
the host? Is it for salvation personified, as Jesus seems to imply [18:9a]?
Or is it for Abraham and his sons in a family reunion [18:9b]? If so, is
Lazarus—the beggar who once sat at Dives's gate—there alongside of Jesus and Zacchaeus at Abraham's banquet? Both Jesus and Zacchaeus face
criticism for their mutual association. Zacchaeus stands and solemnly
promises a reformed life and restitution for his crimes. Jesus recognizes
the good-faith pledge of his host and calls him a son of Abraham.

Both Jericho cases, the blind man and Zacchaeus, face numerous
obstacles in discipleship. Both cases show someone "standing" to recognize the shortcomings of their situation [18:40; 19:8]. Through "standing" true discipleship begins: it requires perseverance through difficulties
in both situations. For the blind man it was difficulty in his blindness,
difficulty of persisting in his prayer, difficulty in Jesus's question; for

---

1. Did you notice how much fun I had in my word choice, Theophilus? The ety-
mology of "being a sycophant or swindler" (συκοφαντέω, sykophanteō [19:8]) sounds
like something silly: "putting on a fig appearance" (sykon, "fig"+ phantasia ["fantasy"]).
The tree itself (συκομορέα, sykomorea) sounds like "fake fig" (sykon+ mōros ["fool"]).
If you give me a moment of poetic liberty, Theophilus, and if you remember what I
said about the fig tree and its fruit standing for Israel's promise of messianic fruitfulness [13:6–9], well, we have quite a visitation between Jesus and Zacchaeus! Maybe
something like Jesus calling the "fig pretender" down from a fake fig tree?

Zacchaeus it was difficulty of his physical circumstances, difficulty of his profession and character.

There is even more to Zacchaeus than his shortness suggests. When Zacchaeus hosts Jesus at banquet, there is at least partial uncertainty about whether he will actually make good on his promises—for one must remember that Zacchaeus spent his life climbing "sycamore" trees and his career out of "swindling" clients—my pun tells you a little about what kind of character we are dealing with. Remember, Theophilus, the "fig tree" (συκῇ, *sykē*) represented Israel's task to bear fruit or a time of messianic peace.

Then, almost to confirm this oily personality, we next find Zacchaeus giving a speech, using hyperbolic pledges to repay his debts and using rhetorical present tense verbs to impress the reader about something he has not yet done! After all, the *archōn* was told he had to give up everything, while Zacchaeus gives away only half of all his abundance, leaving him with security and abundance. At least you should wonder about Zacchaeus's claims to live a reformed life—and perhaps pray he follows up his promise with a fruitful life.

Still, both men of Jericho were once totally lost and blind, but now they show us a path forward to Jerusalem. Perhaps I mean them to represent you and me, Theophilus, as we enter the difficult last phase.

1. Consider both the blind man and the short man in Jericho: what obstacles do I face in being a disciple? Wealth? Some personal blindness? Character flaws or blind spots from the past?

2. Do I know people like Zacchaeus, self-promoting, assertive, pushy, and insecure due to past experiences?

3. Do I trust Zacchaeus-like people's resolve when they claim to have changed? Does Zacchaeus give me hope for their conversion? Do I know anyone like Zacchaeus? What role does Jesus (or God) play when it comes to their conversion? How does 19:10 offer comfort?

"Spoiler Alert" Parable: Fake News about a Happy Ending

Luke 19:11 As they heard these things, he proceeded to tell a parable, because he was near to Jerusalem, and because they supposed that the Kingdom of God was to appear immediately. 12 He said therefore, "A nobleman went into a far country to receive a kingdom and then return. . . . 14 But his citizens hated him and sent an embassy after him, saying, 'We do not want this man to reign over us.'

15 "When he returned, having received the kingdom, he commanded these servants, to whom he had given the money, to be called to him, that he might know what they had gained by trading. . . .

26 "'I tell you, that to everyone who has will more be given; but from him who has not, even what he has will be taken away. 27 But as for these enemies of mine, who did not want me to reign over them, bring them here and slay them before me.'"

As the crowds in Jericho wonder about this feast that Zacchaeus gives as a foreshadowing of some bigger banquet for Abraham and his family reuniting in Jerusalem, Jesus gives them a reality check: "Things are probably going to be different than what you think when we finally arrive. Jesus recognizes that everyone is on edge, anticipating some kind of upheaval now that the pilgrimage is at its end. In the parable (which I only sum up here), a lord goes away to get legal backing for his claims to land and wealth. He leaves the operation of his estate in the hands of ten servants, of which three representatives claim the spotlight. He knows he is taking a chance by going away—he could lose everything to rivals who would move in and take over. But now he has returned to get an accounting from his servants, especially the three representatives he left behind.

Two of the three have reinvested the master's wealth to show a return on their deposit. The third, though, does not take chances. He would rather leverage his money lest he be identified too closely with his master. In real history, taking sides could get a person killed if the wrong group comes to power! Rather than being inspired by his lord who left it all behind, this third servant hunkers down in mediocrity.

Now the joy comes when the master is given the authority: all the servants who took the chance with him get the spoils of his victory. They truly "enter the joy of the master." Instead of a beating or punishment from the opposition, they get tremendous payback for taking their chances with the master.

Are we leveraging our investment or our discipleship? Do we have part of our stock in the world? The servant who did not risk shows indirectly that he does not want to trust the master and does not want to identify with him. He is more or less identifying with the opposition, or at least that he refuses to commit himself. Thus, he should count it as mercy that he is not slain before the master's eyes, like all the rivals who defied the master from the beginning.

Now apply this parable to what I have been hinting at in Jesus's teachings about the Kingdom. Earlier he had said rather plainly, "Will the son of man find faith on earth when he returns" [18:8]? This is the recurrent theme to address the crowd's expectations. All those feasts and banquets Jesus attended may point to something beyond his arrival in Jerusalem and his exodus from there. It is an open question about what will happen when Jesus goes away.

More generally, what is the lesson apart from Jesus's departure? It involves the high cost of discipleship. All along Jesus has been talking about the cost of discipleship, and it is a cost exacted from him as well. He too is on his way to Jerusalem where he will face extreme opposition and trial and death. Then he must go away to receive recognition that he is the legitimate king, no matter what the opposition has plotted against him.

More specifically, how does this parable speak to everyone? The people he has met along the path to Jerusalem are the servants to whom he will entrust his estate and wealth if they will receive them and invest them. How has the Pharisee and the tax collector in the first parable invested their share of the estate [18:9–14]? How about the little children, or the disciples who have been shooing off their parents [18:15–17]? How about the "rich ruler" [18:18–23]? Or how about wealthy people in general or the disciples who say they have left everything [18:24–30]? Jesus then forewarns the Twelve what the ultimate cost could be for servants of his Kingdom: death [18:31–34]. And then they run into Zacchaeus and the blind beggar just before their arrival in Jerusalem [18:35—19:10]. How do they size up to the parable's categories?

Finally, one must reckon with the ending of the parable: the opposition is slain before the nobleman's eyes. In other words, the very climate against even being a servant of the nobleman, or any kind of disciple, is hostile. No wonder that so few join up with a full investment. What should be our attitude toward the various candidates that appeared so far in the *Memoirs*? Should we judge them compassionately because they still come to Jesus—in contrast to the opposition? They may not give all because they do not understand what a full investment entails. Or they may give a limited amount, yet still receive a reward. They may "eke" their way into the Kingdom and escape being slain before the noble man's eyes.

I will leave it at that for these embedded questions, Theophilus. Go back and read the parable, then answer the questions I pose above.

Visitation to the City

Luke 19:28–40 And when he had said this, he went on ahead, going up to Jerusalem. 29 When he drew near to Bethphage and Bethany, at the mount that is called Olivet, he sent two of the disciples, 30 saying, "Go into the village opposite, where on entering you will find a colt tied, on which no one has ever yet sat; untie it and bring it here. 31 If anyone asks you, 'Why are you untying it?' you shall say this, 'The Lord has need of it.'" 32 So those who were sent went away and found it as he had told them. 33 And as they were untying the colt, its owners said to them, "Why are you untying the colt?" 34 And they said, "The Lord has need of it." 35 And they brought it to Jesus, and throwing their garments on the colt they set Jesus upon it. 36 And as he rode along, they spread their garments on the road.

37 As he was now drawing near, at the descent of the Mount of Olives, the whole multitude of the disciples began to rejoice and praise God with a loud voice for all the mighty works that they had seen, 38 saying, "Blessed is the King who comes in the name of the Lord! Peace in heaven and glory in the highest!" 39 And some of the Pharisees in the multitude said to him, "Teacher, rebuke your disciples." 40 He answered, "I tell you, if these were silent, the very stones would cry out."

The conclusion of the pilgrimage has come [cf. 9:51], and the realization hits Jesus that the age-old scripts must now be performed. One of these texts comes from a prophet named Zechariah [Zech 9:9]. He envisions a hero riding into Jerusalem unconventionally—not on war horse after a military victory, but on a lowly donkey. What kind of a performance is that to stir up the people? On the other hand, it is possible that the crowds would know that Israel as a nation of shepherds envisioned kings on donkeys and mules and not war steeds.

Whatever the case, Jesus rides in like Zechariah predicted. The point is not whether Jesus already knows or arranges this event, but it happens just like the visitations that I have described from the beginning, unnoticed by institutional powers, unconventional by worldly standards. Is this what Moses and Elijah spoke with Jesus about in their consultation with him on that remote but glorious mountain? Jesus performs his unique staging of this text by specifying that the animal has never had anyone ride it: he is no ordinary hero carrying out the script, but unique in Israel's history. Not even Zechariah's vision of lowliness captures Jesus's performance of the truth. Simply, "the Lord has need of it" is enough to justify the whole scheme.

The rest of the scene describes a king's arrival and a pilgrim's destination. Whatever goods the people have at hand, they make available to Jesus as acclaimed king—little realizing that much more than one's own garments (my own detail [19:35]) are required to enroll in the Kingdom Jesus is bringing. Whatever is at hand is required, just as the stones of Jerusalem would otherwise testify [19:40]. Jesus allows himself to be mounted on the donkey as king—even in this makeshift way. The crowds are caught up in the unfathomable drama, though all the events fulfill some divine plan, recognized only later. The Pharisees protest its staging [19:39], but they cannot prevent or forestall it.

As they draw near to the temple, suddenly it is clear that this is a pilgrimage festival, and Jesus is both the reason for the pilgrimage and the pilgrim. Adding to the festive refrain that Jesus earlier had quoted [13:35], "Blessed is the one who comes in the name of the LORD," is the identification of this pilgrim as a "king." He is not just Zechariah's hero, but he is the psalmist's king. Even though we have encountered this crucial psalm [Ps 118] earlier in the *Memoirs*, we again see the uniqueness of Jesus's performance.

The final detail of my account goes back to the beginning where the angels announce, "Peace on earth and good will toward men." Now it is the throng who represent the earthly component already prefigured by the vision of the shepherds [2:14]. They unconsciously repeat to the angels what the shepherds had heard, "Peace in heaven and glory in the highest" [19:38]. Heaven to earth, now the earth to the heaven: who could have laid out such parallels of chorus, such choreography of activity, such a perfect performance?

As he makes his way up the road from Jericho, it is not only the people who welcome him. It is Jerusalem at her best that turns out to welcome him, her most fervent aspirations and ideals as found in her buildings, her streets, and her temple. As Habakkuk prophesied, stones can speak, perhaps more honestly than prayers [Hab 2:11, 14]. All must play their role in the ancient scripts that predict this day. While all will not understand his mission, and some oppose him (so we will find out soon enough), all will unconsciously carry out what God has ordained for the purpose of the life of Jesus.

1. Have I ever sensed that I am a part of a bigger whole, one that is way outside of my ability to execute on my own?

2. How would I describe the Kingdom in the Gospel of Luke? How does Luke tie together the idea of the Kingdom expressed in the people's cry here to what was said by angels (2:14) in the beginning of his Gospel? How do the themes of both beginning and end help to bring confidence to the success of the mission of Jesus?

3. Keep a record of all the prophecies that Jesus seems to be aware of fulfilling in his visitation to Jerusalem.

Visitation Results Predicted

> Luke 19:41–44 And when he drew near and saw the city he wept over it, 42 saying, "Would that even today you knew the things that make for peace! But now they are hid from your eyes. 43 For the days shall come upon you, when your enemies will cast up a bank about you and surround you, and hem you in on every side, 44 and dash you to the ground, you and your children within you, and they will not leave one stone upon another in you; because you did not know the time of your visitation."

Finally Jesus reaches the summit of winding road between Jericho and Jerusalem. From here, he can see the city of Jerusalem. Then it dawns on him: he is now on the verge of fulfilling God's plan for his life. Intuition and Scripture tell him that the imminent rejection of his visitation will result in the destruction of the city.

Moreover, it will result in a cataclysm of a magnitude that marked the destruction of Jerusalem by the Babylonians centuries ago: children dashed upon the ground, walls overturned. Probably his mind is riveted on the dirges and grief associated with this catastrophe for his people. He imagines the repercussions of missing the time of "visitation," and he weeps.

Theophilus, let us put ourselves in the place of Jesus here: Can we weep (or rejoice) over what we see in the divine plans for the world around us? Can we see the circling of Jerusalem or the invasion of Babylon in our own context? Do we read Scripture in the same fashion?

Jesus addresses the city directly in its history and its totality. He is in effect speaking to Jerusalem in an intercessory way, in a prayerful way. Do we also speak to our world in this way? Do we let the ancient Scriptures be a guide to our intercession?

FIGURE 7: *Jesus Weeps over Jerusalem* (by Garrett Shireman)

1. When I see someone rejecting sound wisdom or good advice, I can often predict bad outcomes. Have I ever been able to predict a failed marriage, or job demotion, or bad health, or perhaps a jail sentence on such grounds? When the bad outcome hurts those close to me, how do I react?

2. How close am I to God's counsels when I give advice? How do I or can I participate in a visitation of God? How can I be a part of God's grace so that a cataclysm can be avoided?

3. Do we weep at the gloomy prospects of rejecting God's word—or rejoice at the acceptance of God's visitation?

Visitation Performed

> Luke 19:45–48 And he entered the temple and began to drive out those who sold, 46 saying to them, "It is written, 'My house shall be a house of prayer'; but you have made it a den of robbers." 47 And he was teaching daily in the temple. The chief priests and the scribes and the principal men of the people sought to destroy him; 48 but they did not find anything they could do, for all the people hung upon his words.

In case you haven't noticed, Jesus does not cite the ancient Scriptures like some sort of master archivist. He is not just interested in quoting them as clinching arguments. No, his best use of them is when he performs them, bringing them to life and reimagining them. You saw that, right, when he entered the city on the back of a never-saddled donkey—his representation of Zechariah's vision?

Let me give you another good example: suddenly, he decides to visit Jerusalem's temple. The suddenness of his visitation makes me think that Jesus has in mind another text, one spoken by another prophet named Malachi [Mal 3:1–2]. Earlier [13:34–35] when his pilgrimage had barely begun, he spoke to Jerusalem directly with words that might have come out of the mouth of Jeremiah, but these warnings about the temple dumbly floated over our ears. Just now, he wept over the city when he looked down on it from a distance. Again we had vague recollections of the days of Jeremiah, when the city that rejected him as prophet. But these were only words, heartfelt and evocative, yes, but mostly stirring up deep-seated emotions and memories. Mostly, we wondered about what these words could possibly mean, waiting for circumstances to play out some familiar routine of history.

Now Jesus takes action as if to declare that the visitation is at his command. He storms the temple and drives out those whom he [19:46] and Jeremiah earlier [Jer 7:1-15] call "robbers." Just as this largely token act brought rebuke and violence to Jeremiah from the temple and royal authorities, so now for Jesus suffering and retribution lie in wait. For both men, the authorities (chief priests, the scribes, and the leaders of the people [19:47]) are already conspiring to stop such performances of defiance. While in the past the Pharisees served as foil and fodder for Jesus's teachings, now it appears that more deadly forces are arrayed to bring him down.

I find it interesting, Theophilus, that Jesus is in trouble for what he is performing from Jeremiah's script. When Jesus says, "It is written . . . ," you have the sense that Jesus knows the book and gleans from it what he is supposed to do. His own rendition of Jeremiah's story, though, is more than working toward a reformed temple; for Jesus also remembers words that go back to Isaiah about "*a house of prayer for all nations.*" I emphasize these words because they trump what Jeremiah stood for in his temple visitation speech. I added the words "for all nations" to give you a sense about what Jesus undoubtedly understood by citing Isaiah. Although Jesus has so far not explicitly universalized his mission, yet I hope that you have drawn out from my careful record of his acts and speeches ample applications to something much bigger than his hometown, his home region, or his own people. After all, Theophilus (Θεόφιλε, "lover of God"), I wrote you! In your very name is a hint about a much bigger audience than those in front of Jesus.

Jesus's actions speak as loud as his words when he finally arrives at his destination. He carries out his performative role in two ways: a David-like king with cosmic scope (riding on a donkey [19:35], "blessed is the king who comes in the name of the Lord," promising a reign of "peace in heaven . . . and glory in the heights" [19:38]) and a Jeremiah-like prophet with a worldwide message (weeping over the city [19:41], predicting its doom [19:43–44], "the stones [of Jerusalem] will cry out [19:40]," condemnation of the temple). Whatever Jesus represents, it keeps getting bigger and bigger as his mission unfolds.

1. What is the difference between Jesus *speaking* prophecies from the past and *doing* them? What lesson do I get from this distinction between my words and my deeds?

2. Look up some of the passages that Jesus fulfills in the last few passages. What new things can I learn about Jesus's mission by taking a look at these Scriptures?

3. How can I begin to take small steps toward fulfilling the call that God has on my life?

4. How does the prophetic mission of Jesus encourage me to be a prophet? How does the kingly call of Jesus give me confidence?

5. How do these latest passages encourage me to read the Bible in a new way?

Visitation Dialogues

> Luke 20:1–8 One day, as he was teaching the people in the temple and preaching the gospel, the chief priests and the scribes with the elders came up 2 and said to him, "Tell us by what authority you do these things, or who it is that gave you this authority." 3 He answered them, "I also will ask you a question; now tell me, 4 Was the baptism of John from heaven or from men?" 5 And they discussed it with one another, saying, "If we say, 'From heaven,' he will say, 'Why did you not believe him?' 6 But if we say, 'From men,' all the people will stone us; for they are convinced that John was a prophet." 7 So they answered that they did not know whence it was. 8 And Jesus said to them, "Neither will I tell you by what authority I do these things."

Now begins a number of public challenges posed by Jesus's antagonists, many of whom gravitated toward Jerusalem because of the Jewish temple there. These people were riled up by Jesus's teachings, especially as he played them out when he entered the city. The first group to pounce on him were the temple officials, most likely the Sadducee faction (who often served as priests). They have much to lose if Jesus's warnings materialized. His self-declared kingdom authority flies in the face of his rank and upbringing compared to the other highly placed residents of Jerusalem.

I will leave out a verbatim narrative and simply observe that Jesus finds a way to turn their question inside out. If these officials could not sort out who John the Baptist was, how could they understand Jesus? After all, John had attracted vast crowds and stirred up interest at the highest levels of Jewish society. I reported to you that his audiences "were in expectation" [3:15] at his words—just like they "hung on" Jesus's words [19:48]. Too much is at stake for them to take a stand on such a politically sensitive figure—no comment served their purposes for now.

"Get serious," Jesus seems to say. Once you get serious with my message, then I will deal with you as the others who have come to me. I will answer your question directly if you are direct in your coming to me— just as the rich ruler, the tax collector, the blind man, and so on.

The next story illustrates what Jesus thinks their stand-offish attitude really implies about their position toward Jesus and the Kingdom he represents. They will never accept his authority, and the "fallen stone" (see below [20:18]) of Jerusalem and its temple will crush them rather than be a building block his disciples will use.

> Luke 20:9–19 And he began to tell the people this parable: "A man planted a vineyard, and let it out to tenants, and went into another country for a long while. 10 When the time came, he sent a servant to the tenants, that they should give him some of the fruit of the vineyard; but the tenants beat him, and sent him away empty-handed. 11 And he sent another servant; him also they beat and treated shamefully, and sent him away empty-handed. 12 And he sent yet a third; this one they wounded and cast out.

> 13 "Then the owner of the vineyard said, 'What shall I do? I will send my beloved son; it may be they will respect him.' 14 But when the tenants saw him, they said to themselves, 'This is the heir; let us kill him, that the inheritance may be ours.' 15 And they cast him out of the vineyard and killed him.

> "What then will the owner of the vineyard do to them? 16 He will come and destroy those tenants, and give the vineyard to others." When they heard this, they said, "God forbid!" 17 But he looked at them and said, "What then is this that is written: 'The very stone which the builders rejected has become the head of the corner'? 18 Every one who falls on that stone will be broken to pieces; but when it falls on any one it will crush him."

> 19 The scribes and the chief priests tried to lay hands on him at that very hour, but they feared the people; for they perceived that he had told this parable against them.

Jesus conceives something like a play about a vineyard, complete with dramatic parts for the owner and his sharecropper tenants. The parts for both line up completely with the two main antagonists, Jesus and the temple authorities. In this case, God (the owner) is "away," but takes pains to lease the land (Israel) to the sharecroppers (leaders like the ones questioning Jesus now) to take care of it. In the play, God wants to see what the tenants have done with the vineyard.

There are three rounds of visitation—the visiting agents are presumably the prophets. At every turn, they are beaten up; the abuse intensifies into humiliation, then bloodshed, and then expulsion.

The owner thinks aloud, "Maybe I can send someone who carries my own authority. Oh, I know: I will send the person closest to me, my own son. For sure, this will get their attention." The obvious reference here is to the words spoken from heaven at the baptism of Jesus and at the mountain of transfiguration. These words commissioned Jesus to announce the Kingdom, and he has been doing so ever since.

The tenants, on the other hand, see the son, and they tell themselves, "If we kill him, we get his inheritance." I presume they think that when there is no heir, they get the land by Roman law. So this one, the final visitation agent, they lynch after they have abused him.

So Jesus now tells the audience what the moral of the story is: the owner (God) will come again to kill the tenants and lease out the land to others—maybe the Gentiles? The people hear this presentation and immediately object, perhaps imagining that they are the ones killed.

As I said, Jesus is most likely addressing the Jerusalem leaders—or at least they deduce so by the end of the story [20:19]. They are "the builders" looking for the stones to construct a prosperous city or temple, and they are afraid that Jesus will in fact upset their plans. Jesus implies that he is the building stone for Jerusalem, rejected by the city builders. Thus, they will either be crushed by the rubble of a destroyed Jerusalem or they will be crushed by the rebuilding of Jerusalem, rejected by history for their stance. To my mind, this makeshift play recalls the rocks and stones that cry out when they recognize Jesus entering the city, and they imply that the new Jerusalem will be built around them and not around the current "stone" structure.

By the way, Theophilus, I suspect that Jesus likes wordplays, too, for I am told the Aramaic words he uses in his speech for "son," "stone," and "builder" all sound alike. Jesus also knows well the psalm quoted [118] since he cites it so often [13:35, 19:38]. The master at giving speeches, he shows himself here a word-crafting artist—keeping us entertained and on our toes.

1. What does Jesus imply about ownership or design of the divine plan in the two images or parables represented above?

2. The passage to which Jesus may refer about the vineyard may be Isa 5:1–7. How does Jesus slightly adjust his parable to apply to the tenants of the vineyard and not to the vineyard itself? If Jesus is the one "singing" in this parable, who is the "beloved" he sings to and what is the implication of his song in the parable?

3. The passage that Jesus quotes is Ps 118:22, the story of a man on his way into a city to visit (or possibly build) the temple. [See 13:35, 19:38 for comments.] How has Jesus in some sense reconfigured what the temple of Jerusalem means? In other words, how has he become a new cornerstone or cornerstone for fellowship with God? What would this imply for the personnel of the temple?

4. What do cornerstones do for buildings? What is the function of capstones for arches or domes? If I consider my life direction as a building or a structure, what kind of cornerstones mark out the placement of my life? What capstones are responsible for the shape or beauty of things? What happens when I try to rearrange such building materials? How has God set up these kinds of stones in my life where I can say that my life changed or shifted to a new perspective?

5. Have I ever struggled with the placement of cornerstones or boundaries that mark my life's course? What about struggles with the design or shape of my life as God has built it with a capstone? Can I understand why the audience would have reacted to the pronouncement of Jesus in this passage?

Reacting Game Excursus: Ideas for Developing a Game (Luke 20:9–19)

This exercise is an opportunity for creativity and game design. Below are the conditions for two leads on "reacting" Bible studies.

1. One team constructs the story from the sharecroppers' point of view, based on how much work the tenants put into the project. (No wonder the people react with horror to the story, saying, "God forbid!") In fairness to the tenants, they have simply concluded that the land should be theirs, because they put all their "sweat equity" into the vineyard—and no one claimed it while they worked it. The other team plays the part of Luke and Theophilus, who listen to the sharecroppers and then discuss among themselves a good response based on the Gospel of Luke. Discussion could revolve around the questions below:

   a. How do both sides construct arguments for ownership of the land?

b. Which side is more just? Based on the Gospel of Luke, which side is more justified? Which side do I feel more drawn to? Why?

2. 20:17–18 has the makings of yet another parable by Jesus. Take Jesus's ideas one step farther by creating your own play based on the elements Jesus refers to, such as building, materials, how to build, and builders (the contractors), and so on. Which groups and activities in Jerusalem would these elements represent for Jesus?

   a. Who is the target of both Jesus's play and yours?

   b. Why should they bear the punishment Jesus implies for them?

Concluding Game Questions

1. Who loses when the tenants and the building contractors somehow squeeze out the ones they are supposed to be benefiting?

2. Why are they not paying attention to the priorities that were originally given to them by the owners?

3. What is the moral of the overall story, from Jesus's perspective? Is it fair to say that the owner is someone other than the sharecroppers and building contractors? How are these hirelings not paying attention to the owner?

Dialogue about Caesar

Luke 20:20–26 So they watched him, and sent spies, who pretended to be sincere, that they might take hold of what he said, so as to deliver him up to the authority and jurisdiction of the governor. 21 They asked him, "Teacher, we know that you speak and teach rightly, and show no partiality, but truly teach the way of God. 22 Is it lawful for us to give tribute to Caesar, or not?" 23 But he perceived their craftiness, and said to them, 24 "Show me a coin. Whose likeness and inscription has it?" They said, "Caesar's." 25 He said to them, "Then render to Caesar the things that are Caesar's, and to God the things that are God's." 26 And they were not able in the presence of the people to catch him by what he said; but marveling at his answer they were silent.

What high drama even in the midst of what look like innocent dialogues! I use a playful vocabulary in the passage so that you immediately sniff out that a spoof is at hand. So I say that his antagonists "pretended to be sincere," literally, "they put on the masks" of sincerity. They are staging a mock play, and Jesus recognizes their "craftiness" (πανουργίαν, *pan-ourgian*), another word that hints at their gambit. This is a deadly game they want to engage in, so Jesus himself is alert to the danger of the place and the moment.

What happens here is that Jesus turns the table on his antagonists by using their words against them. They put a question to him—a good question in fact, an age-old question about how much allegiance the Chosen People (the Jews) should give to their non-Chosen People (non-Jewish) overlords. What is our obligation to society and government? To bait the trap, they gush out with obsequious praise for Jesus: "We know that you speak and teach rightly, and show no partiality, but truly teach the way of God." Note that word "partiality," a word which literally means "face." Jesus, they assert, does not pay attention to a pretty face, but only does what is right. Ironically, nor is he influenced by pretend faces or masks!

But Jesus does not dance to their tune. He turns the tables on their question by seizing on that notion of "face." Responding, he uses a synonym for "face" in his answer: "Show me a coin. Whose likeness and inscription has it?" Herein the trap springs back on the hunter: he asks them to produce the coin, for he does not have it. And really you need to recognize that the word I use is not "coin," but "denarius"—a particular coin you know well, Theophilus. Whose *face* (therein lies the pun) or image is on the coin? Well, the inscription tells you *Augustus filius divi*, "Augustus, son of God."

So Jesus does not have the denarius, yet the questioners do. Very interesting. . . . Jesus does not respect pretty faces, but apparently they do! Their possession of the coin proves that at least some of their allegiance reflects an obligation to Augustus Caesar. How do they explain this? Thus, with one verbal *touché*, the antagonists are vanquished. They swallow their words and are silent. What more can be said?

In this performance, Jesus has escaped. The antagonists are exposed as interlopers and spies in God's realm, and they must regroup and plot another way. Now, what is the lesson for us? Note the word I use for "spies" (ἐγκαθέτους, *egkathetous*): literally, those who are embedded/encamped with the residents. Thus, these spies are asking the very same and seemingly innocent questions their fellow Jews are asking. How often do we run into people who love to play games with the demands of disciple-ship? How often do I play games with decisions that I take—finding ways of justifying what I want—rather than going directly to Jesus for what I must do for being a good disciple? What "embedded" questions are in all of our minds, Theophilus? What internal spies are even now getting our priorities misdirected?

Jesus's answer is deceptively (should I say playfully?) simple: if you identify with Caesar, then you should follow through; but if you identify with the Kingdom of God, then you must follow through with the de-mands of the Kingdom. We are too far along the path toward Jerusalem for you not to notice, Theophilus, that being a disciple of Jesus is what the Kingdom is all about. Thus, the answer to the age-old question of conflicting allegiances must begin with following Jesus.

1. Whose image do I admire and raise up? How does this image take away from my fundamental allegiance to God?

2. Whose inscription—or whose ideas—do I buy into? How do these ideas take away from my allegiance to God?

3. How can I conform more to God's image in my life? To whom would I compare myself if I had to find a role model in my life?

4. How can I be more in conformity with the truly divine inscription? Where would I find such an inscription that gives me identity?

Dialogue about Marriage and the Afterlife

Luke 20:27–40 There came to him some Sadducees, those who say that there is no resurrection, 28 and they asked him a ques-tion, saying, "Teacher, Moses wrote for us that if a man's brother dies, having a wife but no children, the man must take the wife and raise up children for his brother. 29 Now there were seven brothers; the first took a wife, and died without children; 30 and the second 31 and the third took her, and likewise all seven left no children and died. 32 Afterward the woman also died. 33 In the resurrection, therefore, whose wife will the woman be? For the seven had her as wife." 34 And Jesus said to them, "The sons of this age marry and are given in marriage; 35 but those who are accounted worthy to attain to that age and to the resurrec-tion from the dead neither marry nor are given in marriage, 36 for they cannot die anymore, because they are equal to angels and are sons of God, being sons of the resurrection. 37 But that the dead are raised, even Moses showed, in the passage about the bush, where he calls the Lord the God of Abraham and the God of Isaac and the God of Jacob. 38 Now he is not God of the dead, but of the living; for all live to him." 39 And some of the scribes answered, "Teacher, you have spoken well." 40 For they no longer dared to ask him any question.

Another dialogue challenge, just like the earlier ones about Jesus's authority and the paying of taxes. This time it is the Sadducees, probably allied with the group that was ready to pounce earlier. It is good to remember, Theophilus, that the Sadducees do not have a canon of inspired texts beyond the first five books of Moses and base their denial of the afterlife on the silence of those texts about the resurrection of the dead. Thus, you understand why Jesus would carefully choose a passage that they have studied and know in detail.

He clearly says that marriage is of "this age" [20:34], when a person must be concerned about continuation of life and name and place. However, these present realities have no relevance for the age to come—and all along Jesus has been inviting discipleship without attachments to precisely these other and different elements. A whole new order is coming, where divine relationship takes the place of human connections. His disciples are preparing for that even now as they follow in his steps.

Interestingly, his antagonists try to give Jesus a dose of his own medicine by weaving their own captivating story, though one I'm sure you heard before if you ever read the book of Tobit [Tob. 6:14–15]. Here is how it goes: Seven men lay claim to the same woman, but they all die before they can cement the relationship. So if there is another "age" after this one, who would be married to this woman?

Jesus does not employ his usual strategy of story-telling, but he relies on an analogy that even the Sadducees would accept, at least in theory: angels. For they are in the first five books of Moses. They are defined by their access to and placement before God. For angels, property and family mean nothing.

Notice how Jesus calls his disciples for the only time I know of in my sources and the records, "sons of God" [20:36]. Why does he use this term? I would say there are two reasons: first, according to our way of thinking, "sons" refers to those who are adherents to a discipline. Go back and notice this use of the term in other Jewish writings, like Proverbs—or even in the first five books of Moses where Jews are collectively called "sons of Israel." What we mean is that "sons" follow a father or way of life. Thus, Jesus implies that he represents a discipleship based on those who are students of God, not this age and its priorities. To enter heaven, one starts now with a life of detachment, a lifestyle that avoids dependence on things that this age values (marriage, property, wealth). His use of this term casts down the gauntlet to the audience: Whose disciple are you, God's or this world's?

Then he also suggests that this notion places human destiny in a higher realm than angels, who never have to taste death. Angels are not like God, humans are. Why? Because God has allowed his being to be touched—compromised?—by death, death of the first Adam, and the up-coming death of Jesus (whom I implied earlier is Second Adam). Angels have yet to experience this reality firsthand.

Finally, Jesus stretches back into those five books of Moses, called the Torah, and finds the burning bush passage [Exod 3:1–6] sufficient to illustrate the afterlife. Thus, the reference to the God of Abraham, Isaac, and Jacob shows that he is alive to them just as he was speaking to Mo-ses. He can hold a relationship with them in the present, though none of them is present in the conversation with Moses. If he can do it with those who have passed away, then he can do it with anyone: "all live to him." No one is lost, no matter how they met their end. By our reckoning they are dead and gone, never to return to this life; but God evaluates them by his ability to keep them in play, to keep them in an eternal and angelic world of some sort.

The amazing thing is that God holds every event, every person, ev-ery creature in his consciousness, much like the burning bush. He never loses any memory or any reality—it is like a fire that burns constantly yet never consumes. It throws off heat and light, yet it never uses up its source.

In contrast, the Sadducees think that people who die are gone, never to return. They are used up as fuel for a fire of survival. Survival for them is like looking at the stubble left behind by a mountain blaze: nothing survives except for the seeds buried deep below the charred remains, like some kind of organic tribute to posterity after all has died. Theophilus, you might compare their understanding of "afterlife" to a philosophy called Epicureanism. Not that it is intrinsically evil or pleasure-seeking at all: It simply seems like an entirely wasteful project of nature to save a species by such rampant destruction. Nothing is intrinsically dignified or peculiarly beautiful or individually valuable. Exactly the opposite: it is studied only if it passes on survivability to its progeny.

For Jesus the focus is exactly *not* on the future, but on the present. Progeny is not important, for our survival is already guaranteed. No offspring are needed and are quite irrelevant. While the Sadducees may promote a natural reality "on the ground" of the material world, this forward-looking process is not a part of what Jesus represents. Rather he is searching backward to find Abraham, Isaac, and Jacob. God reaches toward us in the fiery reality of Jesus: he seizes us and tells us that we are not wasted material, that we are not too unfit to survive, that all of vitality (as it were) stops with us.

So the Sadducees believe that Abraham, Isaac, and Jacob are dead forever, and they only live on in their descendants. This makes God connected with dead and not with the living, a problem even more difficult than the one about marriage. One might expand this thought to the Romans (and other ancients) who considered that the living continue only when they build monuments or cities or win battles. Either approach falls short of God's eternality. God holds everything near to his consciousness, and thus everything is supercharged with significance. Everyone is as important as Abraham, Isaac, and Jacob. Everything is held in place but not consumed in the burning bush that so attracts Moses.

In addition, Jesus seems to be arguing for the unity of doctrine throughout the whole of Jewish Scriptures, and so he has no problem in finding meaning beyond the scope of the writer's imagination in Exodus about the burning bush. He takes liberty in reinterpreting the bare basics of earlier passages in terms of new realities. This should be instructive about how we interpret those same inspired writings as well.

1. How does this passage pass on dignity to my spiritual life? How does it help me to consider that I am on par with Abraham, Isaac, and Jacob? How does this comparison help me to imagine what Jesus means by "sons of God" and "equal to angels?"

2. What access do I have to God in light of what Jesus says about my destiny? How should this destiny influence the way I think about daily life?

3. Think about the life of the resurrection. What kinds of things come to your mind when you think about being a "son [or daughter] of God, son [or daughter] of the resurrection"?

4. What does this passage indicate about my identity and heritage shared with Abraham, Isaac, Jacob, and Moses?

5. How does this interpretation that Jesus gives help me to interpret passages in the Bible? How does it help me, like Jesus, to correct misinterpretations of the Bible?

6. Darwinism teaches that individuals die and pass on genes as an organic memory to its progeny. The value is not in a particular individual but in the survival of the species. How would this passage address the topic of Darwinism and survival of the species?

Dialogue Follow-up

The next thing to happen in these dialogues is that Jesus turns on all his challengers, and here is how I reconstruct now what he was trying to say [20:41–44]:

"Now that you have run out of questions, I have a question for you. Why are the people calling me "son of David"? How did David refer to the Messiah? He referred to this figure as "my Lord." And he sits at the right hand of the Most High. So he cannot be lower or lesser than David.

"There is something fitting in their title, I don't deny, but it is only a smidgeon of who I am. This title smacks of politics and manipulation and control. Control is given to me by the enthronement that the Father has promised me, an enthronement that far outstrips David's. I have been invited into it by divine call, whereas David comes through the invitation of a human anointing. We both sit and wait until our enemies fall under our feet, that is true. So I bear with the ignominy that you subject upon me now, sitting and waiting for the fulfillment of this prophecy."

Then he draws out the implication of this counter-challenge for his disciples [20:45–47]. Soon his antagonists—like the scribes—will be theirs. If he sits and waits for the footstool to be put in place, so must they. Meanwhile their enemies seemingly have all the resources and prestige. They can easily demand public respect, and everyone wants to be their client or friend. Their clothes are dandy, their contacts are many, and they love to be seen and noticed. They have the best seats in the assemblies and festive gatherings. They even appear to be religious with long and impressive prayers.

When he searches for a way to measure the kinds of contributions these scribes give in terms of personal investment and self-sacrifice, he sees a poor widow give two coins in the temple collection [21:1–4]. He uses her as the ideal of self-giving for his disciples instead of the temple authorities. If there were a balance to weight what everybody gave that day as their contribution, her two coins pulled down the scale, while theirs barely budged it. Hers came out of her life, while theirs came out of their position.

1. What things do I commit my resources to? Which things involve mere "paying my dues," and which things require sacrifice? How does it show my priorities?

2. What social events or organizations am I part of where I feel outclassed or inferior to others? Why do I still keep attending or membership? What might be a constructive way of dealing with my feelings?

3. Make a list that shows how I am committed to what Jesus stands for as I read in the Gospel of Luke.

4. What is Jesus's title in this passage? What does it imply about his authority? What does it imply about his patience and forbearance?

5. What does Jesus's position imply about the disciples' position and attitude about patience and forbearance?

6. What does it imply about those around us who undermine our confidence with accusations and threats?

Dialogue Conclusion: Jesus's Parting Prediction

Luke 21:5–18 And as some spoke of the temple, how it was adorned with noble stones and offerings, he said, 6 "As for these things which you see, the days will come when there shall not be left here one stone upon another that will not be thrown down." 7 And they asked him, "Teacher, when will this be, and what will be the sign when this is about to take place?"

8 And he said, "Take heed that you are not led astray; for many will come in my name, saying, 'I am he!' and, 'The time is at hand!' Do not go after them. 9 And when you hear of wars and tumults, do not be terrified; for this must first take place, but the end will not be at once."

¹⁰ Then he said to them, "Nation will rise against nation, and kingdom against kingdom; ¹¹ there will be great earthquakes, and in various places famines and pestilences; and there will be terrors and great signs from heaven.

¹² "But before all this they will lay their hands on you and perse-cute you, delivering you up to the synagogues and prisons, and you will be brought before kings and governors for my name's sake. ¹³ This will be a time for you to bear testimony. ¹⁴ Settle it therefore in your minds, not to meditate beforehand how to answer; ¹⁵ for I will give you a mouth and wisdom, which none of your adversaries will be able to withstand or contradict. ¹⁶ You will be delivered up even by parents and brothers and kins-men and friends, and some of you they will put to death; ¹⁷ you will be hated by all for my name's sake. ¹⁸ But not a hair of your head will perish. ¹⁹ By your endurance you will gain your lives."

[21:5–6:] Against the backdrop of the temple, I present the final words of Jesus as one long swan song. The people may have thought his visitation to Jerusalem was all about the restoration of the temple. He tells them that he *did not* come for the beauty of the stones or the stateliness of its architecture. He even predicts its demise, no matter how impressive its structure or its history.

Curious, respond his disciples. We thought we came here for con-firming the temple's place in Israel. So, if this is not the culminating visi-tation, when will your prediction unfold?

Jesus answers with a broader sweep of history that includes not only the current generation but a vision of what will end the whole age and bring about a new one. In this respect, many in his audience recognize that his predictions are not targeting exact details or specific events. Rather they are symbolic and provocative, echoing what other visionar-ies ("apocalyptics") have presented in the holy writings. The whole point is not to give mastery to those who know the future, but to equip the knowers with hope that will get them through the challenges leading to the fulfillment of the vision.

[21:8–19:] Thus at the beginning Jesus says that the endtimes will in-volve a lot of prognosticators and prophets of gloom and doom. It will in-volve false messiahs along the way, and no end of wars and insurrections. One must expect that history will always stir up the human tendency for antagonism and strife. Plus there will always be events and wonders that baffle human explanations and understanding—earthquakes and natural disasters. Yet these facts are merely the sticks and stones of history, when the final visitation will reveal the gold and silver of the Kingdom. Expect these times, but they do not yet signal the countdown period. The Kingdom is not yet visible to everyone.

Let me now paraphrase the "Teacher": "Closer to the crucial moments is a time of persecution, when your faith will end you up before courts and serving jail time. People will start seeing you as 'one of those people' because of your 'testimony.' Don't worry about their charges and their hostility, because I will tell you what you are to do in such situations. 'I will give you a mouth and wisdom' [21:15] that foils their plots, meaning that courage will not fail you to do the right thing; and a higher plane of thought will inspire you (and maybe your persecutors).

"You may even be killed for this testimony. Your opponents may think they are ridding the earth of a problem, but really they have not gotten rid of you, 'for not one hair of your head' [21:18] will be lost. In fact, the opposite: you purchase your souls by facing up to their hostility. Martyrdom is an ultimatum that is complex, so not all of you will be so summoned. But all will see the martyrs as a public testimony."

1. Consider ebbs and flows of human history. How would the words of Jesus fit such a broad outline?

2. What kind of hope does Jesus give in this passage? Does it give me hope?

3. So far, do the words of Jesus offer comfort or dread for what is ahead?

> Luke 21:20–28 20 "But when you see Jerusalem surrounded by armies, then know that its desolation has come near. 21 Then let those who are in Judea flee to the mountains, and let those who are inside the city depart, and let not those who are out in the country enter it; 22 for these are days of vengeance, to fulfil all that is written.
>
> 23 "Alas for those who are with child and for those who give suck in those days! For great distress shall be upon the earth and wrath upon this people; 24 they will fall by the edge of the sword, and be led captive among all nations; and Jerusalem will be trodden down by the Gentiles, until the times of the Gentiles are fulfilled.

25 "And there will be signs in sun and moon and stars, and upon the earth distress of nations in perplexity at the roaring of the sea and the waves, 26 men fainting with fear and with foreboding of what is coming on the world; for the powers of the heavens will be shaken. 27 And then they will see the Son of man coming in a cloud with power and great glory.

28 "Now when these things begin to take place, look up and raise your heads, because your redemption is drawing near."

Jesus continues: "As for Jerusalem, as for your curiosity about my pilgrimage to the city and the temple, here is the answer. Jerusalem will be surrounded and taken, and horrible carnage will result. Don't get caught there when it happens, for the vulnerable will be the first to experience its disastrous consequences. This is what you may know as the 'time of the Gentiles.'[2]

[21:25–28:] "Now comes the more immediate cosmic events that will astound the world and show that this time really I am near. And I will come on the clouds, just as was predicted in Daniel [Daniel 7]. And in the way I will leave ('on a cloud'), so I will return [21:27]. Now is the time to realize that you have conquered and you are now ready to receive your reward. 'Straighten up and raise your heads' [21:28], for you will see it with your own eyes!"

I think I will hold my questions for now, Theophilus, until we see a bigger picture.

Luke 21:29–38 29 And he told them a parable: "Look at the fig tree, and all the trees; 30 as soon as they come out in leaf, you see for yourselves and know that the summer is already near. 31 So also, when you see these things taking place, you know that the Kingdom of God is near. 32 Truly, I say to you, this generation will not pass away till all has taken place. 33 Heaven and earth will pass away, but my words will not pass away.

34 "But take heed to yourselves lest your hearts be weighed down with dissipation and drunkenness and cares of this life, and that day come upon you suddenly like a snare; 35 for it will come upon all who dwell upon the face of the whole earth. 36

---

2. You may have read what others have written about this season, especially from prophets like Zechariah [12:3] or Daniel [8:13]. You may have even read some of Paul's references to the reign of the Gentiles [Rom 11:7–32; also see Rev 11:2], though I do not make mention of his ideas on it in my second volume [Acts of the Apostles].

> But watch at all times, praying that you may have strength to escape all these things that will take place, and to stand before the Son of man." 37 And every day he was teaching in the temple, but at night he went out and lodged on the mount called Olivet. 38 And early in the morning all the people came to him in the temple to hear him.

So as the temple teaching comes to a close, Jesus has answered the question about what to expect now that he has completed his pilgrimage to Jerusalem. Clearly the coming Kingdom will not come immediately: the perspective his disciples must take begins with the broad context of the ages, then the ages, then the seasons, then the generation, then the very day. With the fig tree he is speaking about a particular time in the season when the fruit appears. We are to be like those who look at the tree and evaluate when the harvest will occur.

[21:34–35:] What if we don't figure out what nature is telling us? Without a vision, the people perish—perhaps not at once but slowly and dangerously.

So what is the vision Jesus lays out? First, "dissipation" refers to our past bad decisions that come back to haunt us. Guilt and painful consequences now tie our hands and our hearts so that it is very hard to respond to the day. Second, "drunkenness" refers to our penchant for escape from our boredom and drudgery. Our tendency is to drown our sorrows by cheap thrills and entertainment. Third, the "cares of this life" is literally in the Greek "dividedness." It is how the priorities of life divide our hearts and attention—that is the sense that we are fearful of what the future holds and spend our time worrying and self-centered. We miss what God is unfolding for the whole universe. I would classify this as past, present, and future distractions that slowly kill our ability to "stand" before the Son of Man.

[21:36:] "Watch at all times" refers to staying focused and alert rather than napping and escaping. One must nourish a spiritual life if one is "to stand" instead of cowering and cringing before the Son of Man. How does one do this, but by depending on those around us to rouse us from drowsiness? How can we stay focused but by continually referring back to these words of Jesus?

[21:37]: What of Jesus as he faces his own day of reckoning? He is focusing on his daily life teaching at the temple and spending his nights camping out on the Mount of Olives—always prepared to fulfill his call to preach in the temple. His life is on stand-by, as he is totally consumed with one last appeal to the public, a run of temple performances that goes back to his first appearance in the city.

[21:38]: I have presented to you, Theophilus, these dialogues as one long master performance in front of the city's residents and visitors. Even though Jesus's foes have tried to trip up his presentation repeatedly, he has in fact dazzled the public temporarily as his safeguard against official action. They have flocked to him for a few days of peace as storm clouds gather. At the beginning of the dialogue, "all the people hung upon his words" to prevent his arrest [19:48]. Now at the end, "all the people came to him in the temple to hear him," starting "early in the morning" [21:38]. Together these statements show that his listeners reorganize their schedules and reprioritize their thoughts at his words. It reminds me again of Jesus in the Nazareth synagogue—how often I come back to this opening of his public mission!—when all eyes were upon Jesus as if transfixed into another world.

Jesus will soon finish this performance, just as he did at Nazareth, and the public will have to make a decision about him. Note the words I use to describe the public preoccupation with Jesus: You can only "hang on" to a ledge for so long! You can only come to the temple "early" so often before you have to go back to daily routines. There are three options among the groups who made themselves known in the dialogue.

One group is the one that he targets here: they do not pay attention to the fig tree and cannot figure out what is going on. So they spend their lives in dissipation, drunkenness, and life's anxieties. Throughout his swan song, Jesus has attempted to rouse them out of lethargy to make them consider joining his troupe of disciples.

The second group are his followers in the present audience: Jesus tells them to fix their minds on his words, more dependable than the heaven and the earth itself [21:33]. Theophilus, if we are to "obtain our souls" [21:19] and "escape" and "stand before the Son of man" [21:36], we will have to be in this second group—this goes without saying.

Finally, there is yet a third group in the dialogue [19:47–48; 20:1; 19, 20–26; 46–47], and Jesus has encountered them throughout this prolonged public finale: the temple authorities, the scribes, the Sadducees. These are the ones who lurk around and occasionally show how they oppose him. Their impact will soon to be told in the next phase of my narrative, the demise of Jesus.

1. Do I sense a quickening of events of the sort Jesus describes? What things would I look for? How would I describe for someone the events that would persuade me and them about the second coming of Jesus?

2. What kinds of things past, present, and future are distracting me from noticing the fig tree or hearing the word of God? How am I divided in heart?

3. How can I stay awake with all of these tempting and distracting things going on around me? What practical things must I do to help me stay focused on the coming of the Son of Man?

CHAPTER SEVEN

The Final Act

Part One: Spotlight Theater on Three Characters

WHAT I WILL DO first of all in this chapter of my *Memoirs of How It All Began* is have you focus on the three main actors—Judas, Jesus, and Peter. That is *Part One*. I intend for you to study them carefully, even though events surrounding them still fit into my overall literary plan for the book.

After that I will slightly redesign the details I recorded so that you can imagine the finale in two spiritually different ways. Of course I want you to see the finale with the eyes of faith, but not with eyes that do not see the realities of life's struggles. Anyway, Theophilus, I subtitle this latter section, *Part Two: Farce or Tragedy?*

Spotlight: Judas

Luke 22:1–6 Now the feast of Unleavened Bread drew near, which is called the Passover. 2 And the chief priests and the scribes were seeking how to put him to death; for they feared the people. 3 Then Satan entered into Judas called Iscariot, who was of the number of the twelve; 4 he went away and conferred with the chief priests and officers how he might betray him to them. 5 And they were glad, and engaged to give him money. 6 So he agreed, and sought an opportunity to betray him to them in the absence of the multitude.

The story suddenly turns dark as we enter the final act in the life of Jesus. The visitation mission accomplished, now comes the *kairos* moment when Satan senses his chances. The last time we encountered Satan was in the wilderness at the conclusion of the three temptations before the mission of Jesus, and well before the moment of his transfiguration that sent him to Jerusalem. There I wrote that when "the devil had ended every temptation," he "departed from him until an opportune time (*kairos*)" [4:13].

The *kairos* moment here is when there is a convergence of supernatural plotting and natural self-interest. At no other time was such a moment possible, for though Jesus was surrounded by hostile forces—whether early on, the Pharisees and their allies, or later on, the temple authorities and their Sadducean clients—he marched on safely in the vanguard of popular support. With all eyes fixed on him, Jesus could preach to his heart's content from the start of his mission in Galilee to the end of his dialogues in Jerusalem.

Now Satan personally probes the perimeter of the vanguard and finds there an outlier who is vulnerable. Before, Jesus was tempted by an opponent who had the generic title of the "slanderer" or devil [4:2–13]. In his first confrontation, the devil hit upon a soft spot: Jesus's identity as son. On that occasion all three attacks aimed at undermining who Jesus was, and ultimately they were poised to raise the devil's status above God's. The lesson learned in the desert was that slander could not undo the dedication and determination of Jesus.

So the devil goes to work again, this time identified by his personal name Satan or "Adversary." The devil has been named only two other times in my account, once when Jesus saw Satan fall like lightning from heaven [10:18] and the other time when Jesus says that the representative of the people, a "daughter of Abraham," was bound up by Satan for eighteen years [13:16].

Perhaps it is the case that Satan, now displaced from his abode in heaven and dismissed from the "daughter of Abraham" on earth, realizes that his time to fight is now or never. If his slanderous attack as "devil" against Jesus did not work, perhaps this strategic move as "Adversary" against a key supporter of Jesus would work. He finds his moment and means in Judas, one of the Twelve chosen and groomed by Jesus. Perhaps we are to notice the clue to this disciple's downfall: the plotters "engaged to give him money." Was that Judas's weak spot? Did Satan capitalize on what he knew about Judas's strength as treasurer? I have heard it said that tests come in the area of our strengths.

Let us focus on the background strategy of Satan. His methods involve attacks on solitary individuals. Jesus was alone in the first attack in the wilderness, and now Judas is conspicuously isolated from the vanguard of Jesus's support. The culmination of Satan's attack will be Jesus all alone in the upcoming passion story.

Thus, let us ask ourselves how vulnerable we are in our moments of solitude. We cannot avoid such moments, and in fact they are necessary for assessments of our hearts and lives. Are we ready for such ultimate tests that will come in such vulnerable moments? For if there is danger at such times, we also see in the life of Jesus unimaginable grace and glory to hold our ground. Nonetheless, we should probably echo Jesus's prayer that we be preserved from conclusive "temptation" [11:4].

Satan looks for the right moment to find vulnerability. He did not attack Jesus earlier—and the reader must not misinterpret confrontations and hostilities I have described so far as overtly satanic. What seems to be dangerous moments earlier—the healings, the preaching, the visions and spiritual encounters—are child's play compared to what the passion of Jesus involves. Satan had not personally entered into the thick of things, even if everything looked hostile to the Kingdom that Jesus announced. Let us similarly not think that what everyone predicts about the defeat of the Kingdom of God is true.

Since you have heard so much about Elijah in the life of Jesus, let me tell you one more story about him. Elijah went through terrible anguish, believing that he was the last godly Israelite left [1 Kgs 19:11]. It turned out to be a greatly exaggerated and pessimistic diagnosis of reality, but it nearly succeeded in defeating Elijah. All the while throughout my story, Satan has been biding his time as if seeking the Elijah syndrome to spring upon Jesus. So far Jesus has not been truly forsaken, though circumstances have been tense; nor was Judas Iscariot—until now. Now is Judas's time of solitary challenge.

So there are three words that sum up this first scene in the final act of Jesus: Satan, *kairos*, and strategy. The bottom-line questions are: How aware am I of the spiritual Adversary? How prepared am I to face the Adversary in my times of solitude? How distracted am I by the public commotion that I fail to notice when the *kairos* of Satan arrives? I leave you with these thoughts.

Spinning Things Differently

Luke 22:7–13 7 Then came the day of Unleavened Bread, on which the passover lamb had to be sacrificed. 8 So Jesus sent Peter and John, saying, "Go and prepare the passover for us, that we may eat it." 9 They said to him, "Where will you have us prepare it?" 10 He said to them, "Behold, when you have entered the city, a man carrying a jar of water will meet you; follow him into the house which he enters, 11 and tell the householder, 'The Teacher says to you, Where is the guest room, where I am to eat the passover with my disciples?' 12 And he will show you a large upper room furnished; there make ready." 13 And they went, and found it as he had told them; and they prepared the passover.

If Satan intervenes to unleash his plot, so Jesus devises his own counterplan that measures up to his Adversary. And it is a surprising one that I will devote the rest of this chapter to explain.

He dispatches his closest confidants Peter and John—the two men who so often form a working team later after Jesus has already made his "exodus"—to make the preliminary arrangements for his plan. The *kairos* for Jesus somehow revolves around the Jewish feast of Passover and the whole seven-day period called Unleavened Bread, though he alone perceives its potential for turning the tables on the Adversary.

His strategy involves a corporate approach as opposed to Satan's targeting individuals. Rather than bracing himself or withdrawing mentally and physically, Jesus brings together his closest disciples, the Twelve. Jews know that this time of Passover is all about the community and solidarity, but Jesus—as usual—will take things much farther. His *kairos* is on the cusp of a new era, the history I narrate in my sequel *Memoirs of an Unfinished Tale*.

Passover also involves a dramatic staging of something Jews have done for centuries. Jesus performs Jewish seasonal routines faithfully and deliberately as his response to impending evil. Passover observance involves both sober joy and sweet sorrow in its reenactment. While the adversary works cloak-and-dagger and treacherously, Jesus plans out a banquet with its holiday practices bearing larger-than-life meaning. He is by my estimation still actor, reading an ancient script that only he can perform.

1. What would I do if the doctors said that I have a terminal condition that surely will take me in five days? How would I make my peace with this bad news? How does this grim picture mirror what Jesus is facing?

2. What is my attitude toward upcoming events that I cannot avoid?

The "Hour" to Celebrate?

> Luke 22:14–23 14 And when the hour came, he sat at table, and the apostles with him. 15 And he said to them, "I have earnestly desired to eat this passover with you before I suffer; 16 for I tell you I shall not eat it until it is fulfilled in the Kingdom of God." 17 And he took a cup, and when he had given thanks he said, "Take this, and divide it among yourselves; 18 for I tell you that from now on I shall not drink of the fruit of the vine until the Kingdom of God comes." 19 And he took bread, and when he had given thanks he broke it and gave it to them, saying, "This is my body which is given for you. Do this in remembrance of me." 20 And likewise the cup after supper, saying, "This cup which is poured out for you is the new covenant in my blood. 21 But behold the hand of him who betrays me is with me on the table. 22 For the Son of man goes as it has been determined; but woe to that man by whom he is betrayed!" 23 And they began to question one another, which of them it was that would do this.

Now we see the *kairos* for the strategy that Jesus employs, which I call "the hour." Its context is the feast of Unleavened Bread and Passover. He makes a surprising announcement though: contrary to public expectation, the object of his pilgrimage was not the Jerusalem temple per se. Rather, he set his heart on celebrating Passover with his disciples! Something important will take place in this observance, something involving how his disciples will keep together and how they will advance the Kingdom when Jesus is gone. Unless he eats the Passover meal with them, his visitation is not really concluded.

But where are the rubrics of the Jewish feast? Where the blood to sprinkle on the door lintels? Why does Jesus seemingly abstain from the meal? All these are questions that I invite you to speculate about. Is he the lamb? In fact, Jesus seems to put it both ways: earlier he said, "Go and prepare the Passover . . . that we may eat it,"—and then turns around and says, "I shall not eat it until it is fulfilled in the Kingdom of God." Thus, it

sounds like he will eat it in the future with his disciples, and he is eating
with them now in some broader sense. What is this corporate meal but a
foreshadowing of what we now call Eucharist?[1] What is this future meal
but the messianic banquet so often prefigured in these *Memoirs*, when
there will be no more need for the Passover sacrifice?

This meal is at the intersection of present and future, and Jesus is the
point of intersection. He is the host in both contexts, for he has set up this
meal and pledges a future one. He is careful not to violate the protocols
of the first meal, so his attentiveness to ritual is important to notice. The
ceremony allows him to stress two things: First, together they are sharing
the blessings of the meal as if they are one family. So now this little band
is tied together from a human point of view in love and mutual care and
from a divine point of view as a people given identity and grace.

Second, he directs the entire focus of the meal toward "remembrance"
(ἀνάμνησις, *anamnēsis*, "re-presentation" [22:19]), as if it performs an
installment of the Passover event. It is not the fullness, but neither is it
simply formality. After all, what is *anamnēsis*? It is the re-presentation,
the reengagement with some past event that imparts real-time meaning
and power. It offers an existential choice at every performance to every
participant, whether to immerse oneself more fully into the Kingdom or
to adopt an alternative explanation for reality.

What Jesus does is superimpose his interpretation of Passover on
the dinner so that the disciples can enter into this new perspective. This is
typical Jesus, is it not? All along you have seen that when Jesus performs
any prophecy, text, or (now) ritual, he redefines it according to a tran-
scendent standard. Thus, he tells them it is *his blood* and *his body*. "The
fruit of the vine" [22:18] is an intervention of joy that comes from Jesus's
mission accomplished. There are two cups of festive wine passed around.
One celebrates the joy of the Kingdom, the other a "new covenant in"
his "blood." (Contrary to what you may have heard from others, I say
Jesus shared *two* cups of wine, not just one outside the meal.) It was as
if Jesus deliberately defied his adversary's gloomy *kairos* and now raised
a glass to celebrate his victory. Yes, I'd say he performed Passover in an
unprecedented way!

Nonetheless, he is mindful of Satan's strategy involving the betrayal
of one of his select inner circle. This is how remarkable is Jesus's own
response: he epitomizes the words of that famous passage that goes: "You

1. See *Unfinished Tale*, 95, 120–21, 159–60.

prepare a table before me in the presence of my enemies. You anoint my head with oil. My cup overflows" [Ps 23:5]. Here is he is mindful of his imminent departure ("exodus"), and he is celebrating and inviting his friends together for a last hurrah with them.

Moreover, his cup is so full and overflowing that he, incredibly, shares it with Judas, his betrayer and human agent of his Adversary. He would welcome the client of Satan to his table [22:21]! The role that Judas plays in this dark moment of the performance was done secretly and in isolation. No one but Jesus is aware of who the villain is and what is his tactic—so the intrigue plunges the rest of the invited guests into a game of self-analysis [22:23]. "Who is the culprit? Not I—it must be you!" So they carry on with their challenges and self-defenses. All the while, Jesus knows and somehow relishes his counterstrategy: invite them all (guilty and innocent) to a Passover party!

Remarkable is his composure as he deliberately prepares his disciples for what is ahead. His strategy involves teaching at this party—no hand-wringing, no competitions, no scrutinies, no accusations. He has more to perform that they must take in before he departs at the end of the evening. They must learn to do parties like this one, sharing what they have, accepting false friends as guests, and pledging joy and contentment in the midst of prowling wolves. God himself will take responsibility for the flock.

You could shrug off Jesus's strategy as ritualistic or naïve about the dangers ahead. He seems to calculate that these actions are the "ancient paths where the good way is" [Jer 6:16], just like his ancestors who anticipated some final end to their own exoduses. The assumption of his prediction is that he will survive and celebrate once again. When he says, "From now on I shall not drink of the fruit of the vine until the Kingdom of God comes," he assumes he will survive and celebrate once again. It was an audacious hope in the face of the dangers ahead.

1. How tight is the fellowship that I maintain with fellow believers in the Kingdom of God?

2. How do I respond to my adversaries? How do I imitate Jesus's attitude?

3. What is my thinking about what the Lord's Supper is all about?

ODE TO THE PARTY

Who shall come and sit with me,
Who shall share my food?
Who shall be my friend and foe,
To whom does my invitation go?
Judas, come, and sit right here;
Join Peter and John and James.
Be family for Seder hour,
Be partakers of my name.
Pay no heed, all you guests,
That dark plots cause dismay.
Take up the joy, and the rest,
Take up this Passover day.
I regard you all as friends;
I regard you all my brothers;
Parlor here to sit and praise
The coming Kingdom days.

Party Games

Luke 22:23–30 And they began to question one another, which of them it was that would do this. 24 A dispute also arose among them, which of them was to be regarded as the greatest. 25 And he said to them, "The kings of the Gentiles exercise lordship over them; and those in authority over them are called bene-factors. 26 But not so with you; rather let the greatest among you become as the youngest, and the leader as one who serves. 27 For which is the greater, one who sits at table, or one who serves? Is it not the one who sits at table? But I am among you as one who serves.

28 "You are those who have continued with me in my trials; 29 and I assign to you, as my Father assigned to me, a Kingdom, 30 that you may eat and drink at my table in my Kingdom, and sit on thrones judging the twelve tribes of Israel."

The sordid side of the disciples' corporate life now comes out in double dose. First, they dispute among themselves as to how anyone could possibly think of betraying the Master. As if Judas's bitterness were an exotic disease that no one could imagine! Then their show of indignation erupts into a dispute about who is the best disciple! They make sport about what-ifs and make-believe games: in the world of such competition, the ego is the center of attention. Who is the worst disciple and who is the best disciple? Like most parties, everyone sits around and banters: "Who has done the most for Jesus? I can offer him the most devotion of all his followers!" Such conversations revolve around that word, most—most talent, most popularity, and so on.

Jesus intervenes like a breeze blowing through a stuffy room: the task of those who advance the Kingdom is to put on feasts like today's where even one's enemies sit at table to be served. Jesus had already told his disciples that among his invited guests there sat at the table his own betrayer. Jesus had invited him, arranged his accommodations, and then waited on him this very night!

So what is discipleship, Theophilus, but the kind of self-denial where we pour out ourselves for the ones who are most likely to take advantage of us? Or what about when we are not even noticed as we serve as table waiters for ungrateful guests? What kind of leadership and seniority is this? Jesus's. Who rewards it? Jesus. Just as the Romans and Judas and even Peter (later) did not really understand who Jesus was, God recognized him and promised a hero's share when the Kingdom is no longer a mere visitation but a full presence. Such is the call—paradoxical is the only way to describe it—Jesus gives.

If they survive the upcoming "trials" [22:27], they also share a hero's welcome [22:29–30]. They will sit at table—not just serve all the time; and they will receive a throne to judge Israel.

1. How do I put myself at the center of my fantasies? What kind of fantasies do I have?

2. How am I involved right now in serving or arranging things for others?

3. Recount times when I have worked very hard for some communal event or project and *not* received recognition by the group for my efforts? What would help me to envision being recognized by Jesus for unnoticed service?

Game Losers

Luke 22:31–34 "Simon, Simon, behold, Satan demanded to have you, that he might sift you like wheat, 32 but I have prayed for you that your faith may not fail; and when you have turned again, strengthen your brethren." 33 And he said to him, "Lord, I am ready to go with you to prison and to death." 34 He said, "I tell you, Peter, the cock will not crow this day, until you three times deny that you know me."

All alone, Simon will soon know the ultimate face-off with Satan, that very Adversary who earlier had taken Judas down. The outcome of these struggles rebound toward grace and glory, or they are times of defeat and disaster. Satan's strategy, so successful against Judas, will unfold in due time for Simon Peter.

Satan has "demanded" access to Simon Peter and the other disciples (the "you" is plural [22:31]). This implies that he has some right to them. And so for us all: God allows some one-on-one access to disciples apart from their communal fellowship in the Passover meal. Were it not for Jesus's prayer, who knows what would have happened to Peter? (Why did he not pray for Judas?)

The ordeal that Simon Peter undergoes and barely escapes is a teaching moment for him. Jesus now bids him to own up to his failure like a drunkard who has binged against all advice, or a pet dog who has returned to the pack for the night. For him, the only way to cleanse himself is to go public and try to help others. In helping others, Simon Peter again sets himself on a path of serving at table instead of sitting at table.

The irony is that the focus here vacillates between communal and individual: Jesus addresses Simon by name (using his given name instead of "rock" or Peter), yet speaks to the whole group. Everyone individually must go through this sifting and shaking along with Peter. Yet the corporate is affirmed even more when Simon is told to "strengthen his brethren."

The ludicrous party game the disciples played at table now shows its ugliness: Simon could have been "the greatest" [22:24] among all the disciples, but instead he will betray Jesus just like Judas. That's the problem, Theophilus. We all have Judas in our breasts, were it not for prayer and grace. Peter and the rest of us will eventually be all alone and fail—but for prayer and grace.

1. Should it frighten me that Satan himself may have access to my spiritual life? What should I do?

2. Recall some moment of awful failure. What sustained me in this hour of despair?

3. How are there times when I can recall Judas in my own heart? How did I recover from such a realization?

My Soul's "Et Tu, Brute" Moment [Jesus]

All of you I do invite,
To sit together as one.
Think anew the Kingdom route—
Look at what we've done.

So Peter, John, sit near me now;
And, James, put aside your rage;
For I would bid you enter in,
The joys of Kingdom age.

How often you pass the time
In jousting up foul moods;
How you fancy and you pout
Like princes over measly broods.

Stop playing games of who did what!
Stop saying you're the best!
And see that Satan waits for all—
Judas lurks in your very breast!

Learn my trick to join you all,
On this Seder joy and feast.
Passover's crown I grant to all,
Especially to those who are least.

Come sit with me, Judas, my friend.
Fear not, I know you pretend.

Come share with me my cup and bread;
Come stay until the end.

Since long ago I planned this time,
This feast in Jerusalem's shade,
Once I turned from my trusty home,
To confirm the mission God made.

Seder with its peculiar joys
Serves as end for dusty roads,
As prize for spite and petty games,
As throne for heavy loads.

Luke 22:35–38 And he said to them, "When I sent you out with no purse or bag or sandals, did you lack anything?" They said, "Nothing." 36 He said to them, "But now, let him who has a purse take it, and likewise a bag. And let him who has no sword sell his mantle and buy one. 37 For I tell you that this scripture must be fulfilled in me, 'And he was reckoned with transgressors'; for what is written about me has its fulfilment." 38 And they said, "Look, Lord, here are two swords." And he said to them, "It is enough."

Let me paraphrase the party dialogue I now see it:

[Jesus:] The script is changed. What worked in the past will not work in very near future. Before I sent you out with nothing, thinking that you would meet resistance but not violence. Now it is different, for you will meet what requires new and practical responses—even to the point of reckoning with a sword. Why? Because you will see me not only as a public reformer, a harmless and innocent teacher, but as a publicly condemned criminal. You must be ready.

[Stunned Party Guests:] Here are two swords to protect you, Lord—will this work?

[Jesus:] Enough. You have missed the point yet once again.

Spotlight: Jesus

Luke 22:39–46 39 He came out and went, as was his custom, to the Mount of Olives; and the disciples followed him. 40 When he reached the place, he said to them, "Pray that you may not come into the time of trial." 41 Then he withdrew from them about a stone's throw, knelt down, and prayed, 42 "Father, if you are willing, remove this cup from me; yet, not my will but yours be done." 43 Then an angel from heaven appeared to him and gave him strength. 44 In his anguish he prayed more earnestly, and his sweat became like great drops of blood falling down on the ground. 45 When he got up from prayer, he came to the disciples and found them sleeping because of grief, 46 and he said to them, "Why are you sleeping? Get up and pray that you may not come into the time of trial."

The word "trial" or "temptation" only appears here and three other times in my original narrative: when Jesus was in the wilderness at the beginning of his ministry ("when the devil had finished every test" [4:13]), in the prayer he taught us ("lead us not into temptation" [11:4]), and when the seed falls into soil that succumbs to temptation and ultimately rejects faith ("in a time of testing, they fall away" [8:13]). It is not surprising then that just after Satan has successfully tempted Judas Iscariot and Jesus has warned Simon about Satan's attack, that he should himself be put to the test. It is now the "hour" for Satan and the *kairos* moment for Jesus as he too enters into his own solitude.

The last temptation of Jesus finds its target precisely when it appears that the mission has fulfilled what no one could ever have dreamed just weeks ago: Jesus has arrived in Jerusalem, he has reached the temple, he has performed Passover ritual with his friends. All these things accomplished, now he takes his customary repose in the hillside just outside the city. He has been camping out here of late to prepare himself for his daily public scrutinies. Tonight, though, instead of refuge, the Adversary waits in ambush. This time fasting and quoting the Bible will not do. Only true grit will serve as ticket for his survival.

And what is Jesus's plea? "Remove this cup from me." The cup? Why the cup? It is the cup he did not drink at the Passover. Here he is, the Father's invited guest, and he must drink the cup that parallels what his disciples drank at his table. That cup unified them. It was a source of joy, it was a symbol of covenant, and—paradoxically and chillingly—it was a cup of "blood" (suffering) [22:20]. All these things would pave the way for the Kingdom he "performatively" preached to find its fulfillment. Thus, this is a cup of communion with the Father, a Passover portion with his Father, so to speak. His fellowship is a strange one to human reckoning.

Only the angels at this point would understand the feast to which Jesus was invited in this prayer time on the Mount of Olives. The Father has "earnestly desired" this time with his Son, who has fulfilled all the scriptural directives that described the Messiah and who has proven to be the consummate disciple. Thus, he enters into fellowship with Father God in a way that humans never will understand and not witness "until the Kingdom of God comes" [22:18]. It is a mystery that brings angels to serve as acolytes [22:43].

How demanding the cost of this fellowship is illustrated in the "drops of blood" [22:44] that I describe. That is, the cup of suffering is already imbibed, he is already drinking the potion of this feast. He is totally immersed in "anguish," as my evidence shows.

And the disciples? They adopt a strategy of avoidance "because of grief" [22:45]. They had heard what the Teacher said about a new approach—the taking of knapsack, money bag, and sandals for their ongoing pilgrimage—and yet now they have decided to sleep instead of travel. The idea that Jesus gives them new strategies of resistance or defense because he would be numbered with criminals *grieves* them. Easier to sleep away the new worries about the upcoming struggle than to prepare for it right now.

Jesus once again tells them what we all need to hear: sleep will not deter the devil from testing us. Better to pray what the Lord taught: "Lead us not into temptation" or "Do not put us to the test," for it is too fearful and dangerous to experience without the help of angels and divine grace.

1. How does this picture of Jesus at the hour of his last temptation help me to consider my own temptation?

2. How does his humanness in this picture help me to identify with him and turn away from my own cares and concerns?

3. Describe any "cup" that seemed divinely ordained for me to swallow. How did I go through this time? What were the sufferings and the blessings that were connected to this cup?

4. What does this passage teach me about prayer and intercession?

The Angel in the Garden

Tremble, tremble, who see this man!
Yonder sleeping you miss God's plan.

A cup descends, and foamy brine
Mix sorrow, pain, and joy divine.
A Seder's cup for light and power
Must cope with Pharaoh in this hour.
Grasp, then gulp its bracing brew;
Fear not its taste, its task for you.
From throne above let agent bring
What only he and God can sing.

Luke 22:47–53 While he was still speaking, there came a crowd, and the man called Judas, one of the twelve, was leading them. He drew near to Jesus to kiss him; 48 but Jesus said to him, "Judas, would you betray the Son of man with a kiss?" 49 And when those who were about him saw what would follow, they said, "Lord, shall we strike with the sword?" 50 And one of them struck the slave of the high priest and cut off his right ear. 51 But Jesus said, "No more of this!" And he touched his ear and healed him. 52 Then Jesus said to the chief priests and officers of the temple and elders, who had come out against him, "Have you come out as against a robber, with swords and clubs? 53 When I was with you day after day in the temple, you did not lay hands on me. But this is your hour, and the power of darkness."

Two points stand out: the kiss [22:47] and, once again, the "hour" [22:53]. The kiss drips with irony. It is our regular greeting for family and friends, yet here it is the sign of betrayal to those who are in the dark. Despite the kiss, how little does Judas and his anonymous band know of Jesus! By the same token, how little do the nearby disciples understand of what is soon to take place! Instead of preparing themselves for this moment, they had fallen asleep; and now awake they revert to violent tendencies, apparently not what Jesus intended for them in his last advice about preparing the times ahead.

The "hour" is under another "power" or authority than the Kingdom that Jesus represents: it is dark and short-lived. Yet it keeps everyone, friend and foe, under its grip of oblivion. Still, Jesus resigns himself to it and takes what comes. He does not urge resistance and defiance. Rather he submits and tries to undo the damage his own crew has caused. Thus, he tells his disciples to stop their violent reaction to the apparent set-back to the Kingdom. Then he reverses the damage by healing the injury [22:51]. Rather than taking matters into his own hands, Jesus apparently takes comfort in the fact that the "hour" does not control how the story will turn out. His performance is not determined by this turn of events.

1. How do I get frustrated when things are not going my way? What are constructive ways for me to deal with frustration?

2. How does Jesus react to what seem to be defeats or damages done to him and his name?

3. What public voices or organizations seem to assert that they know Jesus well, yet also seem to miss the true identity of Jesus?

4. How do I see competing kingdoms in these verses? How do I see competing kingdoms in the world today? How does this passage give consolation to those who are in the struggle?

Betrayal with a Kiss

Irony, o irony, how cold your sting!
Judas comes forth to me to cling,
A crowd he brings to find me out;
Yet miss me too, they only doubt.
Yonder sleep, my friends? Give no aid?
You miss the hour, yet come with blade.
You say you know, but no kiss provide;
See Judas's lips and cheek collide.
How dark obscures the face divine
How cold the eyes, how dim their shine.
Evil One, your laugh is cruel,
'Tis "hour" of Dark, your time to rule.
You claim you know, O wily kiss;
Your contact close, but me you miss!
Peter, John, friends, you slumber off;
Confess your love before their scoff.
Tell everyone that this embrace,
Takes body now, but not his face.
Their plot they hatched with fury's fear;
But when I preached, they did not hear.
Still lacking sight and pluck to act?
O foes, o friends, hear this fact:

You who sleep in bushes, be blind;
And you who kiss, will not me find!
You both are seekers who shirk me bold,
Both to leave me, in dark and cold.

Luke 22:54–62 54 Then they seized him and led him away, bringing him into the high priest's house. Peter followed at a distance; 55 and when they had kindled a fire in the middle of the courtyard and sat down together, Peter sat among them. 56 Then a maid, seeing him as he sat in the light and gazing at him, said, "This man also was with him." 57 But he denied it, saying, "Woman, I do not know him." 58 And a little later someone else saw him and said, "You also are one of them." But Peter said, "Man, I am not." 59 And after an interval of about an hour still another insisted, saying, "Certainly this man also was with him; for he is a Galilean." 60 But Peter said, "Man, I do not know what you are saying." And immediately, while he was still speaking, the cock crowed. 61 And the Lord turned and looked at Peter. And Peter remembered the word of the Lord, how he had said to him, "Before the cock crows today, you will deny me three times." 62 And he went out and wept bitterly.

Spotlight: Peter

One disciple, Peter, stealthily slipped away in that hour of darkness. He was determined to prove his fidelity, to fight off the paralysis of the night—for so he had promised Jesus. In the shadowy world between drowsiness and vigilance, he crept unnoticed into the compound where Jesus was held captive. He reported: "I can only say I tried to shake off sleep and stay awake around the nighttime fire in the courtyard. Was I there to keep vigil—I still wonder—or was I only rehearsing brave dreams? Put on the spot three times, I preferred the shadows, the camouflage of night and mental fogginess. It was only after my third denial that a rooster woke me from my delusion. And there was Jesus peering at me as if to signal he was keeping night watch, his own vigil over my soul."

Three times was Jesus's prediction, and now it was Jesus's own prayer that sustained Peter in this thrashing by Satan—also predicted by Jesus. Peter realizes that he has proved nothing about himself except that Jesus was completely right about him.

It is in the vision of Jesus and in the summons of the rooster that hope returns to Peter. For Jesus's glance shows his vigilance, and the rooster's crow that dawn is coming. The hour may belong to Satan, but the certain day is the watchman's. One will surely pass, the other boasts of a divine visitation we heard prophesied long ago by another who was keeping vigil [1:78–79].

1. How have I experienced dark nights of the soul? How did I respond to "temptation's hour"?

2. Describe times when I have given up hope and then found traces of hope to keep me going. Give thanks for such times.

3. Consider the glance of Jesus toward Peter. How have I ever experienced such a glance?

4. How can I identify with Peter?

Peter's Prayer

At midnight I come to keep my pledge
To be true and brave, alert.
In spite of plan, you know my soul,
Its promises nothing but dirt.

For vigil found me creeping in,
To keep watch over you by night;
To lurk, to slink, to sit alone,
Only campfire to give light.

Yet little light means little cost;
Little to keep profile low;
Little the cost to enter in,
Little my pledge also.

I stake myself where nighttime lurks,
And thrice it caught me in fright.
For thrice I said I was not his,
And thrice I proved him right.

Grim was the signal that rooster crowed,
Sharp was the glance his eyes showed.
Bitter were tears that flooded my face,
And stumbling my flight, utter disgrace.

Yet watchful cock signals night flee away.
Come, dawn, bid my soul take its stand!
Jesus had watched to keep Satan in check;
Now sun beams its grace on the land.

If I could but say what I swear I would do,
Could I only fulfill what I say!
The only sure thing to anchor my life
Tells how vigil of Jesus holds sway!

Reacting Game Excursus:
Eavesdropping in the Passion of Luke
(Luke 22:39–62)

Preliminaries (2–5 minutes)

Organize everyone into three teams. Usually, just counting by 1-2-3 is the easiest way to get three random groups. One will be the "Eavesdropper Group A," one the "Eavesdropper Group B," and the final group "Eavesdropper Group C." The facilitator will be the MC who is the lead investigator. Each group is quizzed individually and sequentially with an "interrogation" by the facilitator.

Facilitator's introduction:

1. "We're doing some eavesdropping, compliments of the Gospel of Luke today. Luke gives us (literally) a bird's-eye view of what took place in the crucial moments surrounding the arrest of Jesus.

2. "Since we're eavesdropping we don't have all the facts, so *we have to put the facts together*. I mean, Luke doesn't come out and tell us directly, as if it is plain and simple.

3. "I suggest that he writes us a *mystery* that we need to investigate. Our task here is to put together the facts and devise *an interpretation that fits the facts*."

Small Group Discussion (10 minutes)

Luke 22:39–46 39 He came out and went, as was his custom, to the Mount of Olives; and the disciples followed him. 40 When he reached the place, he said to them, "Pray that you may not come into the time of trial." 41 Then he withdrew from them about a stone's throw, knelt down, and prayed, 42 "Father, if you are willing, remove this cup from me; yet, not my will but yours be done." 43 Then an angel from heaven appeared to him and gave him strength. 44 In his anguish he prayed more earnestly, and his sweat became like great drops of blood falling down on the ground. 45 When he got up from prayer, he came to the disciples and found them sleeping because of grief, 46 and he said to them, "Why are you sleeping? Get up and pray that you may not come into the time of trial."

Eavesdropper Group A Discussion

You are the "angel from heaven" who appeared to Jesus (22:43). Discuss and answer the following questions, and then choose a representative to speak.

1. What did you see in the passage related above?

2. What did you hear in the passage related above?

3. What did you say in the passage related above?

You will want to discuss among yourselves the answers above, because you may be asked further questions, like "why?"

Luke 22:47–54 47 While he was still speaking, suddenly a crowd came, and the one called Judas, one of the twelve, was leading them. He approached Jesus to kiss him; 48 but Jesus said to him, "Judas, is it with a kiss that you are betraying the Son of Man?" 49 When those who were around him saw what was coming, they asked, "Lord, should we strike with the sword?" 50 Then one of them struck the slave of the high priest and cut off his right ear. 51 But Jesus said, "No more of this!" And he touched his ear and healed him. 52 Then Jesus said to the chief priests, the officers of the temple police, and the elders who had come for him, "Have you come out with swords and clubs as if I were a bandit? 53 When I was with you day after day in the temple, you did not lay hands on me. But this is your hour, and the power of darkness!" 54 Then they seized him and led him away, bringing him into the high priest's house.

Eavesdropper Group B Discussion

You are a member of the "crowd" (v. 47). Discuss and answer the following questions, and then choose a representative to speak.

1. What did you see in the passage related above?

2. What did you hear in the passage related above?

3. What did you say in the passage related above?

You will want to discuss among yourselves the answers above, because you may be asked further questions, like "why?"

> Luke 22:54–62 54 Then they seized him and led him away, bringing him into the high priest's house. But Peter was following at a distance. 55 When they had kindled a fire in the middle of the courtyard and sat down together, Peter sat among them. 56 Then a servant-girl, seeing him in the firelight, stared at him and said, "This man also was with him." 57 But he denied it, saying, "Woman, I do not know him." 58 A little later someone else, on seeing him, said, "You also are one of them." But Peter said, "Man, I am not!" 59 Then about an hour later still another kept insisting, "Surely this man also was with him; for he is a Galilean." 60 But Peter said, "Man, I do not know what you are talking about!" At that moment, while he was still speaking, the cock crowed. 61 The Lord turned and looked at Peter. Then Peter remembered the word of the Lord, how he had said to him, "Before the cock crows today, you will deny me three times." 62 And he went out and wept bitterly.

Eavesdropper Group C Discussion.

You are the "cock" who crowed (22:60). Discuss and answer the following questions, and then choose a representative to speak.

1. What did you see in the passage related above?

2. What did you hear in the passage related above?

3. What did you say in the passage related above?

You will want to discuss among yourselves the answers above, because you may be asked further questions, like "why?"

Large Group Discussion (25 minutes)

"Facilitator's Interrogation of Group A"

1. I am wondering why Jesus brought his disciples to the Mount of Olives. What did he expect them to see or learn? When he came back to them, what do you think he was thinking that they should have seen?

2. So let's talk about the "trial" of Jesus, if that is what we call it. Why does Jesus need to pray, if he is so great a leader? What was this "cup" you mention? Did it contain good things or bad things? If good things, why did he wish it away? If bad things, why would the "Father" give it to him?

3. And what exactly did you do for him? Why does it require you to do something, as opposed to asking his disciples to do something? Is it possible that you understand something that the others do not? Is it possible that you know what this cup entails and the others do not know?

4. Just wondering why the disciples sleep: please tell me. (Read 22:45.) What did you hear that they could not face, according to Jesus? (Read 22:46.) You weren't there, but did you know that the disciples had just finished an argument about who was the greatest follow-er—and Jesus warned them that following him would mean public disgrace and struggle?

"Facilitator's Interrogation of Group B"

1. What did you say Judas did to identify Jesus? Why a kiss? What does a kiss normally imply about a relationship?

2. How does Jesus recognize the strangeness of such an action? I mean, do you kiss someone that you are going to betray? Why then would Judas choose this act to signal a person to arrest?

3. Why does Jesus say, "No more of this" [22:51]? Do you think that they might also be doing the same thing as Judas, except doing with a sword what Judas did with a kiss?

4. Why is a sword—or a kiss—useless in terms of what will happen next, at least according to Jesus?

5. Why does Jesus say that the power of darkness is an hour? How short is an hour?

"Facilitator's Interrogation of Group C"

1. You certainly have a unique position in this hearing. I have never interviewed a bird. Tell me, what do you think Peter was trying to prove?

2. You weren't there, but did you realize that the disciples had all fallen asleep while Jesus went through his trial on the Mount of Olives, just a little east of Jerusalem as the bird flies (so to speak)? Were you there when Jesus told his opponents that it was the hour of darkness? What normally happens when it is dark? So what time do you think it was when Peter slipped into the gate of the high priest's compound into the courtyard?

3. You say that you heard Peter deny Jesus three times. And then you crowed. Why? What does your crowing normally mean? So what were you trying to signal?

4. And you saw Jesus turn and look at Peter. What do you suppose Jesus intended to mean by this glance? And then what did Peter do?

5. Do you happen to know what another disciple named Judas did when he betrayed Jesus? So how does Peter's action differ from Judas's? What made them respond differently?

Conclusion to the Interrogation (3 minutes)

The facilitator should sum up what the group learned about Jesus from all three perspectives. Perhaps the facilitator can make the synopsis and read the poems above corresponding to each of the three perspectives. Or the facilitator can simply open the floor for a few comments on what was learned about Jesus's experience from the various perspectives.

Part Two: Farce or Tragedy?

I will try now to present these last events doing my own version of what the Adversary had arranged. Bear with me as I spin this perspective, for I believe it is Jesus's. It is not necessarily a pretty choice, but it is related to the outcome of my story—and hopefully it will help you cope with your own life story. Both the Adversary's take on things and mine are imaginable and thus options for interpretations of the following scenes. I will below call his presentation "farce" and mine "tragedy."

Scene 1

> Luke 22:63–71 63 Now the men who were holding Jesus mocked him and beat him; 64 they also blindfolded him and asked him, "Prophesy! Who is it that struck you?" 65 And they spoke many other words against him, reviling him. 66 When day came, the assembly of the elders of the people gathered together, both chief priests and scribes; and they led him away to their council, and they said, 67 "If you are the Christ, tell us." But he said to them, "If I tell you, you will not believe; 68 and if I ask you, you will not answer. 69 But from now on the Son of man shall be seated at the right hand of the power of God." 70 And they all said, "Are you the Son of God, then?" And he said to them, "You say that I am." 71 And they said, "What further testimony do we need? We have heard it ourselves from his own lips."

Farce: Now Jesus is completely in the hands of his enemies, those who kiss him on one hand, but beat him once the kiss has targeted him on the other hand. Here is how they make mockery of their kiss: How could he be a prophet? How does he know the future if he cannot even make out who will hit him? How could he be a visionary? How can a man blindfolded see anything that clarifies reality? He cannot figure out even the basic questions revolving around himself and his own fate. His claim to have God's point of view is beggared by the blindfold they place on him. Rather, does the blindfold not show him to be someone who is deluded and driven by self-grandeur?

Daylight only brings more assaults against his claim to God-centeredness [22:66]. This time his antagonists are the very ones who tried to scorn and attack his reputation among the people, in the days just before when they stealthily approached him in the temple. The performance of priests and scribes only proves that their kiss meant that they did *not* recognize him as prophet or messiah or of divine origin. They are determined to turn this last act in the life of Jesus into a *farce*, a bad joke about any claim Jesus has made about himself.

Perhaps Jesus didn't know what exactly would happen next and had in his moment of trial imagined the worst of loneliness and suffering. Perhaps this is why he answered so ambiguously as he did, for his words veiled his hopes and fears. While Jesus himself would struggle with his own sense of God's dealings, he was still performing the part assigned to him. His own disciple Judas betrayed him, his intimate table friends abandoned him, and his best disciple denied him. His invisible audience and supporting cast among the angels were his only help.

Scene 2

Tragedy: Jesus's response [22:67–68] reminds me of the lines uttered by one of Israel's ancient prophets, Jeremiah. When Jeremiah was brought before King Zedekiah of Judah, he said: "If I tell you the truth that I know, what good will it do? For you will not change your view of me."[2] Jesus overshadows his predecessor, though, because he was right about his opponents, while Jeremiah was wrong. In addition to Jeremiah, Jesus cites [22:69] yet another dramatic scene that everyone knew from their upbringing: the coronation of someone called the Son of Man who summons the Kingdom of God. This vision was reported from of old in the book of Daniel [Dan 7:1–28].

First prophet, now king. The implications are clear to the assembled opponents that he is making an extraordinary claim to divinity [22:70].

---

2. Get a hold of Jeremiah's scroll, if you can, Theophilus, and read it for yourself. King Zedekiah not only secretly listened to Jeremiah, but even arranged for his rescue more than once [Jer 37–38, esp. 38:14–16].

Their deductions about him fall short because they are not willing to acknowledge the visitation Jesus brings. The light that Zechariah predicted so long ago [1:78–79] as the dawning of day now had yielded (briefly) to "hour of darkness." The high priests and scribes are the ones now blindfolded.

Jesus will make his way through the drama surrounding his exodus [9:31] with a composure based on how Daniel's vision predicts his vindication. Rather than stand for trial before his opponents in this current hour, he will be seated and give judgment. "From now on" [22:69] God will make sure that things will be different. The last act in the life of Jesus will not be directed by the Adversary.

1. How have I ever felt like I was on trial? How does it help that Christ seems to go through his own sense of uncertainty as he faces his end?

2. What are the causes or ideals I stand for that seemingly are overwhelmed by the obstacles in front of them? Try to imagine a time or event in my life when I felt that my efforts were hopeless or that it was futile to continue in a particular direction.

3. Does it ever seem that God or Jesus is "blindfolded" in the way that events unfold in my life? Does it seem I am blindfolded in the way his will unfolds in my life?

4. What title do I think best typifies Jesus in this passage? What title would I give this last act of the story as it so far has played out?

Scene 3

> Luke 23:1–5 Then the whole company of them arose, and brought him before Pilate. 2 And they began to accuse him, saying, "We found this man perverting our nation, and forbidding us to give tribute to Caesar, and saying that he himself is Christ a king." 3 And Pilate asked him, "Are you the King of the Jews?" And he answered him, "You have said so." 4 And Pilate said to the chief priests and the multitudes, "I find no crime in this man." 5 But they were urgent, saying, "He stirs up the people, teaching throughout all Judea, from Galilee even to this place."

We move from the two groups that should have known Jesus, the disciples (now asleep or in denial) and the Jews of Jerusalem (who kissed him, yet misunderstood his identity). He will meet the Romans and their political crony, Herod. Yet another attack on Jesus's identity, this time in front of the Romans about his claim of installing a kingdom. The scene shifts from Jerusalem to Rome, making the new actors Roman instead of Jewish, but so far we do not see much evidence for a reversal the way Jesus hinted at earlier [22:69].

Farce: "Are you the king of the Jews?" [23:3] Either it is not so easy for Jesus to respond to this question, or it is clear that nothing Jesus says will change what happens. It is the ambiguity of the answer that makes Pilate, familiar and fierce when putting down insurrections against Rome, recognize that he is not dealing with the usual bandit or rebel. A threat to Caesar is one thing, but delusion is something else. Learning that Jesus is from an area technically outside his jurisdiction, he evades ruling by giving the case to the local authority, the Jewish king called Herod.

Pilate's attitude seems to be as follows: "Let Herod handle this situation, and it will serve me to be seen as referring Jewish things to him as their overseer rather than interfering as an outsider anyway." It is an unholy collaboration, and wholly unrelated to the Kingdom of God. It is a convenient deal—more about politics than principle.

Scene 4: Which Interpretation?

> Luke 23:8–12 When Herod saw Jesus, he was very glad, for he had long desired to see him, because he had heard about him, and he was hoping to see some sign done by him. 9 So he questioned him at some length; but he made no answer. 10 The chief priests and the scribes stood by, vehemently accusing him. 11 And Herod with his soldiers treated him with contempt and mocked him; then, arraying him in gorgeous apparel, he sent him back to Pilate. 12 And Herod and Pilate became friends with each other that very day, for before this they had been at enmity with each other.

I added this snippet to my account, and it continues to spin things according to the Adversary's perspective. As a Jew, Herod seems like he could be truly concerned for Jesus. His interest though is purely superficial—and at any rate Herod is not really very interested in his religion anyway. His extended family line is mixed in its Jewish pedigree—and he personally tends toward being antagonistic toward Jewish zeal. (Why?

Because it threatens his status as a favored Roman client.) The main thing Herod wants to see now is Jesus perform as "wonderworker" like Elijah or Moses before Pharaoh.

Tragedy: But Jesus doesn't live up to his billing. Why would Jesus waste his breath? Why not wait for things to unfold according to his Father's plan? As events unfold in this last act, perhaps Jesus already is silently rehearsing his part.

Farce: This response leaves Herod irritated to the point of scorn toward Jesus. Who would pay attention to such nonsense about Jesus being someone great? So he dismisses Jesus with his own sideshow [23:11]—as if in sympathy with the Adversary that brought Jesus into the jaws of his human enemies. Herod's contribution to the hour, though, is a little different than Judas's: instead of identifying him with a kiss, he puts him in a costume. Now it is not a farce about "Jesus, play the prophet," but "Jesus, entertain us!" Dress up religion in the garments of politics, while controlling it for political purposes.

Yet Herod implicitly concedes that Jesus is not any danger to him or to the prevailing order. He sends Jesus back with the satisfaction that a political alliance has been cemented. He now recognizes that his patron Pilate has given him his privileges of handling Jesus as a Jewish subject. Something good has come out of this pretender from Galilee!

1. Do we expect too much of our political leaders? Do we expect them to uphold or implement the Kingdom?

2. The Gospel of Luke and Acts of the Apostles is generally favorable in its view of established order and authority as represented by the Roman Empire. How does Luke show this attitude here?

3. How have I seen politicians manipulate the image of Jesus to their own advantage?

4. How again does the resignation of Jesus speak to me about how I should handle myself under pressure?

Scene 5

Luke 23:13–25 Pilate then called together the chief priests and the rulers and the people, 14 and said to them, "You brought me this man as one who was perverting the people; and after examining him before you, behold, I did not find this man guilty of any of your charges against him; 15 neither did Herod, for he sent him back to us. Behold, nothing deserving death has been done by him; 16 I will therefore chastise him and release him." 17 18 But they all cried out together, "Away with this man, and release to us Barabbas"—19 a man who had been thrown into prison for an insurrection started in the city, and for murder. 20 Pilate addressed them once more, desiring to release Jesus; 21 but they shouted out, "Crucify, crucify him!" 22 A third time he said to them, "Why, what evil has he done? I have found in him no crime deserving death; I will therefore chastise him and re-lease him." 23 But they were urgent, demanding with loud cries that he should be crucified. And their voices prevailed. 24 So Pilate gave sentence that their demand should be granted. 25 He released the man who had been thrown into prison for insurrec-tion and murder, whom they asked for; but Jesus he delivered up to their will.

Farce: Jesus is led back and forth, to and fro, yet nothing comes from his lips and no attempt is made for self-defense. The unholy political alli-ance between Pilate and Herod is not only unrelated to the Kingdom of God, but now it is their government authority that catches Jesus in Satan's trap. Despite three attempts to exculpate Jesus, Pilate finally appeases the crowd's desire for the blood of Jesus.

In his place there is one who is released, a murderer and insurrec-tionist, who goes by the name of Barabbas. Ironically, his name means "son of the father." Instead of the one who establishes the real and good Kingdom of God, the one who was called from the skies "beloved Son" [3:22], there is no divine voice here, only silence. The one to obtain favor and freedom a son should expect is the very one who least deserves it. The crowd, the temple authorities, and the spineless political authorities have their kingdom; but unknown to them, it is not run by Caesar or by principle of law but by Satan [4:5–6]. The grim humor of this last act and this scene specifically can only be appreciated by the executioner. In this hour, the one on stage that everyone sees is blindfolded and wearing a costume! Is he defeated by such mockery, or is he waiting?

1. Give examples from history of propaganda campaigns or "fake news" that has misled the public.

2. Give examples of how sometimes I am misled by external trappings or by disinformation.

3. Say you are a lawyer for the accused before this crowd. Describe what is going through your head as you would try to defend this man Jesus and his claims, even while he stands silent and costumed before you.

Scene 6: Which Interpretation?

> Luke 23:26–31 And as they led him away, they seized one Simon of Cyrene, who was coming in from the country, and laid on him the cross, to carry it behind Jesus. 27 And there followed him a great multitude of the people, and of women who bewailed and lamented him. 28 But Jesus turning to them said, "Daughters of Jerusalem, do not weep for me, but weep for yourselves and for your children. 29 For behold, the days are coming when they will say, 'Blessed are the barren, and the wombs that never bore, and the breasts that never gave suck!' 30 Then they will begin to say to the mountains, 'Fall on us'; and to the hills, 'Cover us.' 31 For if they do this when the wood is green, what will happen when it is dry?"

Farce: The farce is not complete. It now twists away from mocking Jesus to mocking his disciples. Instead of Simon Peter, now there is another Simon who is told to take the cross and follow Jesus. (Where have you heard this line before [9:23]?) Instead of a crowd exalting his triumph as king of healing and deliverance as when he entered Jerusalem, now there is a procession of stragglers who lift up a dirge at his downfall. Everything is staged in dramatic fashion, as if to entertain a watching world. The Adversary directs this hour of darkness [23:26–27].

Tragedy: Or does he? Time now for me to interject with my own uptake of the presentation. It begins right here as Jesus encounters "the daughters of Jerusalem." For the first time since he has been arrested, Jesus opens his mouth to set things straight about what really is going on. From now on, Theophilus, events will increasingly show an alternative interpretation, as if there is a preferable version about what is happening. And the next few scenes suggest that the hour is yielding and the darkness fading.

The first encounter with these poor women allows Jesus to assert that God is totally in control. He had already observed that Jerusalem did not recognize the day of divine visitation [13:34–35; 19:41–44] now or in the past. Now he speaks about future visitations that will bring about grim prospects for Jerusalem and for the world. He predicts what amounts to an apocalyptic scenario—a taste of what things would be like at the end of time as we know it.

The women are gripped by the emotions of this hour, the tragedy of an innocent man's death. Jesus urges them to look at a bigger picture. Future events will show the real-life invasion and destruction of Jerusalem. For the "daughters of Jerusalem," sadness will surround their family life and children, so bleak that only celibacy can avoid what is at stake [23:29]. If we could capture their sentiment as lines uttered in the play Jesus imagines, it would be: "Why did I bring my offspring into such a world? Why invest my life energy in raising children?"

The real tragedy Jesus describes involves a topic I have earlier raised: divine visitation [23:30–31]. It will be so fierce that they will flee away from the city in an attempt to find sanctuary. Better to die in the countryside than to be slaughtered with their families in the city. But then come the cryptic words of Jesus that this is only the "green" wood phase of the coming conflagration. In other words, the fire that John the Baptist had predicted [3:7, 9, 17] will come. At first it will be only like a smoldering fire burning up the green branches (perhaps the destruction of Jerusalem itself), but later it will be an inferno to consume everything in its path (the consummation of the universe as we know it).

1. How does Jesus imply that his dying will impact our lives? What is the chain of events that Jesus implies his death will cause?

2. Is there any preparation I can make that will respond to the coming events Jesus implies?

3. Do some research on the Roman invasion of Judea and Jerusalem by Titus and Vespasian around the year 70. How do these events tend to confirm the words of Jesus? If this is the "green" word, what does it mean for the dry wood?

4. What does it mean to "weep for yourselves and for your children"? How are our children affected by our behavior and our attitudes?

Scene 7: Which Interpretation?

Luke 23:32–43 Two others also, who were criminals, were led away to be put to death with him. 33 And when they came to the place which is called The Skull, there they crucified him, and the criminals, one on the right and one on the left.

34 And Jesus said, "Father, forgive them; for they know not what they do." And they cast lots to divide his garments. 35 And the people stood by, watching; but the rulers scoffed at him, saying, "He saved others; let him save himself, if he is the Christ of God, his Chosen One!" 36 The soldiers also mocked him, coming up and offering him vinegar, 37 and saying, "If you are the King of the Jews, save yourself!"

38 There was also an inscription over him, "This is the King of the Jews." 39 One of the criminals who were hanged railed at him, saying, "Are you not the Christ? Save yourself and us!" 40 But the other rebuked him, saying, "Do you not fear God, since you are under the same sentence of condemnation? 41 And we indeed justly; for we are receiving the due reward of our deeds; but this man has done nothing wrong." 42 And he said, "Jesus, remember me when you come into your Kingdom." 43 And he said to him, "Truly, I say to you, today you will be with me in Paradise."

Tragedy: So far as I know, Theophilus, I am the only one to speak about the dialogue Jesus had with the convicts crucified with him. When I say they were "put to death with him" [23:32], I want you to consider the literal meaning: they were "lifted up" [ἀναιρέω, *anaireō*]. Remember that I like puns—for they give meanings that can only be grasped with a little afterthought. Imagine if you can then, that the cross is not a gruesome place of execution (the way the Adversary sees it), but a seat of enthrone-ment.[3] It was from this elevated position that Jesus would utter powerful words and make rulings to stir his comrades on their crosses. From his throne, therefore, let us imagine that Jesus holds court with advisers to his right and left in his castle called "Skull."

First, Jesus notices how his human antagonists (Pilate, the priests, Herod, and so on) have been hoodwinked into their mockery. So he prays for God's pardon upon them due to their ignorance about what is really going on. In some sense, his prayer for them represents what he

3. I am the only one that I know of to use this word for the execution of Jesus. I used this a lot, Theophilus, as you may remember—but almost always in regard to figures who are authorities or pretenders—so my word applies not to any ordinary death but to those who are executed because of some high status they claim. I use it in regard to Jesus, Theudas (an insurrectionist), Moses, James, Stephen, Paul, and so on. The only other time I use the word in my story about the life of Jesus is in regard to the plan of the Jerusalem authorities and Judas Iscariot to defeat Jesus [22:2]—and the pun works well here: all their efforts to bring him down in fact only lift him up!

had sought earlier for his chief disciple Peter: deliverance from Satan's hour. It is spiritual darkness that has been foisted on them (Judas, Simon Peter, the Romans, even the priests) unawares. Only Peter has so far been aroused from his slumber of night to see the enormity of his crime. As for the rest, they blithely go about their affairs as if they were at a carnival: gambling, taunting, gaming. As the brutal scene wears on, though, others will be stricken by their guilt. This we will see in due time.

Farce: Meanwhile, the spiritually blindfolded actors relish this great irony of Jesus holding court on the cross. They scoff at what Jesus has led the crowd to believe about him. Messiah? What nonsense! Soldiers also join in, just as the nations and their rulers "set themselves and take counsel together against the LORD and his anointed one" [Ps 2]. Their final joke is to offer Jesus a mock royal banquet, replete with rancid wine. Then the perpetrators hang a title on the whole comic affair they have pulled off: "[Look everyone!] This is the king of the Jews!" So reads the banner over Jesus as the byline for all to appreciate.

And Jesus has mostly been silent. It is as if he is recalling heroic deeds performed long ago and internally rehearsing the scripted words. Only the weeping women and the bamboozled crowds have so far stirred Jesus to give his own commentary. Now the chief "advisers" on right and left enter the fray. One demands that the audacious claims he heard about Jesus now be fulfilled—now or never! This man is at his wit's end [23:29], outraged at the ridicule Jesus has foisted on him.

Tragedy: The other, though, recognizes the reality of what is at stake. Rather than falling into the abyss of darkness, he senses something different about the "Kingdom" Jesus represents. The focus in this interchange is on "paradise," not an earthly throne. Really, he realizes, it is Jesus who acts and recites on this stage before the crowd—even at this nerve-wracking climax of the plot—flawlessly and gracefully [23:41]. As for this "good thief," he knows he has bungled his lines, his acting, his timing. He deserves to be condemned by the critics for his failings—but not Jesus.

Now he turns to Jesus, the one he will die with. He senses his last chance for dignity at performance in life. For him, Jesus is the true representative of the Kingdom that will offer him a new beginning [23:42].

Jesus immediately connects the request to the original human condition, when Adam and Eve lived in "paradise," a garden [23:43]. Jesus now is the new Adam (remember Luke's genealogy of Jesus as son of Adam, son of God [3:38]), the good thief now the first family member of

Adam. It is the final line Jesus addresses to another human being, and he has singled out a man whom society has sentenced to execution.

1. Think about times when the good thief versus bad thief conversation gets played out in my head. What were the situations that caused me to give up hope completely and castigate God? What were the simple and unassuming moments when I recognized that God's intervention would not conform to my expectations or hopes?

2. Why or why not do I find the words of Jesus to the "good thief" a good answer for the dire conditions facing him?

3. What would it be like to die with Jesus, shamed and humiliated on the cross? In the face of such ignominy, is it possible to see myself as dying like the bad thief?

4. How can I pray for a good (and noble) death?

5. What kind of paradise do I imagine in light of what transpires here?

Scene 8

> Luke 23:44–49 44 It was now about the sixth hour, and there was darkness over the whole land until the ninth hour, 45 while the sun's light failed; and the curtain of the temple was torn in two. 46 Then Jesus, crying with a loud voice, said, "Father, into thy hands I commit my spirit!" And having said this he breathed his last. 47 Now when the centurion saw what had taken place, he praised God, and said, "Certainly this man was innocent!" 48 And all the multitudes who assembled to see the sight, when they saw what had taken place, returned home beating their breasts. 49 And all his acquaintances and the women who had followed him from Galilee stood at a distance and saw these things.

Farce or Tragedy? Jesus resigned himself to this end, yet he gave new meaning to this awful outcome. The Adversary can no longer keep it camouflaged. Jesus's perspective threatens to swallow up the whole plot in a reversal of his original expectation.

Nevertheless, the curtain falls on today's theater—and its two representations. So now is the time to return to a semblance of reality. However, this new condition is not a routine reality, for the world has witnessed the death of Jesus.

Darkness oozes its presence over everything, "darkness over the whole land . . . while the sun's light failed" [23:44–45a]. It is an oily darkness as if painted in black pigments on white canvas. The darkness is everywhere felt. It is one that brings us as an audience back to the original darkness before creation [Gen 1:2a]. On an earthly level, all of our human efforts at atoning ourselves with God come to life, as it were, and face their infinite limitations. As if to emphasize the charade of the Jewish temple and its priests, the curtain guarding the inner sanctuary shreds as if in anguish [23:45b]. Then Jesus announces that the Son is coming back home, but in the form of breath instead of body, spirit instead of flesh [23:46]. Thus, the divine Spirit or breath that once hovered over the chaos to bring forth a new world [Gen 1:2b] now returns to the Father and bides its time.

If there is to be triumph in these *Memoirs of How It All Began*, it will not come because of his efforts or intervention. Intervention must come from his Sponsor, the Father who recognized the sonship of Jesus at his baptism [3:22] and at his transfiguration [9:35]. The exodus spoken of so long ago was a cooperative effort: Jesus had completed the pilgrimage to Jerusalem and had conducted the Passover dinner with his disciples. The current darkness between the sixth and ninth hours also reminds us of that first exodus when nighttime allowed the children of Israel to escape Egypt under the leadership of Moses [Exod 14:20].

In this current darkness, not much remains: his disciples have fled, the crowd turned against him, and it seems like the only things left are the helpless "daughters of Jerusalem" and the dying "good thief" next to him. All else is gone.

Or is it? The Roman soldier now publicly attests to what Pilate thought (and did nothing about): Jesus is innocent [23:47]. It is a token, a small token that his performance was not as laughable and lame as everyone seemed to think. Yes, Jesus was innocent! He measured up as a hero, not vindicated but at least recognized. In the fashion of a tragedy, it is this recognition that will stir up second thoughts and new insights.

The turning point gains momentum as the crowd witnessing the ghastly scene recognizes their complicity in doing away with such an innocent one. They beat their breasts as a sign of repentance. Darkness is not as complete as it first seemed.

A few of his fellow Galilean pilgrims also see what transpires. They piece the clues together, like perceiving one's face reflected in a broken mirror. They had been cautioned at the Passover to stay alert, and now they are coming to their senses. The women of Jerusalem also see the scene, those whom Jesus had told to pray for themselves that they would survive their upcoming trials. Something is stirring . . .

1. Describe any times when God sovereignly intervened in my life. Have I ever experienced a reversal of expectations or events due to what seems to be supernatural influences?

2. How does the sonship of Jesus not preserve him from humiliation in this story? How does my sonship not preserve me from similar outcomes?

3. What does the tearing of the temple's curtain say to me?

4. What does the breathing out of the Spirit of Jesus suggest?

Final Scene: Sabbath

> Luke 23:50–56 Now there was a man named Joseph from the Jewish town of Arimathea. He was a member of the council, a good and righteous man, 51 who had not consented to their purpose and deed, and he was looking for the Kingdom of God. 52 This man went to Pilate and asked for the body of Jesus. 53 Then he took it down and wrapped it in a linen shroud, and laid him in a rock-hewn tomb, where no one had ever yet been laid. 54 It was the day of Preparation, and the Sabbath was beginning. 55 The women who had come with him from Galilee followed, and saw the tomb, and how his body was laid; 56 then they returned, and prepared spices and ointments. On the Sabbath they rested according to the commandment.

The moment of recognition has passed, at least in the sense of theater. "Today" for paradise and Joseph of Arimathea and the good thief [23:45] and Zacchaeus [19:9] and so many others I have mentioned in these *Memoirs* is over, and history has moved on. At least that is what the Adversary would like us to think. Even for those of us aroused from our slumber and remorseful for our conduct, the workweek is over, and the sun sets on it to signal that the Sabbath is upon us.

Rest from the labors of the mission comes upon Jesus, his disciples, and my narrative. Jesus goes into repose in a place not ever inhabited by human flesh. While he lies in state and in silence, there is yet more mention of witnesses seeing what was taking place. This account is filled with eyewitnesses [23:35, 48–49, 55]. It is time simply to observe and reflect on what happened in these last few days. Nothing can be done now—the last act is over. We once acclaimed him with cheers and high hopes, but now we can only wait and reflect.

By means of all the witnesses I mention, I stress that Jesus is really dead. The corpse of Jesus lies in the new tomb. Soon the women will return for anointing a dead body. The story I told allows you, Theophilus, two lines of interpretation—the farce or the tragedy. One came at the instigation of the Adversary, the other directed by Jesus. Either we have walked away by now, or we simply beat our breasts in repentance for our complicity.

Either way, everyone takes a Sabbath break.

CHAPTER EIGHT

The End Game

Reacting Game Excursus: Theophilus Wants a Report about What Happened after Jesus Died and Was Buried (Luke 24:1–48)

Preliminaries (2–3 minutes)

DIVIDE EVERYONE UP IN the usual fashion into three or four groups, depending on how many are participating. Have each group read and then discuss the passages assigned to them below. Explain to everyone that Theophilus is visiting and wants an explanation of what happened after Jesus died and was buried. So he is conducting a follow-up interview with Luke's sources for the benefit of retelling the story for everyone. The groups must meet separately to rehearse what they originally said to Luke. The following introduction may be helpful.

Moderator: "I am Theophilus. Thank you for coming out to me to go over the document that Luke sent me to understand how important the life of Jesus was. We are near the end of the *Memoirs*. So I have called you together to help me understand what happened after Jesus died and was put in the tomb. I have divided you into three groups, and you will get together and read particular passages that our brother Luke put together about events that happened after the death of Jesus. In your group you will carefully read together a snippet from Luke's report, discuss it among yourselves, and then come back to answer my questions about what Luke meant. I need help in understanding, and I am so grateful you are here to help."

Small Group Discussion (10 minutes)

Group One: The Women

Luke 24:1–11 But on the first day of the week, at early dawn, they went to the tomb, taking the spices which they had prepared. 2 And they found the stone rolled away from the tomb, 3 but when they went in they did not find the body. 4 While they were perplexed about this, behold, two men stood by them in dazzling apparel; 5 and as they were frightened and bowed their faces to the ground, the men said to them, "Why do you seek the living among the dead? 6 Remember how he told you, while he was still in Galilee, 7 that the Son of man must be delivered into the hands of sinful men, and be crucified, and on the third day rise."

8 And they remembered his words, 9 and returning from the tomb they told all this to the eleven and to all the rest. 10 Now it was Mary Magdalene and Joanna and Mary the mother of James and the other women with them who told this to the apostles; 11 but these words seemed to them an idle tale, and they did not believe them.

The women describe among themselves what happened while they walked to the tomb of Jesus. Tell them as a group: "*The passage above is the only information you have* for this preparation session, so you must stick to the above account and not incorporate other voices from outside sources! Choose someone to be two of the women on the scene, and rehearse with them answers to the following questions so that they can report to Theophilus and to everyone":

1. Carefully describe what happened.

2. Give an explanation for what happened based on what you know.

3. What should we do?

Group Two: The Walkers

Luke 24:13–27 That very day two of them were going to a village named Emmaus, about seven miles from Jerusalem, 14 and talking with each other about all these things that had happened. 15 While they were talking and discussing together, Jesus himself drew near and went with them. 16 But their eyes were kept from recognizing him.

17 And he said to them, "What is this conversation which you are holding with each other as you walk?" And they stood still, looking sad. 18 Then one of them, named Cleopas, answered him, "Are you the only visitor to Jerusalem who does not know the things that have happened there in these days?" 19 And he said to them, "What things?" And they said to him, "Concerning Jesus of Nazareth, who was a prophet mighty in deed and word before God and all the people, 20 and how our chief priests and rulers delivered him up to be condemned to death, and crucified him. 21 But we had hoped that he was the one to redeem Israel. Yes, and besides all this, it is now the third day since this happened.

22 "Moreover, some women of our company amazed us. They were at the tomb early in the morning 23 and did not find his body; and they came back saying that they had even seen a vision of angels, who said that he was alive. 24 Some of those who were with us went to the tomb, and found it just as the women had said; but him they did not see."

25 And he said to them, "O foolish men, and slow of heart to believe all that the prophets have spoken! 26 Was it not necessary that the Christ should suffer these things and enter into his glory?" 27 And beginning with Moses and all the prophets, he interpreted to them in all the scriptures the things concerning himself.

Cleopas and his companion describe what happened while they walked to the town of Emmaus. Tell them as a group: "*The passage above is the only information you have* for this preparation session, so you must stick to the above account and not incorporate other voices from outside sources! Choose someone to be Cleopas and someone to be his companion, and rehearse with them answers to the following questions so that they can report to Theophilus and to everyone":

1. Carefully describe what happened.

2. Give an explanation for what happened based on what you know.

3. What should we do?

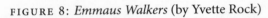

FIGURE 8: *Emmaus Walkers* (by Yvette Rock)

Group Three: The Diners

Luke 24:28–35 So they drew near to the village to which they were going. He appeared to be going further, 29 but they constrained him, saying, "Stay with us, for it is toward evening and the day is now far spent." So he went in to stay with them.

30 When he was at table with them, he took the bread and blessed, and broke it, and gave it to them. 31 And their eyes

were opened and they recognized him; and he vanished out of their sight. 32 They said to each other, "Did not our hearts burn within us while he talked to us on the road, while he opened to us the scriptures?"

33 And they rose that same hour and returned to Jerusalem; and they found the eleven gathered together and those who were with them, 34 who said, "The Lord has risen indeed, and has appeared to Simon!" 35 Then they told what had happened on the road, and how he was known to them in the breaking of the bread.

[This group is optional and can be combined with "the walkers" above, or can be separated as "the diners" due to the length of the whole account (24:13–35).]

Cleopas and his companion describe what happened when they arrived at Emmaus. Tell them as a group: "*The passage above is the only information you have* for this preparation session, so you must stick to the above account and not incorporate other voices from outside sources! Choose someone to be Cleopas and someone to be his companion, and rehearse with them answers to the following questions so that they can report to Theophilus and to everyone":

1. Carefully describe what happened.

2. Give an explanation for what happened based on what you know.

3. What should we do?

Group Four: The Disciples

Luke 24:36–49 As they [Cleopas and his companion] were talking about these things, Jesus himself stood among them [the disciples], and said to them, "Peace to you!" 37 But they were startled and frightened and thought they saw a spirit. 38 And he said to them, "Why are you troubled, and why do doubts arise in your hearts? 39 See my hands and my feet, that it is I myself. Touch me, and see. For a spirit does not have flesh and bones as you see that I have."

40 And when he had said this, he showed them his hands and his feet. 41 And while they still disbelieved for joy and were

marveling, he said to them, "Have you anything here to eat?" 42 They gave him a piece of broiled fish, 43 and he took it and ate before them.

44 Then he said to them, "These are my words that I spoke to you while I was still with you, that everything written about me in the Law of Moses and the Prophets and the Psalms must be fulfilled." 45 Then he opened their minds to understand the Scriptures, 46 and said to them, "Thus it is written, that the Christ should suffer and on the third day rise from the dead, 47 and that repentance for the forgiveness of sins should be proclaimed in his name to all nations, beginning from Jerusalem. 48 You are witnesses of these things. 49 And behold, I am sending the promise of my Father upon you. But stay in the city until you are clothed with power from on high." [ESV]

The disciples gathered in Jerusalem describe what they remembered when the above event happened. Tell them as a group: "*The passage above is the only information you have* for this preparation session, so you must stick to the above account and not incorporate other voices from outside sources! Choose two people to be spokespersons for the disciples, and rehearse with them answers to the following questions so that they can report to Theophilus and to everyone":

1. Carefully describe what happened.

2. Give an explanation for what happened based on what you know.

3. What should we do?

Large Group Session: Debriefing with Theophilus (15 minutes)

Group One Debriefing: The Women

Luke 24:1–11 But on the first day of the week, at early dawn, they went to the tomb, taking the spices which they had prepared. 2 And they found the stone rolled away from the tomb, 3 but when they went in *they did not find the body*. 4 While they *were perplexed* about this, behold, two men stood by them in dazzling apparel; 5 and as they were *frightened* and bowed their faces to the ground, the men said to them, "Why do you seek the living among the dead? 6 Remember how he told you, while he was still in Galilee, 7 that the Son of man must be delivered into the hands of sinful men, and be crucified, and on the third day rise."

8 *And they remembered his words.* 9 and returning from the tomb they told all this to the eleven and to all the rest. 10 Now it was Mary Magdalene and Joanna and Mary the mother of James and the other women with them who told this to the apostles; 11 but *these words seemed to them an idle tale,* and they did not believe them.

Debriefing: Theophilus, the moderator for this larger group discussion session, goes over the three questions briefly with the group. Then he conducts a "debriefing," a more penetrating analysis of what the group interview should show using the italicized phrases above from their passage. Note how the women do not get to see Jesus, although they have a supernatural experience related to him at the burial site. Their own words and experiences, though valid, are not enough to overcome the apostles' tendency to put more stock in the flesh than in the faith. After all, perhaps these women were simply overcome by emotion (Luke says that they were "perplexed" and "frightened"), as the disciples might have believed. One thing that the women have in addition to the angelic visitation is the very words of Jesus ("they remembered his words")—thus, the beginning step of the Church to compile the Scriptures in the form of the New Testament, recording the very words of Jesus.

Group Two Debriefing: The Walkers

Luke 24:13–27 That very day two of them were going to a village named Emmaus, about seven miles from Jerusalem, 14 and talking with each other about all these things that had happened. 15 While they were talking and discussing together, Jesus himself drew near and went with them. 16 But *their eyes were kept from recognizing him.*

17 And he said to them, "What is this conversation which you are holding with each other as you walk?" And they stood still, looking sad. 18 Then one of them, named Cleopas, answered him, "Are you the only visitor to Jerusalem who does not know the things that have happened there in these days?" 19 And he said to them, "What things?" And they said to him, "Concerning Jesus of Nazareth, who was *a prophet* mighty in deed and

word before God and all the people, 20 and how our chief priests and rulers delivered him up to be condemned to death, and crucified him. 21 But *we had hoped* that he was the one to redeem Israel. Yes, and besides all this, it is now the third day since this happened.

22 "Moreover, some women of our company amazed us. They were at the tomb early in the morning 23 and did not find his body; and they came back saying that they had even seen a *vision of angels, who said that he was alive.*

24 "Some of those who were with us went to the tomb, and found it just as the women had said; but *him they did not see.*" 25 And he said to them, "O foolish men, and slow of heart to believe all that the prophets have spoken! 26 Was it not necessary that the Christ should suffer these things and enter into his glory?" 27 And beginning with Moses and all the prophets, *he interpreted to them in all the scriptures the things concerning himself.*

Debriefing: Theophilus, the moderator for this larger group discussion session, goes over the three questions briefly with the group. Then he conducts a "debriefing," a more penetrating analysis of what the group interview should show using the italicized phrases above from their passage. The debriefing lays out the following questions:

- Is it possible that Jesus walks beside us, but we don't understand the Scriptures well enough to recognize him?

- Are we so tied up in our own plans to restart our life that we don't stop and contemplate the *Memoirs* that are from previous generations?

Group Three Debriefing: The Diners

Luke 24:28–35 So they drew near to the village to which they were going. *He appeared to be going further,* 29 but they constrained him, saying, "*Stay with us,* for it is toward evening and the day is now far spent." So he went in to stay with them.

30 *When he was at table with them, he took the bread and blessed, and broke it, and gave it to them. 31 And their eyes were opened and they recognized him;* and he vanished out of their sight.

32 They said to each other, "*Did not our hearts burn within us while he talked to us on the road, while he opened to us the scriptures?*" 33 And they rose that same hour and returned to Jerusalem; and they found the eleven gathered together and those who were with them, 34 who said, "The Lord has risen indeed, and has appeared to Simon!" 35 *Then they told what had happened on the road, and how he was known to them in the breaking of the bread.*

Debriefing: Theophilus, the moderator for this larger group discussion session, goes over the three questions briefly with the group. Then he conducts a "debriefing," a more penetrating analysis of what the group interview should show using the italicized phrases above from their passage. The debriefing lays out the following questions:

- Were we too busy with our lives to notice that our hearts "were burning within us" when we once listened to the words of the Bible? Maybe we never made the change back then that our hearts were urging?

- Why did Jesus choose this event to reveal himself to them? What would have "clicked" for them when he did what he did at the dinner? (See 22:7–23.)

- Now with the added event, they can put things together and say it was Jesus, both in the Scriptures and in the ritual.

Group Four Debriefing: The Disciples

Luke 24:36–49 As they [Cleopas and his companion] were talking about these things, Jesus himself stood among them [the disciples], and said to them, "Peace to you!" 37 But they were startled and frightened and thought they saw a spirit. 38 And he said to them, "Why are you troubled, and why do doubts arise in your hearts? 39 *See my hands and my feet, that it is I myself. Touch me, and see.* For a spirit does not have flesh and bones as you see that I have."

40 And when he had said this, he showed them his hands and his feet. 41 And while they still disbelieved for joy and were marveling, he said to them, "*Have you anything here to eat?*" 42

They gave him a piece of broiled fish, 43 *and he took it and ate before them.*

44 Then he said to them, "These are my words that I spoke to you while I was still with you, that everything written about me in the Law of Moses and the Prophets and the Psalms must be fulfilled." 45 *Then he opened their minds to understand the Scriptures,* 46 and said to them, "Thus it is written, *that the Christ should suffer and on the third day rise from the dead, 47 and that repentance for the forgiveness of sins should be proclaimed in his name to all nations, beginning from Jerusalem. 48 You are witnesses of these things.* (ESV)

Debriefing: Theophilus, the moderator for this larger group discussion session, goes over the three questions briefly with the group. Then he conducts a "debriefing," a more penetrating analysis of what the group interview should show using the italicized phrases above from their passage. The debriefing should illustrate out the following points:

- This is the crowning demonstration of the resurrection—the third testimony to Jesus being alive. After the implicit endorsement of the women who had the vision of the angel at the tomb, the urging of Cleopas and his companion to read the Bible, and then the promotion of the ritualized meal, now Jesus appears physically to the disciples.

- The resurrection thus is real, and this time he comes to them by appearance like a "spirit" and by sensory impressions like a corporeal person.

- He uses this occasion of the assembled church to launch them on a mission: to spread the good news of forgiveness beginning from where they are in Jerusalem (not Emmaus) to the rest of the world's peoples.

- To launch them (women, Cleopas and his companion, the disciples), Theophilus reads the next and final line:

  Luke 23:49 "And behold, I am sending the promise of my Father upon you. But stay in the city until you are clothed with power from on high."

Conclusion

[Back to Luke:] This is where I leave you, Theophilus, at the end of *Memoirs of How It All Began*. It leads directly into my next account of how things went after Jesus rose, and you can read my review of it called *Memoirs of an Unfinished Tale*.

Index

Abraham (bosom of), 158–61, 178,
  195–97
Adam (Jesus as Adam), 25–26,
  39–40, 54, 238–39
afterlife, 196
Agamemnon, 106
Ahimelech, 38
Alexander the Great, 93
angels (outside the nativity and
  parables), 195, 219, 225–26,
  230
Anna, 13–16
Antiochus IV Epiphanes, 92
apocalyptic vision (of Jesus), 200–
  205, (236)
apostle(s)
  definition, 42
  exhausted, 81–82
  on mission, 79–80
  twelve, the, 41, 163
  vs. the seventy, 93
archon [rich man], 75, 109, 172–74,
  177, 179, 188

Babylonian destruction of
  Jerusalem, 184
baptism
  of Jesus, 23–25, 240
  of suffering, 124–25
Bar mitzvah (of Jesus), 17–18
Barabbas, 234
Babel, tower of, 10
Bethsaida, 92, 107
birds, 115, 120–21
blessing (or curse), 137–38

blind man (of Jericho), 177–78, 188
burning bush, 196

Caesar, 19–20, 94, 105, 156–57,
  192–94
Capernaum, 92, 106
catachesis, 3
centurion
  at cross, 239–40
  in Galilee, 50
charis ("credit") [see "Anglicized
  Words" below], 44–46, 51,
  106
children, 171–72, 173
Chorazin, 92, 107
chorus (Greek), 166
church, 123, 162
Cleopas, 245–47
client-patron relationships, 50–51,
  79, 232
coin (lost), 146–48, 192–94
corrections, 163
criminals crucified with Jesus, 236–
  39, 240–41
crowds, 126–27, 144–46, 176, 188,
  204, 226, 234
cup (Passover), 211–12, 217, 218,
  220

darkness, 239–40
daughter of Jairus, 77–78
daughters of Jerusalem, 235–36, 240
David
  and Ahimelech, 38
  Jesus imitating, 187

Son of, 198
Dead Sea (salt), 146
Decapolis, 75
denarius, 193
devil (also see "Satan")
    demons, 71–73
    spiritual warfare, 102–3
    temptations in the wilderness,
        26–29
devious business agent ("dishonest
        steward"), 155–58
dialogues (of Jesus in the temple),
        188–205
Diogenes the Cynic, 105
disciples
    as friends, 114, 125
    at resurrection table, 247–48,
        251–52
    competition, 214
    excuses preventing training, 98
    high cost, 181
    Peter, James, John, 86–89
    private lessons, 119–21
    seventy vs. twelve vs. trio, 98
    Simon (Peter) and disciples, 215
    "tests" of disciples, 117
    training, 83–85
    training the seventy, 91
    vs. Caesar and Herod, 94
dives, 158–61, 165
door (closed), 133–35, 138–39
dropsy (victim), 138–41

Elijah, 33, 54–55, 86–89, 182, 208,
        232
Elisha, 33, 56
epiphany (vs. theophany), 23–25
Epicureanism, 196
Elizabeth, 5, 7–8
Emmaus walkers, 245–47, 249–51
Eucharist, 211

face (of actor, of coin), 193
farce (vs. tragedy), 85, 229–241
fasting, 37
fig tree, 127–30, 178, 202–3
finger (of God), 102–3
flowers, 120–21

funeral (of Nain), 53

Gabriel, 5–6
Galilee (Jesus leaving), 89
gap between scholarship and
        practice, xi
Gehenna, 114, 116
Gerasenes, 72
Golden Rule, 45, 96

Haftarah, 32
hair, 115
Halakah, 5
Herakles (Hercules, demigods), 75
Herod, 79–80, 94, 135–37, 231–34,
        237
Holy Spirit, 23–24, 27, 32, 113, 116,
        240
hospitality, 142–44

infants, 171–72, 173

Jairus, 78
Jeremiah, 186–87, 230
Jericho, 176–79, 180
Jerusalem visitation, 182–85
Jewish-Gentile relations, 71
Jonah (sign of), 105–7
John the Baptist,
    baptism vs. Jesus's baptism, 124
    crowd's expectations of, 58
    expectations of Jesus, 56–57
    meaning of his name, 5
    preaching of, 20–23, 188, 236
    vs. Caesar, 19–20
Joseph of Arimathea, 241
Judas the betrayer, 207, 212, 230
judge ("unrighteous"), 167–68

kairos ("opportunity") [see
        "Anglicized Words" below],
        207, 209, 210
key (of knowledge), 111
kiss, 220–21, 230, 231
King of the Jews, 238
Kingdom of God, 36–37, 43, 47, 78,
        81–82, 106–7, 122–23, 124,
        126–27, 130–32 138–41,

156–58, 171–72, 173–75,
179–82 , 202

Last Supper, 112, 115, 125
lawyers, 110
Lazarus, 158–61
leaven, 130–32
Legion, 72–73, 103
lepers, 165–67
Levi (Matthew), 36
loaves and fishes, 81–82

Maecenas, 105
mammon, 155
marriage feast, 122–23
martyrdom, 110, 112, 115, 117, 125,
201
Martha (and her sister Mary), 97–99
Mary
    and Gabriel, 6
    and Elizabeth, 7
    "blessed", 8
    epitomizing the Jewish people, 6
    in the temple at Passover, 17
Memoirs of an Unfinished Tale, xi,
    19, 34, 42, 102, 123, 162,
    166, 209, 211, 253
Midrash, 38n5
mission (of Jesus), 135–37, 187
monuments, 110
Morning Star [see "Dayspring"], 10
Moses, 86–89, 103, 182, 194–97,
    232, 240
multitudes [see "crowds"], 126
mustard tree/seed, 130–31, 163
mystery, 67, 69

Naaman [see "Elisha"], 56, 107
narrow gate, 133–35
Nazareth, 31–33
Nineveh, 105–7

Odysseus, 106
orderly account, 1, 4, 106, 120

patience [see "persistence"], 67
parable(s), 67, 95–96, 99–101, 102–
    3, 117–19, 126–27, 128–32,

141–52, 155–57, 158–61,
    164–65, 166–71, 179–82,
    189–91
paradise, 238, 241
paradox, 31, 33, 35, 37, 40, 51–53,
    88,
Passover, 209–12
performance
    Bible study concept, xi–xiii
    dialogues of Jesus in temple,
        188–205
    of Jesus to project meaning, 40,
        111, 136–37, 138–41, 182–
        85, 186–88, 190, 211
    Spontaneous, 165
persistence [see "patience"], 67,
    69–73, 74–81
Peter, Simon, 83, 85–89, 123, 125,
    173–75, 209, 215–17, 222–
    24, 235
Pharaoh, 103
Pharisees, 35, 36, 38, 40, 108–12,
    135, 138–41, 146, 149, 151,
    169–71, 173
pigs, 72, 140
Pilate
    (His execution of Galileans),
        127–30
    Interrogation of Jesus, 231–34,
        237
pilgrimage, pilgrim(s), 169, 182–83,
    186–87, 202, 210, 240–41
prayer (of Jesus), 34, 40–41, 84–85,
    100–105
presentation, 14–15
Prodigal son (parable of), 149–52,
    156–57, 159
prophets, 135–38, 189
Psalm 118 (used by Jesus), 135–38,
    183, 188–90
pun(s), 5, 10, 140, 178, 190, 193,
    (235), 237

reacting, xi–xiii
    games, 62–66, 74–76, 152–55,
        190–92, 224–29, 243–53
remembrance, 211

Roman judicial hearing [rhetoric],
    108
rooster, 223, 226–27

Sadducees, 188 194–97
salt, 144–45
Samaritan(s)
    grateful leper, 165–67
    Parable, 95–97
Satan, 207–9, 212, 215
seating (at banquet), 141–42
Sermon on the Plain, 42–49, 96
servants ("unworthy"), 164–65
Seven Wise Men of Greece, 105
seventy
    return, 94
    sent out, 90–92, 107
Shabbat/Sabbath, 34–38, 138–41,
    241
sheep (lost), 146–49
shepherds, 12–13
sign (of the times), 126–27
silence (of Pharisees), 138–39
Simeon, 13–16
Simon of Cyrene, 235
skull, 236–39
Sodom and Gomorrah, 21–22 93,
    107
Solomon (and the queen of the
    South), 105–7
Solon (of Athens), 105
Son of Man, 35, 39, 116, 168, 175,
    202–3
Sons of God, 195
spies, 192–94
Sukkot (Jewish feast), 86
sword, 217
Sycamore tree, 177–79
sycophant, 178
symposium, 142–44

Tables (of the Law), 172–73
tax collector, 35–36, 169–70, 171,
    173, 188
taxes, 192–94
Temple, 169–70, 186–91
temptations (of Jesus), 27–29, 218
tenants, 189–91

tender mercy, 9
Theophany (vs. epiphany), 23–25
Theophilus (as actor), xii, 1
thief in the night, 123
tithes, 109
tower
    building, 144–46
    of Siloam, 127–30
tragedy, 85, 166, 229–41
Transfiguration, 86–89, 190, 240
twelve ("the Twelve") [see "Apostle"],
    42, 70–80, 81–82, 93, 107,
    163
Tyre (and Sidon), 92–93, 107

unleavened bread, 209

visitation(s), 4–19, 156, 168, 176,
    182–85, 186–87

wealth, 172–73
widow
    in city, 167–68
    in temple, 198
    of Zarephath/Nain, 33, 50, 52,
        78, 107
wilderness, 26–30
wine, 37, 56–57, 211–12
wisdom (of God), 59, 64, 111
woman with flow of blood, 77
women
    as disciples, 60–61, 99
    at the tomb, 245, 248–49

Zacchaeus, 177–79, 241
Zechariah, 5, 9, 231
Zikkaron, 5

Scripture Index

JEWISH SCRIPTURES

Torah

Genesis
19:1–29   21, 92

Exodus
3:1–6   22, 196–97
14:20   240

Prophets

1 Kings
10:1–13   108
17:17–24   55
17:20   55
17:8–24   56
19:11   208

2 Kings
1:9–16   88
19:21   7

Isaiah
1:8   7
5:1–7   190
23   93
37:22   7
53:7   140
60:13   10
61:1–11   33
62:11   7

Jeremiah
6:16   212
7:11–15   137
7:1–15   186

Malachi
3:1–2   186

Zechariah
2:10   7
9:9   7, 182
12:3   202

Zephaniah
3:14   7

Habakkuk
2:11, 14   183

Writings

Psalms
2   238
6:6–7   135
6:8   134
9:14   7

Psalms (*continued*)

23:5	212
24	164
34:18	78
49:12, 20	140
107:3	134–35
110:3	10
118:22	137, 191
119:63	29

Proverbs

13:12, 19	15
14:10	78
16:31	115
18:24	ix
26:11	104

Daniel

7:1–28	230
8:13	202

NEW TESTAMENT

Matthew

5:3–10	43
5–7	42

Acts

4:23–32	106
10:1–20	5
17:28	45

Romans

11:7–32	202

Revelation

11:2	202

OTHER

Tobit

6:14–15	195

SELECT ANGLICIZED GREEK, HEBREW, ARAMAIC, AND LATIN WORDS

Achreioi	165
Agalliaō	94
Allogenēs	166
Anaideia	101
Anaireō	237
Analēpsis	88
Anamnēsis	211
Anatolē [ex hypsous]	10
Apologia	116, 118
Apostolos	41
Acharistous	45
Aphrōn	118
Archōn	74–76, 109, 172–74, 177, 179
Asbetsos	22
Augustus filius dvi	193
Bar-nasha	39
Boulē	74–76
Carpe diem	109
Charis	44, 96, 99, 106, 143, 166, 176
Chrēstos	45–46
Daimones	75
Deinos	112
Do ut des	118
Douleuō	151
Egkathetous	193
Ekstasis	35
Epistatēs	166
Eschaton lepton	127
Eulogemēnē	8
Euphoreō	118
Exodos	86, 111
Halakah	5
Hypōpiazō	168
Imperator	23

Kairos	28, 126, 134, 207
Katēcho	3
Makarios	8, 143
Mystērion	67, 80, 96
Neaniske	54
Pais	54
Panourgian	193
Paradoxia	31, 88
Pax	11
Rakham	9
Shalom	11
Splanchna [eleous]	
	9
Stigmē	27
Zikkaron	5